THE GRAND TOUR IN ITALY
(1700 - 1800)

PAUL FRANKLIN KIRBY

With 16 Illustrations

S. F. VANNI (Ragusa)

Publishers & Booksellers

30 West 12th Street, New York

Per la Tittera

*Gli inglesi non sono gente
insoffribilmente cattiva.*

—JOSEPH BARETTI

CONTENTS

PREFACE

In Florence near the place of the Ponte Santa Trinità there is a little coffee-house, which during the last months of the war in the Spring of 1945 was much visited by some of the English and American officers stationed in the city. One afternoon I found there a book entitled *The Enchanted April*. The frontispiece, reproduced from a water color original, showed a cypress, a gulf of blue, and a misty lilac-colored mountain. The story itself concerned a plain London woman named Mrs. Wilkins, who had endured the insipidity of her life and of her husband for a respectable time — about eight years — when one day as she sat in her humdrum club reading the *Times,* she noticed an advertisement. "To those who appreciate flowers and sunshine. Small medieval castle on the shores of the Mediterranean to be let furnished for the month of April." She laid aside the paper, stood up, walked to a window and looked out into the rainy street. There she saw milling umbrellas and splashing taxis. But she was looking beyond and through them into the depths of a vision where eternal summer was filled with golden light. She had to speak of it to someone. "Think of getting away for a whole month — from everything — to heaven!" The severe looking lady to whom this outburst had been addressed pretended for a moment the kingdom of heaven was within her; but she soon admitted that for years and years she had been happy only by forgetting her ideas of true happiness. And then the story tells how, after doubts, these two escape to shores where they are beautified by beauty, washed through with sunlight and raised above themselves by the austerity of sheer bliss.

For many months I had observed that for a certain class of Englishman Italy was something like a heaven. At least it seemed to be the not quite real land of poetry — a kind of other England illumined by inexpressible, tormenting magic. I began to think of some of the British officers I had met during the war. At Catania a few days after the Germans had withdrawn I remember going to speak with the rosy faced Town Major, a very large gentleman with a loud voice. Before

I left I had the impression that there was something immemorial about him — that he had been in Catania for many ages. He seemed to know every alley and building in the city. Then there had been a young Lieutenant Colonel, who, during almost the whole of a flight from Catania past Aetna, and Taormina, through Scylla and Charybdis, and over the wilds of Magna Græcia to San Spirito on the Adriatic, knelt on the metal floor of the aircraft so as to have a better view through a porthole. I will never forget the expression on his face as we climbed over gigantic grey mountains and peered down into lands that for ages have been abandoned to the sun and lost in a voiceless dream. As we swept alongside pearl-hued stone cities high among the clouds in upland niches, I saw that he knew those hidden places. He called them by name; and above valleys where columns of wood smoke hung in the air as though time itself had been suspended, for him the ever-living past of Italy and the Mediterranean was just beyond the glass.

Everywhere we had gone in Italy, it had been the English who had taken us to see the sights, the English who really knew it and governed it. And they not only knew it, many of them; they possessed it and loved it with an intensity hardly to be surpassed by any fervor of patriotism. They footed it along old roads in Tuscany as though they were in paradise. In the little village of Assisi they were fortunate enough to have their own inn, and they sat on the terrace of it by the hour gazing down into the shadowy vale of Umbria. They requisitioned the most picturesque villas, pitched their tents where there was a fine view, and whenever possible made use of castles. They always seemed to have been there before, whenever the chance of war brought us.

In a way they had, because there is something atavistic, something perennial and Phoenix-like about Englishmen in Italy. In this Holy Year when Englishmen, Scotsmen, and Irishmen are arriving in Rome by plane, by train, by bus and truck, and even by bicycle and on foot — it was only a few days ago that I stopped on the windy road to Mont' Amiata to have a word with a boney red-bearded Englishman in sandals, walking to Rome and sleeping in fields by the way — in this year it is easy to remember the pilgrimages of far off Medieval times, so long ago that many of the wonders now known in Italy had not yet appeared. But the roads, lowlands and mountains would have been much the same, and watch kept by the same gray company of strongholds that look to each other from high places still. In the country in the Spring when the fields are green and the cuckoo sings, it is easy to imagine Englishmen of the Crusades trotting on with armed companies and their colors flaming among the little leaves.

And then came English scholars of the Renaissance to learn Italian and attend universities, to converse with distinguished Italians, but not to see pictures or to take any notable delight in Italian landscape. Perhaps they had pre-occupations. Travel was an adventure for men of courage in Shakespeare's time. In an excellent book by E. S. Bates, *Touring in 1600,* you may read of frozen corpses on Mt. Cenis, wayfarers murdered by keepers of inns — and even at one inn served up pickled! You may read of ambushes on the road, not to mention beds, where tourists of both sexes congregated according to chance. Money was a serious problem. Coin or jewelry had to be carried. If lost, credit was almost impossible to establish. And those were times when the punishments for debt were as severe as they were for heresy.

Eighteenth century travels in Italy were more like our own — less difficult, and less serious. Scholars did not go to learn Greek because they could learn it at home. The study of Italian as a polite language was generally a thing of the past. Englishmen went to Italy with much more curiosity about classic and Renaissance art, and began to notice the land of Italy itself— wistful, luminous, plain, its grain and olive trees, the stones of its buildings clear in prodigal light. They began to see what we who have travelled see even better, that Italy is a land apart.

This book is an account of adventures on the road — hence the geographical division of the experience — an account of a great discovery more valuable to the human spirit than the discovery of Eldorado could possibly be. No theories have been demonstrated. It should be evident that the Grand Tour in Italy had a profound effect not only on the individual, but that it was a chief cause of the altered tastes of England and other eighteenth century nations.

For me, however, the tour itself, the accounts of it, and the people who made it are interesting — more interesting than the results. Most of the thousands of imitations of Mediterranean architecture which are scattered all over Northern Europe, England and North America are just as depressing as most English Romantic poetry. These things lack light, just as Romantic poetry for my taste lacks something clean, veracious, simple and cheerful, something as severe and honest as an old villa in the gently-composed Tuscan country-side. I have focused on the tour and not on the results.

Thus, like the travellers themselves I have passed lightly over the names of æstheticians — Riedsele, Volkmann, Mengs, Lessing and even the erudite and original Winckelmann. There is no discussion of the "ruins of Rome" theme in eighteenth century poetry, or of themes of topographical poetry, or of early uses of the word "sublime" to describe great things in nature and art. This would make another kind of book. Although the methods of exact historical research have been used a certain *disinvoltura* of style is permitted with the hope of echoing the charm of a departed civilization.

Some authors are quoted often and others, whose works are listed in the bibliography, only once or twice or not at all. This could be remedied by substitution if there were any cogent reason for rejecting natural choices in order to include a few words from authors who were dull.

I am happy to take this occasion to thank Mario Bowinkel of Naples and Comm. Giuseppe Giosi of Rome for directing me in certain antiquarian and art matters. I must also acknowledge debts of gratitude to the Philadelphia Library Company, the Rare Book Room at the Library of Congress, and to the staffs of the libraries at Yale, Columbia, Rome and Harvard universities. Many are the courtesies and suggestions received from Professors James L. Clifford, Marjorie Nicolson, Maurice Valency, and Giuseppe Prezzolini. Miss Marion Thompson carefully and skillfully prepared the text. And last I wish to record with loving thanks the patience of my wife, who watched and waited while I wrote of "the land of lands," her home.

PAUL FRANKLIN KIRBY
Siena, September 21, 1951

Castel del Monte "Watch of Puglia."

CHAPTER I

BOUND FOR ITALY

Far to the right where Appenine ascends,
Bright as the summer, Italy extends.

Oliver Goldsmith

I

Italy has always been the traveller's favorite land. During the Renaissance, in Medieval and early Christian times, and during the Græco-Roman centuries, even in those remote ages of fable when Ionian wanderers sailed out to its blue coasts, Italy was the land of the blest, a place of eternal youth, where hills and valleys yielded perpetual harvests, fruits dropped from the trees in all seasons, and where all beautiful and happy things might be seen. Travellers returning have cast a glamour about it. They have talked about it and have written about it. Years after, when the petty troubles of their tours have been forgotten, the vision of it has returned. They have seen again its great mountains tumbled in savage and majestic disorder, looking down upon the gray "garden of the world," — castles, temples, villages and cities, like dots in a map — all bordered by the sea.

During the eighteenth century this classic and fabulous ground was the grandest part of the Englishmen's Grand Tour. Tens of thousands went through Italy, and sent their sons to see what they had seen. It was evident, as Joseph Addison had said after his own tour, that there was "no place in the world where a man may travel with greater pleasure and advantage than in Italy." There is something more particular in the face of the country, and something "more astonishing in the works of nature, than can be met with in any other part of Europe." And as Addison explained, Italy is also the school of painting, of music, of architecture, and of sculpture and letters. The number, variety and refinement of political states in Italy would alone justify the travels of future statesmen there. No part of it was without its historic fame. Scarcely a "mountain

1

or river that has not been the scene of some extraordinary action."[1]

II

To seek the very beginning of British travel to Italy one must go far beyond the limit of history. Among the mists and tides and the crying gulls of northern seas there surely dwelt spirited men willing to quit native trackways and sail south with ancient Mediterranean traders who had passed the Pillars of Hercules for cargoes of British pearls and gold and tin. Long before Rome or Athens flourished, British eyes scanned the Mediterranean. After the time of Caesar, bearded, cross-gartered military adventurers from Britain must have been no uncommon sight in the Imperial City.

The first unforgettable image that history or tradition gives of Englishmen in Rome is that of the golden-haired boys in the market place. "Non Angli, sed Angeli," remarked the great Gregory, then a priest, and he vowed that the English would be Christian. Ten years later St. Augustine landed on the Isle of Thanet and Gregory's promise was fulfilled. For a thousand years, as a result of this conversion, an untold number of English men and women of all degrees followed the Pilgrims' Way across the Chalk Downs to the Channel, and traversed Merovingian, Carolingian, and Bourbon France and the long roads of Italy until they came to Roma Sacra.

Arthur was the earliest Christian King of Britain who took the road to Rome and the only king who slew a dragon on the way. Caedwalla, King of Wessex, went to Rome and died there in 688. Offa, King of the West Saxons, and another king, Coenred, journeyed to Rome together in 709, and they too, having retired from brutal tribal bloodshed, remained in sunny Italy and died there. King Ina went to Rome about 725 and died there.[2] Alfred the Great, while still a youth, had been twice to Rome, and who can doubt the effect of these experiences on his deep intelligence? Who can doubt that his serious efforts to improve the knowledge of the English clergy received their initial stimulus in his contact with the civiliza-

---

[1] Addison, *Remarks on the Several Parts of Italy*, preface, pp. [i-ii].
[2] Lassels, *The Voyage of Italy*, part II, p. 256; see *Encyclopedia Brittanica*.

2

tion of the south? During the Crusades every adventurer who could leave home seems to have gone down to the Mediterranean. Richard Cœur de Lion was there, of course, and spent an uneasy winter at Messina, where, according to some accounts, he presented King Arthur's famous sword Excalibur to Tancred as a peace offering.[3] One grim Crusade story tells how Guy de Montfort, son of the powerful Earl Simon, set upon young Henry of Cornwall in the church of Viterbo and hewed him to pieces as he clung to the very altar.[4] And a little later, history records the marches and countermarches, the beating of drums and blowing of battle-horns, the raids and victories and defeats of the English *condottiere*, Sir John Hawkwood, renamed Giovanni Acuto, as he led his White Company through the turmoils of Tuscany and Lombardy.

Chaucer went down to Italy twice during the dawn of the English Renaissance. Then after the Wars of the Roses, young English gentlemen of the new nobility and scholars of promise were sent abroad, especially to Italy, "the elder sister of all other countries,"[5] and were maintained there at royal expense to add worldly and courtly experience to the academic training of Oxford and Cambridge.

Discounting Chaucer's business journeys to confer with the merchants of Genoa in 1373 and with Barnabo Visconti at Milan in 1378, the first learned intermediaries to bring the civilization of Renaissance Italy to Medieval England did their work a century after Chaucer and a century before Sidney's time. Then came Erasmus, who had been tempted to stay for life in Rome, where he revelled in the clear sky, the fields, the libraries, the pleasant walks and charming conversations of educated men, and who had worked so hard with Aldus Manutius at Venice that they "scarce had time to scratch their ears." Tunstall, Colet, and Lily brought classic learning and Greek ideals to sixteenth century Oxford. Dr. Edward Wotton learned Greek at Padua and lectured there in zoology. Dr. Caius of Cambridge studied anatomy under Vesalius at Padua.

---

[3] Northall, *Travels through Italy,* p. 17.

[4] Mrs. Trevelyan, "The Wandering Englishman in Italy," *Proceedings of the British Academy,* (1930), p. 62; see Charlotte Yonge, *The Prince and the Page* (1865).

[5] Lassels, *op. cit.,* p. [1].

Sir Thomas Wyatt lived in Italy. Thomas Hoby went to see Tuscany and even to live in Sicily to observe the country and to get completely away from Englishmen for a while. From 1545 to 1550 William Thomas lived and travelled through parts of Italy and returned with a knowledge of Greek and enough historical lore to write his very good *Historie of Italie*.

Sir Philip Sydney was the ideal aristocratic traveller. He learned Italian so he could appreciate the Italians; he conversed with men who had distinguished themselves in various ways; he listened to the music he heard on all sides; in spite of his tutor, he contrived to mingle familiarly with the people of the country; and still he maintained his self respect and returned with a respect for Italy. It is said that he also brought back a portrait of himself painted at Venice by Paolo Veronese. Unfortunately the painting has disappeared.

Some early Englishmen remained in Italy. The tomb of one of these may be seen in the church of San Gregorio in Rome. Sir Edward Carne was ambassador to the Holy See from Henry VIII. He first resided in the capital from 1530 to 1533 when the operations of Henry, relative to Anne Boleyn and the Pope, brought about his reluctant return to England. But in 1555 he was sent again to Rome by Mary. When Elizabeth came to the throne, Sir Edward had not the least inclination to leave Italy. Moreover his feelings had always been with the Catholic religion, and he greatly doubted the convenience of visiting England, although he had some properties there, which might be confiscated at any time the Queen decided he was a recalcitrant subject. With this possibility in mind he caused to be circulated a report that the Pope was detaining him. And though it was learned that he had concocted this sad tale himself, he still managed to remain in Rome, and to keep both his religion and his English estates.[6]

Another early Italianate Englishman was the famous Sir Robert Dudley, son of Queen Elizabeth's Earl of Leicester by an unrecognized marriage. He crossed the Channel in 1605 after all efforts to prove his legitimacy had been thwarted by his father's final wife. With him travelled in true romantic style, a "page," Elizabeth Southwell. They went to Florence as their land of heart's desire, and were married, notwith-

---

6 Mrs. Trevelyan, *op. cit.*, pp. 64-66.

standing the fact that he had a wife and seven daughters in England. The rest of Dudley's life is part of the history of Tuscany. It was he who refurbished the Grand Duke Cosimo's fleet, and who drained the marshes between Pisa and Livorno in 1621, and who suggested that Livorno be made a free port, which rendered it one of the most important mercantile centers of Europe, and in the eighteenth century something like an English colony. While he lived in Florence, Sir Robert enjoyed a grand palace; he died at his Castle of Carbello, three miles from the city.[7]

Among other seventeenth century travellers, aside from a considerable number of the nobility, were James Howell, George Sandys,[8] Milton — and later — Evelyn,[9] John Ray,[10] the botanist, Bishop Burnett,[11] and Richard Lassells, originator of the phrase "Grand Tour."

III

The eighteenth century ways to Rome were as long and as arduous and as expensive as they had ever been. They were in fact more arduous than they had been in antiquity. Nevertheless it was part of the traditional duty of a nobleman, as much a part of the mold that formed a gentleman as were public schools and Latin grammar, Horace and Cicero, and boxing and fagging. A young cavalier still travelled to enlarge his comprehension of manners, customs, and government, and to see *classic lands*; but his journey was also a quest. He was expected, as in the days of chivalry, to inure himself to weariness, hunger, perils, darkness, high winds, women, nakedness, death and so on. He did this by going over the seas to

---

[7] *Ibid.*, pp. 72-77.

[8] Sandys in 1615 published *The Relation of a Journey Begun an Dom. 1610, in Four Books.* This work was well known to Thomas Gray. See the Toynbee and Whibley edition of *The Correspondence of Thomas Gray,* (1935), I, 163, 175.

[9] Evelyn went abroad in 1643 and returned to England in 1647 after more than a year in Italy. He went abroad a second time in 1649 and returned in 1652. See Toynbee, *Dante in English Literature,* p. 137.

[10] Ray, *Observations . . . made in a Journey through Italy,* 1673; see also Harris, *Collection of Modern Voyages,* II, 641-658, "Travels . . . through the Dominion of the States of Venice, Lombardy, Tuscany . . . Naples."

[11] Burnett, *Some Letters, Containing an Account of what seemed most remarkable in Italy,* 1686.

ascend difficult hills and struggle through sloughs and over broiling deserts in Italy, where he encountered the monsters Pope and Pagan, and a hundred "carnal Cogitations," as he stalked among stupendous shells of antiquity or advanced with unflagging courage through the labyrinths of art.

Italy two centuries ago was more than just another foreign land. It was every man's second home. It was the mother country of Europe. It was the home of many of the most famous men of history. It lay in the very navel of human experience, the Mediterranean. The natural beauty of it was a byword. The very words picturesque and romantic meant Italy. "The man who has not been in Italy," said Dr. Johnson, "is always conscious of an inferiority from his not having seen what it is expected a man should see. The grand object of travel is to see the Mediterranean."[12]

IV

Getting to Rome was no very mysterious matter. It is conceivable that one might start out with not so much as a glance at a guidebook or a map and still arrive safely at all the salient points, and ultimately find himself in the broad plains of Latium hurried by a unique attraction into the glimmering grey jumble of the Eternal City. But, if so, he would have sacrificed the pleasure of travelling over mountains and valleys by seas and rivers in his mind as he sat toasting his feet by the andirons.

During the first half of the century, travellers were most familiar with Addison's *Remarks on the Several Parts of Italy* judging from references to it. Addison's book is still known to the general tourist in Italy, and can be found in the bookshops of Rome and Florence. Addison's manner is a bit cool and aloof, and his matter is, much of it, selected bits of ancient poetry describing famous places of the classic tour. The whole suggests a highly polished and inlaid marble floor, over which reflections of the author move with regulated grace.

Addison himself had recommended Misson's *A New Voyage to Italy* . . . published in English in 1695 at London, four

---

[12] Boswell, *The Life of Samuel Johnson,* ed. Hill-Powell, (Oxford at the Clarendon Press, 1934) II, 458.

years after its first appearance in French at the Hague. To Addison this work seemed admirable because of Misson's "plan of the country," and in fact the curious airview engravings and careful descriptions do convey to the untravelled reader a much clearer impression than it is possible to receive from some of those old works.

The most painstaking guide-book was the squat little volume by Richard Lassells entitled *The Voyage of Italy, or a Compleat Journey through Italy, with the Characters of the People, and the Description of the Chief Towns, Churches, Monasteries, Tombs,* etc., published at Paris and London in 1670. It is in the preface to this work that the phrase Grand Tour first appeared. As the author, a Catholic, had spent many years in Italy, and had conducted five separate tours through the usual cities, it is not remarkable that his book contains more exhaustive accounts of the sights than almost any other general work in English has ever given.

A man like Gibbon, of course, who was one of the most heroic of travellers in books, grappled with whole libraries as he prepared to tread "with lofty step the ruins of the forum." He says[13] that he went through the tomes of Bergier's *Histoire des Grandes Chemins de l'Empire Romain,* Wesseling's *Itineraries,* Strabo's *De Situ Orbis* (17 books), Pliny, Pomponius Mela, catalogs of ancient poets, d'Anville's *Itineraires Mesures,* Donatus Nardini's *Roman Antiquities,* and the coasting voyage of Rutilius, a Gaul who went by sea from Rome along the Riviera to his native land in 417.

The average gentleman probably travelled and died without seeing these old works. His schooling, and the memory of a few conversations, would be enough and more than enough. Some well established families, no doubt, possessed manuscript notes like those from the Stow library, which list a great number of inns in Italy with comments such as "Very good," "Thief," "Make your bargain first," and contains billets-doux to the beautiful hostess of the Tre Re in Siena.[14]

General maps of Italy which could be bought in England

---

[13] Gibbon, Edward, see Oxford World Classics edition of the *Autobiography,* p. 142.

[14] Jones, "The William Robinsons in Italy," *Huntington Library Quarterly,* April 1941, p. 344.

in those days were printed from engravings on thick paper rectangles backed by wear resisting water-proofed cloth. Though not very accurate according to our standards, they showed a great amount of detail, and indicated the relationship of cities and roads well enough. The chief complaint against them was their cavalier attitude towards mountains.[15] If the tourist, following hints from the carte, began peering from his coach window for a great range and found only a plain instead, he usually contented himself with his discovery; and cartographers, understanding the advantages of having too many mountains in their maps and not too few, distributed them freely up and down a peninsula famous for its bold terrain. Local maps could be had in almost every Italian city.

As the years rolled by, the heap of popular travel books increased as the number of travellers themselves increased. During the first half of the century the tour of Italy was still restricted to the exceptionally rich nobleman and his retinue and to a few uncommonly curious individuals and to artists bound for Rome. But from 1763 until the Napoleonic Wars literally tens of thousands of English crossed the channel and a great part of them went on to Italy.[16] An accurate and diverting travel book appeared during this time at least once and often twice each year.

Looking back it seems now that the most useful and the most compact guide book appeared in the year 1777, entitled *The Gentleman's Guide in his Tour through Italy with a correct Map and Directions for Travelling in that Country.* It was sold in London, and by the booksellers in Dover, Margate, Brighthelmstone and all the bathing towns on the coast. The author, Thomas Martyn, says in his preface "It will naturally be asked, why we have more travels into Italy, when we have too many already?" And his explanation is that most books on the subject were written with "a view to be read at the fireside at home," rather than to accompany a man abroad. And of the few intended to inform the traveller on the spot, he writes "their works have been either very partial and defective, or else too voluminous to be carried about with tolerable con-

---

[15] Swinburne, *Travels in the Two Sicilies,* I, 212-213.

[16] Lambert, *Grand Tour,* p. 41. After the peace of 1763 so great was the rush of Englishmen to Europe that Walpole reported 40,000 as the number of travellers estimated to have passed through Calais in 24 months.

venience."[17] These objections are well founded enough. For example Peter Beckford, uncle of the author of *Vathek,* wrote, "Compare Piozzi with Smollett; Baretti with Sharpe; and you will be at a loss what opinion to form of a country of which they all treat so differently."[18] He goes on to say that he will be guided in writing his *Familiar Letters from Italy* by Père Jerome La Lande's *Voyage d'un Français en Italie.* This work though it was excellently complete, certainly would justify complaints of being unwieldy as it was published in nine fat volumes with a large supplement of maps. The well known guide by Nugent, which came out in 1749 and in several revisions, was a work of four volumes. But the "prudent traveller endeavors to bring his baggage within as narrow a compass as possible,"[19] as Martyn says, and for that reason, and for the variety of detailed information it contained, his *Gentleman's Guide* was unrivalled as an actual travelling companion, and as a source of facts about money, routes, hotels, galleries and art works in the second half of the eighteenth century.

V

When at last the traveller had armed himself by reading older tourists, collected his impediments, and had taken leave of his friends, he crossed London Bridge, turned left at St. George's Church and rolled down the old Kent Road,[20] which frequently he would not expect to see again for three or four years. Everyone went well equipped, if not splendidly; and walking abroad, or "rambling" like Goldsmith's was rare in the eighteenth century. One poor adventurer named Joshua Lucock Wilkinson carried, "a few books, two shirts, and a thin cotton jacket." His only protection was a "slender stick." A "small knapsack"[21] contained all his wealth. He was short sighted. He had no knowledge of the languages of the continent. He had no passport. He was of military stature and came near to being impressed several times. He apparently lacked every talent including that of "disputing his passage" by flute

---

[17] Martyn, *The Gentleman's Guide in his Tour through Italy,* p. iii.
[18] P. Beckford, *Letters from Italy,* preface.
[19] Martyn, *op. cit.,* p. ii.
[20] Boorish, *A Mapbook of English Literature,* (Henry Holt: New York 1936) p. 17.
[21] Wilkinson, *The Wanderer;* see preface.

as Goldsmith had done. And he certainly lacked the talent of writing, for even a very careful reading of his book leaves the direction and chronology of his tour well masked. It is possible that he did not know himself where he had been.[22]

Some left London like a shot "through the fortress of dust,"[23] as one tourist expressed it. Some wearied with preparations and farewells, are said to have clapped themselves up in their postchaises and slept to Dover, and sometimes over the channel to Calais, where their first act would be to call for wine from Mr. Dessein, and then set off for St. Omer, "dying of the hyp"[24] until their arrival at Paris. Others would leave town slowly with a heavily loaded coach and take three days to reach the channel, pausing perhaps at the King's Head, Rochester and the Rose Inn, Sittingbourne, and then resting easily at the City of London Inn at Dover until the wind should be just right.[25]

Usually arrangements for the coaches would be made at Calais. Lawrence Sterne was only one of thousands who looked about the yard of Mr. Dessein's inn for a reasonable vehicle. Great lords would hire an entire channel boat to ferry their coaches and equipment across, sometimes inviting the more modest tourists aboard as guests for the passage.

Mr. Dessein, incidentally, was subject of many comments. He was almost the first Frenchman many of the English would see operating on his own French soil, and the usual attitude towards him is suggested in the words of Thicknesse, who described him as bowing and giving "you a side look, as a cock does at a barley-corn."[26] He had the reputation of being rather

---

[22] At the end of the copy of Wilkinson's book which is now the property of the Philadelphia Library Company a disgruntled eighteenth century reader wrote, "La Fin d'Ignorance et Affectation—what better can you expect of an Englishman?"

[23] Walker, *Ideas suggested on the Spot in . . . Italy,* p. 1.

[24] Douglas, *Traveling Anecdotes,* pp. 1-2.

[25] Gardenstone, Francis G., *Travelling Memorandums* . . . Edinburgh, 1792. I, 6-8.

[26] Thicknesse, *A Year's Journey . . .,* p. 9; Gardenstone, *op. cit.,* p. 11, says, "Mr. Dessein appears to me to be a sensible, considerate, unaffected man." But by the time Gardenstone saw him (1786), he had made his fortune and was old and mellow. By 1776 M. Dessein had amassed a fortune of 50,000 pounds (Lambert, *Grand Tour,* pp. 41-42.) some of it by exercising the *Droit d'aubaine,* which he had purchased from the King of France. See the first chapter of *A Sentimental Journey.* Sterne lamented that if he had died of indigestion, even his little picture of Eliza, which he had promised to carry to his grave, would have been stripped from his neck. "Ungenerous!"

10

sharp in exchanging money; and anyone who found a coach to his liking, at a price that seemed reasonable usually mentioned the fact with a mixture of surprise and pride.

According to some of the guide-books, a coach or post-chaise ought by all means be English. Ideally it would be purchased in England and built especially for Italian roads. It should be low-hung and double-perched with well-seasoned corded springs, and axle-trees of iron. It should have as accessories two drag chains with iron shoes, two drag-staffs for hill climbing, and a spare parts chest containing everything necessary to dismount the coach. The chest ought to be padlocked and suspended from the iron work beneath the vehicle.

Reading an elaborate guide-book like that of Marianne Starke[27] one sees that a travelling coach must have been fitted up as for a siege, if not actual pitched battles, the assumption evidently being that when an Englishman left England, he entered areas something like Milton's "chaos and Eternal Night," where none of the amenities and few essentials of life could be found. A well-prepared tourist should carry beds, large leather sheets, two pillows per bed, pillow cases, a change of linen sheets, two blankets and two bedside carpets per bed. Any guide-book recommended swords, pistols, knives, and extra door locks. Miss Starke included silver table spoons, sugar tongs, a silver teapot, and block tin tea kettle, a tinder-box, several block tin lamps, and a travelling *chaise-percee,* adapted to fit over the well of the carriage. She also listed flavorings and spices and — oatmeal, as no one but an Englishman would have porridge.

To resist the chill of brick and marble pavements in the galleries and palaces of Italy, it would be wise to have cork or double-soled shoes and boots; and flannel waistcoats and long drawers would be very useful in high altitudes and unheated houses. If perchance the traveller were making the tour with the hope of improving his health among other things, he should have the use of Buchan's *Domestic Medicine,* and a medicine-chest with scales and weights, a rhubarb grater (rhubarb was considered an excellent safe laxative), an ounce and half-ounce measure for water, a small mortar, and a knife for

---

[27] Starke, *Travels in Italy,* pp. 263-266. Starke is interesting for her dramatic accounts of the conquest of Italy by Napoleon, and his arrivals in Florence and Rome.

spreading blisters, a set of elementary dental tools and some tooth brushes and leaf lead. It is hard to imagine that many actually carried all these things. Still there was more. The well-protected traveller would have Dr. James' powder, castor-oil, hartshorne, æther, pure opium, sal volatile, laudanum, paregoric, emetic tartar (you could never be sure in Italian inns), spirits of lavender, camomile-flowers, calomel, salt of wormwood, essence of peppermint, magnesia, salve, basilicum, caustic and lint. Oil of lavender was particularly useful in clearing up an infested bed, while vitriolic acid had the same effect on bad water. And finally Miss Starke recommended that the bottom of a carriage should be thoroughly pitched without-side, to counteract the spattering of muddy roads, and permit fording rivers without too much seepage. And spare saddles should be carried in the event the coach collapsed.

VI

In speaking of the conditions of travel we have not mentioned expenses. If a nobleman, instead of making his tour, remained at home and enjoyed several London seasons, he might easily have spent near the large sum that he would have laid out in travels. In any case a gentleman was a gentleman precisely because his mind was not clogged with material considerations. On the other hand, a prudent individual, who had not the means of passing for an Englishman of fashion, might certainly live both well and reasonably in Italy. It was not uncommon for officers and others of modest resources to have kept the finest company in such courteous places as Florence and Siena, and to have enjoyed every comfort except a carriage at a cost of less than one hundred pounds sterling per year, including clothes and incidentals.[28] During the second half of the century genteel apartments in Venice were to be had for eight to about eleven lire a day including dinner. The lira was worth about five pence English. And it was estimated that a single man might live well in Venice, keeping one servant for about seventy pounds a year,[29] or that he might live very well indeed with both servant and gondola for about

---

28 Martyn, *op. cit.*, p. xx.
29 *Ibid.*, pp. xx-xxi.

one hundred and twenty pounds per year, there being some expenses which he must add to this, such as theatres, coffee-house, clothes, etc., and other costs a single man might readily undertake in Venice. Boswell during the first seven months of 1765 contrived to rid his father of £460 sterling, which that Scottish gentleman observed was far beyond what his income could afford. He hinted that £460 was too much to pay for the acquisition of a language, which around Edinburgh would be no better than Arabic.[30]

Before a tourist set out on foreign ground, he usually secured his money in the form of circular exchange notes or traveller's cheques given for any sum, from twenty pounds upwards, and negotiable without charges in the principal towns of Europe and in Italy at Leghorn, Nice, Florence, Genoa, Parma, Milan, Rome, Trieste, Turin, Venice and Naples.[31]

With his affairs thus prepared, one might stiffen the sinews, summon up the blood, and take courage from the words of the seasoned voyager Lassels. "Ulysses," he had written, "Is set forth by Homer as the wisest of the Grecians, because he had travelled much, and had seen . . . the cittyes and customs of many men." Then he added with contempt:

> So his son Telemachus is held for a very shallow witted man; and Homer gives us the reason, because his mother Penelope, instead of sending him abroad to see forrain countryes, had allwayes kept him at home, and so made of him a meere Ono-cephalus, and a homeling Mammacuth.[32]

And nothing could be more disgraceful to an Englishman.

30 Boswell, *Private Papers . . . from Malahide Castle*, V, 90.
31 Martyn, *op. cit.*, pp. xii-xlvi.
32 Lassels, *op. cit.*, preface, p. [iv].

Mountains and the sea in the late 18th century. View of Pirano — Capo d'Istria at Gulf of Trieste

CHAPTER II.

MOUNTAINS AND THE SEA

On earth, in air, amidst the seas and skies,
Mountainous heaps of wonders rise;
Whose tow'ring strength will ne'er submit
To reason's batt'ries, or the mines of wit.

Matt. Prior

I

Curiosity concerning the homeland of their long-bearded ancestors undoubtedly hurried some tourists to Germany, whence they passed by way of the Brenner to Bolzano or from Imperial Vienna to Venice and so into Italy. By far the greater part of them, however, drove straight on for Paris, then down the valley of the Loire, and along the Rhone through the tall poplars of Lyon and the vineyards and the villas of Languedoc. The border of the Duchy of Savoy in pre-Napoleonic times lay about fifty miles due east of Lyonnaise, and the tourist frequently went thither to Chamberry and Lanslebourge, and then over Mt. Cenis to Susa and Turin, capital of the Kingdom of Sardinia. This most popular way, from Lyon to Turin, was a journey of 193 English miles.[1]

There were also three main ways from Switzerland into Italy: the Little St. Bernard near Mont Blanc, the Simplon connecting Geneva and the Rhone headwaters to Lago Maggiore, and St. Gotthard some miles to the east, which also led into Lago Maggiore.[2]

Following these routes — any of them — forced the old traveller into long direct contact with the awful power of rude nature and had a tremendous effect on his imagination and on eighteenth century artistic and literary taste.

Oliver Goldsmith went along the Vienna-Venice road,

---

[1] See appendix I on Martyn's Table of Mileages in his *Gentleman's Guide in his Tour through Italy.*
[2] Lassels, *The Voyage of Italy,* pp. 23-72.

15

where he "disputed his passage" with very little satisfaction either to himself or the unbewitched upland peasants. It was there he discovered that

> the rude Carinthian boor
> Against the houseless stranger shuts the door.[3]

There is a good-humoured account of this boorishness in Dr. John Moore's *View of Society and Manners in Italy*. Just what indignities were suffered by the friendless and penniless Goldsmith, we will never know. Twenty years or so later in the same country the Duke of Hamilton, accompanied by Dr. Moore and servants was rolling briskly in the direction of Venice. Coming to a little town — "miserable" as usual — about sundown, the Duke had determined to press on rather than stop. As the carriage rattled into the post-yard, Dr. Moore, spying the master sitting in a cloud of pipe smoke with his chair leaned back against the post-house door, called out to get ready fresh horses, and to lose no time, adding with an air of importance, that he could not possibly stay a moment.

The vehicle stopped. Ostlers immediately began unhitching the horses. Doctor Moore stepped out and was told that if he were indeed in such a hurry, not a finger would be raised to detain him, but that meanwhile there were no other horses to carry him on — that all the horses of the post were reserved for the use of the Archduke, who had set out from Vienna to Venice about the same time.

The Doctor then wanted to know when horses — any horses — would be available, and was told — the next day, or the following day, or the day after that — no one could say! He and the Duke exchanged glances and agreed that it was a great hardship "to be stopped short, so unexpectedly at a little paltry inn," but they resolved to bear their "misfortunes with firmness and equanimity."[4]

The postmaster accordingly was instructed to prepare his beds and a good supper with some of his best wine. Instead of hearing these injunctions with pleasure, he replied that he had no wine except what he would drink himself, that he would

---

[3] Goldsmith, "The Traveller," lines 3-4.
[4] Moore, *View of Society and Manners in Italy*, p. 5.

only give suppers to his family, and that when it came to beds, he only had one for himself and his wife and his child, and that it was doubtful that his Grace and the Doctor could enter it too without some confusion. "I had not hitherto perceived," Moore wrote, "that this man's house was not an inn." *That* — and the postmaster indicated it with the stem of his pipe — was across the street. Very little time was required to discover that all its food had been consumed and that all its rooms were taken. They found the same situation in another little inn, and were refused entry to every private house. The Doctor was annoyed. After all a Duke was a Duke — not to mention that an Englishman was an Englishman. Nevertheless he went gently back to the postmaster, who was still sitting by the door smoking his pipe.

"I informed him of our bad success, and, in a more soothing tone of voice . . . begged to know how we were to dispose of ourselves that night."[5] The postmaster replied that this was more than he could tell. Meanwhile, as rain had begun to fall, and as the evening became disagreeably cold, he wished them a very good night, went into the house, and carefully bolted the door. "No philosopher, ancient or modern, ever supported the distress of others with more equanimity than this man."[6]

The conclusion of this Carinthian story had a moral for tourists in Italy. As a last resort they turned to the Duke's Italian servant. He stood innocently shrugging his shoulders and kept his eyes fixed on the ground, while he said in a low tone, "Cent'ore di maninconia non pagono un quattrino di debito,"[6] and then he walked off into the night with the air of one to whom the situation was quite familiar. Very shortly the superior of a convent had taken them to a little house, where they were served sauerkraut, and salad, and good wine, and afterwards slept in delightful beds. Some days later in Venice this story amused their Royal Highnesses, the Archduke and Archduchess of Austria.

II

The great majority of English travellers, however, had no contact with the "rude Carinthian boor." They went direct through Savoy to the western ports of Italy.

---

[5] *Ibid.,* pp. 5-6.
[6] *Ibid.,* p. 6.

One of the most famous places visited along this route was the Grande Chartreuse, a day's journey from Grenoble. The story of the founding of this remarkable institution, and a fine account of several days spent there, may be seen in William Beckford's *Italy*, which taken altogether is one of the most appealing and poetic of eighteenth century travel books. In no part of the author's writings do his peculiarly evocative gifts shine more than in his pages on the Grande Chartreuse.[7] It was at this place, incidentally, that Thomas Gray left his famous ode in Latin. It was here that Doctor Johnson intended to leave his ode in Latin. It was here that almost every Englishman forced his genius into poetry.

Towards the end of the century a gay traveller by the name of Thomas Watkins went up to the Chartreuse and was treated by the monks "with good breeding and hospitality."

> Whilst dinner was preparing, we diverted ourselves with a book called the Album ... We found on inspection, many of our acquaintance, and such a medly of poetry and prose, as never was collected before. Oh! that some wag would transcribe these books, and publish copies of them in England. Then would you see invocations to the Muses, addresses to the Dryads, odes to the Monks for a dinner, descriptions of the place, and sentiments, Oh what sentiments ... but the best is you would also see who were the authors of these inestimable compositions ... I will answer for the sale of such a book, and must again say, I wish somebody would undertake it.[8]

A few years after this, in 1792, when Robert Gray asked to see "the Album," he was told by the monks that someone had appropriated it recently.[9] Perhaps it is now in England.

However the traveller went, whether by sea from Antibes to Genoa or over the mountains, he would be reminded of the greatness of Rome in its Golden Age, when one could take the Julian Augustan Way at Nice and follow it to Genoa along the Ligurian coast, from Genoa pass through Lucca and Pisa on the Aemilian Way, and from Pisa go straight on to Rome,

---

7 William Beckford, *Italy*, pp. 215-245.

8 Watkins, *Italy, Sicily ... in a Series of Letters*, p. 178.

9 Robert Gray, *Letters during a Journey through Germany, Switzerland and Italy*, [in 1791 and 1792], p. 217.

just as we can today. But in the eighteenth century the fall of Rome was, as Gibbon said, "still felt by the nations of the earth."[10] More than one tourist decided not to acknowledge the lack of a road. Shelley's friend, Harriet Williams, wrote of a large number of oxen, horses, mules and other cattle streaming out of the Alps on a day in 1794. They had dragged a great man's carriage "from the bottom of the mountain that he might have the fame of crossing St. Gothard's in a vehicle with wheels." She added that the monks there had "no difficulty in conjecturing . . . that if it was not the Emperor or the Burgomaster of Berne, the two greatest personages they knew of, it must be an English Lord . . . as our countrymen are known to be the only travelling philosophers who make experiments of this kind."[11] Usually carriages were unbolted, and laid piecemeal on the backs of mules, together with trunks, tool chests, *chaises percees*, lanterns, kettles, swords and beds. This caravan went ahead as rapidly as possible. The tourists themselves were carried over on open chairs lashed to a pair of poles. And they sometimes felt real qualms as the carriers pranced along the edges of precipices and leaped from rock to rock like mountain goats. Almost everyone was amazed at the chasms into which he nearly fell. Some recommended to their friends going by water. Yet Lord Abingdon actually transported his hounds and went hunting on Mt. Cenis and others like John Ray stopped there for days to botanize. Mrs. Piozzi gave the truth of the matter when she wrote that the "portion of terror excited either by real or fancied dangers on the way, is just sufficient to mingle with the pleasure and make one feel the full effect of the sublimity."[12]

During a great part of the year snow lay on the pass. Gray and Walpole speak of being "swathed in beaver bonnets, beaver gloves, beaver stockings, muffs and bear-skins."[13] They even had bandages laid over their eyes to save them from the glare. And at the top they found fat juicy clouds that hung "glouting." A favorite pastime was discharging pistols to start an avalanche. If not a dangerous passage, it was a memorable

---

[10] See paragraph one of *The Decline and Fall*.
[11] Lambert, *Grand Tour*, p. 87.
[12] Piozzi, *Observations and Reflections made in the Course of a Journey through France, Italy and Germany.* 2 vols. London, 1789, I, 42.
[13] Thomas Gray, *Correspondence*, I, 140, note 6.

one and worthy of the land to which it carried thousands of delighted travellers. Speaking of the torrents, crags, snows, blasted trees, the clouds about him and below him, Gray wrote back enthusiastically to his mother, "It is impossible to conceive without seeing them; and though we had heard many strange descriptions of the scene, none of them at all came up to it."[14]

III

A voyage on the blue Mediterranean might be more comfortable. If the wind were right and steady, it would be possible to go along the enchanting coast mile after mile, and scarcely move from the shade of the lateen sail, but the chances were against it. When Addison tried, he had gone as far as Savona, where the water became so rough that he was forced to make the best of his way by land along the *corniche* on a road much more difficult than that over Mount Cenis.[15] John Evelyn had almost been wrecked at Savona. "An Irish Bishop and his brother, a priest, were confessing some as at the article of death,"[16] until unexpectedly the wind fell, and the perfume of orange trees and jasmine streamed out many leagues over the sea.

Smollett also went by sea, and was blown into San Remo. He went to a place which his captain had assured him was the finest hotel in all the Genoese Riviera. It may have been, but he found such misery and dirt in it as would have discredited a foul hedge saloon in England, and he seems to have been surprised that the keeper was out taking a walk instead of sitting in his kitchen waiting for windfalls. After a little delay, during which Smollett had time to be thoroughly agitated by the disgusting state of affairs in Italy, the owner came and assigned bedchambers; and this gave him another subject for a diatribe. In fact the reader cannot help rejoicing in Smollett's misfortunes. When he stayed in a good inn, it was all very dull indeed. But his room at San Remo was somewhat cramped. There was just space for two beds and "an old rotten table covered with dried figs." (This was thoughtful.)

14 *Ibid.,* I, 126.
15 Addison, *Remarks,* p. 17.
16 Lambert, *op. cit.,* p. 23.

There were two "crazy chairs." The walls, once whitewashed, were draped in spider webs and blotched with dirt "of all sorts" he asserts, and the brick floor had not been swept "for half a century." He had supper in another room as bad in its way as his bedroom and he "fared villainously."[17] To add to his vexation, the wind next morning was as high as ever and he was compelled to lie over for another day. The second inn along the Riviera was so terrible that he even wished he was back again at San Remo. When he went to bed there, he had not rested five minutes before he felt something crawling on various parts of his body, and "taking a light to examine, perceived above a dozen large bugs."[18] That was enough. He leaped out, wound his overcoat around him, and remained up the whole night sometime sitting and sometimes lying on a great chest in the hallway. At his next to last stop along the coast, he rested in an inn that was tolerable, and in which he had no good cause to complain of the beds; but what did bother him was that owing to the hot weather "there was a very offensive smell, which proceeded from some skins of beasts new killed, that were spread out to dry on an out-house in the yard."[19] At Lerici, the end of the sea excursion, he claimed that he was almost poisoned at supper, that his rooms were so stuffy that he was nearly smothered until he thought of lying out of his bed again, this time on four chairs, with his leather portmanteau under his head — for two reasons we can be sure, as Smollett was fully convinced by then of the fundamental dishonesty of all keepers of public houses.[20]

Of course this gave an uninviting idea of travel in Italy to those who stayed in England. They would not be likely to imagine after reading Smollett's account that English businessmen moving between southern France and Leghorn along that coast made themselves quite comfortable by carrying their own mattresses and cooking gear, so that at the worst they could run into harbors and sleep on board.[21] Experienced travellers would never stay at a small town inn. Nor would an Italian unless he had been excommunicated. Monasteries were always

17 Smollett, *Travels through France and Italy,* II, 33-34.
18 *Ibid.,* II, , 38.
19 *Ibid.,* II, 48.
20 *Ibid.,* II, 50.
21 Smollett reports this himself; *op. cit.,* II, 50.

open with bedchambers and good food ready; and the appreciative wayfarer paid by leaving money for the performance of masses and saying of prayers.[22] But the fireside voyagers of England, and the blighted, caustic newspaper scribblers in London could not be expected to know this, and it is not surprising to find in the *Critical Review* for May, 1766, some one querying with reference to Smollett's account, "Is not this . . . sufficient to cure our travelling gentry of their itch for novelties? novelties that afford nothing but a variety of wretchedness."[23]

IV

No gentlemen, however, would be deterred by a novelist's tale of trouble. A few years after Smollett, Sir James Edward Smith, M.D., F.R.S., President of the Linnean Society, was stuck at San Remo. "The sea was so rough, the captain would not venture out."[24] So he took up his abode at a small inn. The wind blew hard and was very cold. His room had no chimney, and was warmed only by a brazier, which gave off fumes but not much heat. The windows, except in the upper part, had no glass. The inn keeper, to reconcile him to his suffering, told him that the Duke and Duchess of Gloucester had, the year before, 1785, slept in the very same bed that had fallen to his share. And even that consolation was ill-founded; for he learned afterward, when he had the honor of paying his devoirs to their Royal Highnesses at Naples, that fatigued as they had been at San Remo, they really could not go to bed, and consequently had stayed awake until the wind had died down and they were able to put out again with their sixteen feluccas. Their Royal Highnesses also informed him of what the inn people had concealed, that an English consul resided in the town, who, if he had known, would have taken upon himself all the duties of a host. "This is mentioned," he says, "for the benefit of all whom it may concern in the future."[25] It was more or less expected that genteel tourists would travel across a European web of courtesy, seldom condescending to

[22] Baretti, *An Account of the Manners and Customs of Italy: with observations on the Mistakes of some Travellers*, pp. 26-27.
[23] *Critical Review*, Vol. 21, May, 1766, p. 331.
[24] Smith, *Tour on the Continent*, I, 212.
[25] *Ibid.*, I, 213.

commercial arrangements. And the guide books suggested making up a list of all resident ministers along the itinerary and if possible procuring personal letters of introduction to each one of them.

No gentleman making the Grand Tour, properly speaking, would walk, any more than a Medieval knight would ride in the cart of a peasant. The act lacked dignity. But impatient as he was with San Remo and having no more relish for the sea captains, Sir James took temporary leave of his travelling companion, Younge, and began to scramble over the cliffs toward Genoa. As a botanist he would have more to look at even though it was December, and so he went up and down the rough foot trails and mule tracks for many days, and stayed in places which were not in the least suitable. In approaching the town of Finale, he says that he took a wrong path down a long steep hill to the edge of a stream. When he saw his mistake, it was too late. The only bridge was a great distance away, and to reach it, he would have had to climb up the hill again. So he unlaced his shoes and stripped off his stockings and waded through. As there was a good deal of ice in the water this gave him a chill, and when he arrived at another tumble-down inn, he inhaled such a quantity of fumes from a brazier in the common room that he fell senseless to the floor and had to be carried out and laid on the ground. He suggests this was hardly necessary as the inn had no glass at all — only shutters — which were kept open in the daytime to save oil for the lamps, so that the inhabitants sat in the wind and rain no matter whether they were inside or outside.[26]

V

When the traveller went by sea the worst might be no more than a dash of salt water added to his vermicelli soup aboard a tartane.[27] Or it might be no more than an uncomfortably stiff gale, or glassy sweltering days of waiting. It might be no more than having to stop in out of the way places, like Cap Corse, or Elba,[28] or even more inconvenient and remote little ports. There is no record of anyone's being forced onto the

26 *Ibid.*, I, 224.
27 Lockhart Muirhead, *Journals of Travels*, p. 383.
28 Swinburne, *Travels in the Two Sicilies*, I, 30-40.

Isle of Monte Cristo. But Christopher Hervey, Esq. in 1760 was blown to Capraia, which from the coasts of Corsica or the mouth of the Arno, looks like a jagged blue fin swimming on the sea. There were no hotels, when Hervey landed there, and he went about from house to house, trying to find a room. But the houses were small and well inhabited. Finally he was admitted to one, and shown into "his" room. Shortly a scuffle broke out in another part of the house. There were furious words. Maledictions flew thick and fast, and it seemed that blood would soon follow. The patron, Genoese by origin, had, it seemed, given up the room of his son-in-law, a mere Capraian. The son-in-law threatened to send for the police, who in fact soon arrived, and carried him off to jail. Hervey felt some compunction at being the immediate cause of so much domestic friction. He thought of going to the police to obtain the prisoner's release. And he did — next day.[29] Meanwhile the bed was very comfortable.

One young man on the way to Rome in January 1740 to study painting reported:

> The winds sailed us betwixt Genoa and Corsica; where we were beating about for a week, and truly with continual and imminent danger; for in the day time a calm always came upon us, and storms with contrary winds succeeded in the night. Amidst all this, it was very happy for us, that a south wind did not rise, for if it had, we must have been inevitably driven on the rocks which lye on the coast of the states of Genoa. Tho' the discipline and danger of the sea generally causes in fresh water men various evacuations; yet, to my great inconvenience, it had but half its effect upon me; so that at my landing . . . I was obliged to have the advice of a physician.[30]

Some travellers speak of being weathered in at Monaco, where they were struck by the "romantic"[31] appearance of the rock and its fortress, but found little else of interest. Others were becalmed. This meant rowing, sometimes for whole days or nights. There was a real danger, however, of southern squalls. Most captains absolutely refused to set out when bad weather seemed to be in the offing, and most travellers, with years of voyaging ahead of them, sat down and waited. But

---

29 Hervey, *Letters from Portugal, Spain, Italy and Germany*, II, 381-2.
30 Russell, *Letters from a Young Painter*, p. 17.
31 Smollett, *op. cit.*, II, 31.

not Joseph Baretti on his way back to Italy after ten years of England. His captain had determined to rest at Antibes on the way to Nice. Baretti remonstrated. The captain was firm. A storm was expected. He would not put his life, or his crew or his ship in jeopardy. And that was that. But Baretti had to get on. He would pay well if the captain set out. So they did. But by the time they had gone about four miles Baretti began to regret his handsome payment. A sudden southwest wind, set upon them. Huge waves piled up and foamed against the cliffs. The rowers struggled in desperate silence for about three hours, listening to the roar and boom of the sea, until they came in sight of Nice. Baretti looked through his pocket telescope and saw people ashore watching, as he learned later, to see the vessel crash against an ugly rock called the "Cobbler." What made his case seem past hope was that the Nizzards, unable to imagine how anyone could leave Antibes in such weather, had taken them to be part of a crew of Barbary pirates. So they were left to their own shifts, not because it was unnecessary to rescue infidels, but because it was considered very dangerous to approach an African crew, which he says, was always assumed to have the black plague aboard. The instant it was known that they were Europeans, a bark with twenty-four rowers put out. A line was thrown to Baretti's vessel when it was only forty yards from the "Cobbler." Having recovered from the shock, Baretti went on by sea to Genoa. He had no choice. It was November and snow was already deep on the mountains along the coast.[32]

---

[32] Baretti, *A Journey from London to Genoa*, pp. 132-143.

Maecenus' palace stables — "Of this edifice, once the resort of Augustus and the great men of the celebrated period, nothing more is at present to be seen than the remains of an inferior portico. A brand of the Anio glowing with tumult through the dark and lofty arches of this building, increases the interesting and mysterious character of the place."

Pre-historic cave near Viterbo to show arch.

CHAPTER III

ON CLASSIC ROADS

Then up rose these HEROES *as brisk as the sun,*
Their horses like his, were prepared to run.

Matt. Prior

I

The eighteenth century route through Italy appears on a map in something like the shape of a necklace tying together Genoa, Turin, the lakes, Venice, Rimini, Ancona, Terni, Rome; then Bologna, Florence, Siena, and Rome with Naples and its bay a sapphire pendant deep in the Mediterranean. A small number of adventurers, a very small number indeed, penetrated lower Italy and Sicily, lands lying as it were, in the very heart of civilization, but which were then, and are even now, buried in eternal blue oblivion by an excess of light.

In a land of millennial culture like Italy, and probably more in Italy than in any other, one walks or drives today along roads shadow-laced beneath clear skies among vineyarded and olive-clad hills that have been the same since the age of myth. Compare a map of Roman places of the Augustan age showing the roads through Italy[1] and you will see how amazingly they coincide with the *strade principali* of our own century; but many of the roads are older than Rome, and no one can say for how many centuries white oxen have dragged their wains along them.

By the time English travellers began passing through Italy in great numbers, the main routes were familiar to all touring Europeans and had been since the Renaissance. In 1580, for example, Montaigne made what amounted to a Grand Tour in the hope of easing the anguish of gallstones.[2] Entering by the Lago di Garda, he went through Verona and Padua to

---

[1] Shepherd, William, *Historical Atlas*, Henry Holland Company, New York, 1929, pp. 26-31; see any good contemporary map, *e.g.*, those published by The Touring Club Italiano.

[2] Montaigne, *Journal du Voyage en Italie, passim.*

27

Venice, and from Venice he crossed the Po Valley to Bologna, went over the Apennines to Florence, and dropped down the classic road to Rome by way of Siena, Buonconvento, Acquapendente, past Monte Amiata and the lake of Bolsena, through Montefiascone and Viterbo. At Rome he made what later became standard side trips to Ostia and Tivoli. Then, turning north again, he labored through the high barrier of the Apennines once more to Ancona on the Adriatic coast. Montaigne was an excellent traveller, who according to the diary kept by his servant, would leap out of bed gay as a lark at the prospect of a long wearying day on the road, and who was never so sure he was going the right way as when he knew he was being carried to an unknown town, and who hated reaching a destination as much as reaching the end of a good book. At Ancona therefore, rather than roll along the easy coastal roads and into the plains of Lombardy, he swung back into the mountains and climbed into unvisited hill-places until he came to Florence. From Florence he went down the Arno Valley to Bagni di Lucca where he tried drinking the waters for his gallstones. But neither the waters of Bagni di Lucca or of any other town had the good effects of wandering on new roads, and the greater part of Montaigne's seventeen months in Italy were passed in shifting from place to place in Tuscany and the province of Rome. At last he went North to Turin and climbed over Mt. Cenis.

A little more than a decade later Fines Moryson,[3] the famous Elizabethan maker of itineraries, toured Italy in much the same circuit. He saw Naples and its environs, the only part of the Grand Tour not performed by Montaigne.

II

Two hundred years ago Italian roads would not have been as beautifully paved as many of them are now, and yet the roads were well kept, and for the most part better than the roads of England. Travellers were particularly impressed by the excellence of the highways in Tuscany and in the Dominions of the Pope. In the high Apennines, which had to be crossed twice at least, the ways were rocky and wild, and as

[3] Moryson, *Itinerary*, Glasgow, 1908.

they sometimes become rather tenuous even now, it is likely they did so in the eighteenth century. There are some stretches where the original flints of the Romans crop out, and set on edge as they are, they present very rugged surfaces to the weary hoof and shaking wheel.

During the sad seasons of Winter and early Spring when the gray rain comes down for days, the roads of Lombardy were sometimes flooded. Sterne was detained ten days at Turin by drowned fields.[4] Some writers complain of the lack of bridges, and in fact fording creeks and ferrying over broad rivers appears to have been very common in the Po Valley.[5] It hardly seems necessary to mention the perennial problem of mud. Arthur Young[6] told of trudging through soggy fields beside his coach, which wallowed along at the rate of about one and one half miles an hour with seven struggling horses floundering before it. In some emergencies tall white oxen were added to the horses, and in parts of Italy the still more powerful buffalo would be used to extricate a sunken vehicle.[7]

III

The actual time needed to go from place to place in Italy would vary with the season, the weights of the carriages, and the dispositions of horses, drivers and passengers. A traveller moving about during the Summer or Autumn could always allow a day for the passage of Mt. Cenis, though it was only fourteen miles long, and another day for reaching Turin. From Turin two long days, of ten or twelve hours each would bring him to Genoa. Milan was two days from both Genoa and Turin. From either Genoa or Milan it was a rather long four-day trip to Bologna, a pivotal point of northern Italy. From Bologna one passed over the Apennines to Florence (sixty-three miles without any good inns) in one long hard drive often made by moonlight. From Bologna to Venice was 102 miles or just less than twenty hours. From Bologna it was

---

4 Sterne, *Letters of Laurence Sterne,* ed. Curtis, Oxford, Clarendon Press, 1935, p. 263.

5 Wright, *Some Observations Made in Travelling through France, Italy . . . in 1720-1722,* pp. 33-34.

6 Young, *Travels during the Years 1787, 1788 1789 . . .,* p. 267.

7 Wright, *op. cit.,* p. 32.

three hundred and five miles via the Adriatic and the central Apennines to Rome, a journey requiring about sixty-eight hours travelling, not counting stops of any kind. A week or ten days should be allowed at least for so long and so vigorous an excursion. From Florence down to Rome through Siena was usually done in four or five days. The one hundred and fifty-two miles from Rome to Naples required a little more than one entire day of twenty-four hours and was often done without stopping to sleep, as the only way to lodge comfortably was by obtaining letters at Rome for the Ginetti palace at Velletri or the Convent of St. Erasmo near Mola di Gaeta.[8]

IV

The genteel way of travel was by the post. And it was not inexpensive. It seems probable that touring in this fashion could not have cost less than twenty-five cents a mile or much more than a dollar (of our money) a mile per coach. If a tourist wished to avoid the expense of posting, as Smollett did of course, he could arrange with a *vetturino,* who would furnish carriage and horses, or mules, from point to point at a fixed price, and this was the mode of travelling among the Italians — even those of condition. The price, however, had to be fixed before-hand and in writing or the stranger would be likely to find it not fixed at all. In making these arrangements, the *vetturino* would always ask at least one third more than he would accept, and Englishmen were advised to serve their own and each other's interests by constantly beating down the prices. But even with the best understanding before-hand, a sly *vetturino* sometimes hoped to augment his profits, once he was on his way and had the tourist at his mercy.

One writer relates that in his passage from Loreto into the vast mountains that stood between him and Rome, his two postillions became quite obstreperous. "They took us up those hills and sung and talked all the way as if they had been driving a load of hay." He often remonstrated with them about their speed, which seemed to him to be excessive, but they took no notice and went as they pleased. "Later one of them with a demanding air whisked his hat into the chaise, and looking

---

[8] See appendix 2.

the other way, asked for money." They dashed his hat aside and told him to get about his business. "The fellow then seized our harness, and would scarce let it go, till we showed him a pistol."[9]

The same traveller, Adam Walker, when he was returning North through Lombardy, had arrived at Reggio, travelling by the post. He had paid the postillion. The horses were changed. He was just setting off for Parma, when the postillion who had dismounted, rushed up again and demanded his fare. "We were confounded at the assurance of the man." A dispute arose, and in a few moments several hundreds of people had closed in around them, snarling and siding with the postillion. "The post-master would take out his horses, except we pay the man, which we positively refused, till we were surrounded by thousands, who began to be very riotous," and seemed to be on the point of a serious attack, when a gentleman of magisterial air pushed through the mob, and asked the cause of the trouble. "We told him the plain fact, which satisfied him we were right."[10] The postillion was reprimanded, and then assaulted by the crowd, as the Englishmen rattled out of town.

V

"Italian inns," says Martyn in his guide book, "are generally represented as detestable." And he adds, "Some of them are certainly bad enough; but there are many very good ones, especially in large towns and on those roads frequented by foreigners."[11] Many of the English were partial judges. Some of them were merely unfortunate travellers. Inasmuch as many readers have learned about Italian inns from Smollett, who stopped in poor ones, it is worth offsetting some of the prejudice created by his eloquence by mentioning that Sir James Edward Smith, M.D., who travelled twenty years later never "discovered dirty sheets in Italy, though always very scrupulous in . . . examination on that head." He remarks that "England is . . . the most indelicate of all civilized nations with respect

---

9 Walker, *Ideas suggested on the Spot . . . in Italy,* p. 203.
10 *Ibid.,* p. 366.
11 Martyn, *op. cit.,* pp. iv-v.

to bed and table linen. Our great inns are less to be trusted about sheets than any abroad."[12]

Most tourists were not troubled by the inns, at least along the Grand Tour route, except when they had some particular misfortune that left them with no alternative but to sleep in a bad place.

VI

For a quick summary of all the probable accidents of the road one can do no better than review the tour of Dr. Smollett. His inspection of Italy, one of the fastest on record, was concluded in two months. It was meteoric. The passion he had for speed and economy multiplied his troubles. But Smollett loved suffering. It whetted his acerbity and gave his writing a lively tang. He might well have said, as Mark Twain did, "I make no pretense of showing any one how he *ought* to look at objects . . . beyond the sea — other books do that."[13]

At Buonconvento, not far south of Siena, he failed to give the usual *buona mano* to hostler, who in revenge, put two unbroke young horses in the traces. The party had just got beyond the town walls when both horses and postillion tumbled down together on the road with such kicking and jerking as seemed likely to beat the coach and baggage into a thousand pieces. Smollett, enraged, took his walking stick and went back into the village, where he had an enlightening conversation with an official of the post and received no other satisfaction than a fresh pair of horses, as the hostler, being a practical man, took some pains to keep out of range of his stick.[14] Then having passed safely across the heights of Radicofani, Smollett, was clipping along the undulant plain of Viterbo when his coach shuddered, listed and foundered with a broken axle.[15]

When he left Rome to return to Florence, Smollett decided, why it is hard to say, not to "consult the carte,"[16] as he put it. He wished to avoid a reengagement with the difficult moun-

12 Smith, *A Sketch of a Tour on the Continent,* I, 337.
13 See preface to Mark Twain's *Innocents Abroad.*
14 Smollett, *Travels through France and Italy,* II, 76.
15 *Ibid.,* II, 80.
16 *Ibid.,* II, 138.

tain of Radicofani and with this in mind asked the advice of a banker named Barazzi, the same who told young Gibbon that his father had cut off his allowance.[17] It may be that banker Barazzi had a sense of humor. At any rate he recommended that Smollett go through Terni to Florence. And he did. At first the road was deceptively easy, but afterwards, when it was too late to turn back, the coach began to soar into blue-gray heights among the clouds. And Smollett wrote:

> Great part of the way lies over steep mountains, or along the side of precipices, which render travelling in a carriage exceedingly tedious, dreadful and dangerous; and as for the public houses, they are in all respects the most execrable that I ever entered . . . The houses are abominably nasty, and generally destitute of provision; when eatables were found, we were almost poisoned by their cookery; their beds were without curtains, and their windows without glass . . . The first day we put up at what was called an excellent inn, where cardinals, prelates, and princes often lodged. Being a meagre day, there was nothing but bread, eggs and anchovies in the house. I went to bed without supper and lay in a pallet, where I was half devoured by vermin.[18]

And the last part of the road was so bad, that he did not fail to "bestow a thousand benedictions per diem on the banker Barazzi."[19]

On one of the steepest ascents in Italy into a town of any importance, namely Perugia, Smollett's horses were drawn backward and almost over a cliff.[20] Fortunately someone thrust a stone under one of the wheels and saved him. Two or three days later on the way from Arezzo to Florence, Smollett's postillions scourging the horses through rain and mud with great ferocity, nearly rolled him into a ditch about eight feet deep. He and his wife leaped out just as one of the horses slipped over the edge, where he hung by the neck, "so that he was almost strangled before he could be disengaged from the traces."[21] When Smollett got to Florence on foot about ten o'clock that night, rushing through the pitch dark in what he hoped was the direction of the only open gate, he was swear-

---

17 Gibbon, *Private Letters* ed. Prothero, London, Murray, 1897, pp. 71-72.
18 Smollett, *op. cit.,* II, 138.
19 *Ibid.,* II, 143.
20 *Ibid.,* II, 142.
21 *Ibid.,* II, 146.

ing horribly to frighten away all bad characters. He was covered with mud. His greatcoat was heavy with water. He was sweating feverishly inside it as he strode along with his weeping wife on one arm. Nevertheless, when he had changed his clothes, eaten a hearty supper, and warmed himself by the fire in Mrs. Vanini's English style hotel, he drank a glass of wine to the health of the banker Barazzi as the cause of his delight.[22]

VII

As has already been hinted by the experience of Smollett there was one place in Italy on the main road from Florence to Rome which was not easily forgotten by most travellers. Mt. Amiata, dark with vast forests of chestnut, stands on the southern border of Tuscany. Probably the most famous road in the world, the Francigena, so-called in remembrance of Northerners who have passed along it, twists high over the eastern slopes under the tower of Radicofani — a strange name that Horace Walpole played with, pretending that the Re di Cofano was one of the three kings who went to the birth of Christ.[23] This tower of rusty stone rising like a clenched fist against the sky can be seen at a distance of what was then a long day's trip. It looks down on a desolate waste, strangely shrivelled and treeless, not merely vacant, but oppressed with the dumb violence of gouged-out slag-coloured hills and by the ceaseless wind. A character in Boccaccio's tale of Ghino di Tacco says of this zone, "Messere, voi siete in parte venuto dove . . . le scomunicazioni e gl'interdetti sono scomunicati tutti."

In the highest part of this country is a bare-looking inn. As the modern driver speeds by in a cloud of dust, relieved to have made the hill without engine failure, and darts on to Rome, he might pass the inn without a glance. Usually within the portico, tethered to the pillars, there are half a dozen asses with grain sacks and jars of oil, wine and waters. And here and there is a rough-voiced *barocciaio* with the face of a brigand. As if to symbolize the ageless emptiness of the wind

---

22 *Ibid.*, II, 148-149, 157-158.
23 Walpole, *The Letters of Horace Walpole,* ed. Cunningham, London, Bentley, 1857, I, 51.

blasted summit, that reddish cracked bastion of Desiderius rakes the clouds. No one would stop there now, but in the eighteenth century everyone stopped there, prince or poet, Imperial Majesty,[24] churchmen, women, clerics, and of course their travelling servants and other thieves, because there was no other place to stop — not within a half day's journey.

Gray calls Radicofani "a terrible black hill," and the inn, once a hunting lodge of the Medici, seems not to have pleased him much, for he writes "your cellar is a palace in comparison; and your cat sups and lies much better than we did" there. At night he and Walpole stopped up their glassless windows by hanging the bedclothes on the shutters. And afterward they lay on the bedstraw in their coats. "Such are the conveniences in a road, that is, as it were, the great thoroughfare of all the world."[25]

About seven o'clock one cold and dismal evening the author of *Vathek* toiled slowly up the road to Radicofani. "My heart sank," he says. The wind increased and when he had arrived at the inn, every door and shutter in that hollow carcass of a building was slamming and rattling as though the spirit that dwelt upon the peak was about to exercise some terrible mystery. "My only spell to keep him at a distance was kindling an enormous fire." And for some time he peered along the dark passages, where a "grim fraternity of cats kept whisking backwards and forwards." He pitched his bed near the hearth "which glowed with embers, and crept under the coverlids, hardly venturing to go to sleep." He was scarcely settled when two or three of this mystic cabal came stalking through a little hole under the door of his room. "I insisted on their moving off faster than they had entered, and was surprised, when midnight came, to hear nothing more than their doleful mewings." Next day he writes, "I begin to despair of magical adventures, since none happened at Radicofani, which nature seems wholly to have abandoned."[26]

24 Dutens, *Memoires d'un Voyageur qui se repose,* p. 273.
25 Gray, *Correspondence,* I, 145.
26 William Beckford, *Italy,* pp. 161-163.

VIII

One unpleasant experience which Smollett somehow managed to miss, is reported by Arthur Young, the hard headed agricultural writer. This was a voyage, definitely not part of the Grand Tour proper, a voyage of a hundred and twenty-five miles by public barge from Venice to Ferrara. The passengers were packed in like "herrings in a barrel,"[27] sleeping at night on mattresses which all of the power of language could give no idea of, eating food that would make a dog sick, prepared by a cook who "takes snuff, wipes his nose with his fingers, and his knife with his handkerchief," while he doles out his "greasy treasure."[28] It is interesting to see that Sir James Edward Smith, whom we have already met wading through an icy stream in Liguria, actually enjoyed the same trip only a few months before Young came through. His barge was "very clean." He enjoyed unrolling the mattresses, which occasioned "much merriment" and awkward difficulties. He slept soundly although he admits that the passengers were "piled" rather than "laid" among chests, bales, and tubs. And when he discovered on his arrival at Venice that all the hotels were full, the barge captain undertook to find him a lodging *gratis,* and absolutely refused all subsequent offers of money or any other return for his civility.[29]

IX

The trouble with some who have left accounts of travels in Italy in the eighteenth century is that they were mere writers and consequently too poor to make the trip either in great style or in comfort. A gentleman would change horses at every post, regardless of cost, as he sped from city to city, and would seldom leave his coach for any country inn. And in the cities there were good hostelries, sometimes on the English plan, which of course made them much more expensive. These increased through the century. But a hotel, after all, was only a landing place. Within a few days a travelling gentleman would be someone's guest or would have taken his own villa or lodgings for a season in any of the principal cities, or in the fairy-tale town of Siena, *madre della lingua,* whither he often went first to acquire Italian.

---

27 Young, *op. cit.,* p. 262.
28 *Ibid.,* p. 263.
29 Smith, *op. cit.,* II, 360.

CHAPTER IV

SHINING PROSPECTS

Whereso'er I turn my ravish'd eyes,
Gay gilded scenes and shining prospects rise,
Poetic fields encompass me around
And still I seem to tread on classic ground.

Addison

I

The amazement that came upon old travellers in the Alps was something like a religious revelation. "The immediate sensations conveyed to the mind by the sight of such tremendous appearances," Mrs. Piozzi wrote, "must in every traveller be the same, a sensation of fulness never experienced before, a satisfaction that there *is* something great to be seen on earth — some object capable of contenting even fancy."[1] Among her chairmen on Mt. Cenis was one fellow, who had been in a gentleman's service twenty years in London and Dublin, and who at length had "begged his discharge, chusing to retire and finish his days a peasant on these mountains, where he first opened his eyes upon scenes that made all other views of nature insipid to his taste."[2]

Thomas Gray, writing to his friend West from Turin as he went into Italy, said that he had not yet seen any of those famous works of art that were to change and improve the traveller: "But those of Nature have astonished me beyond expression."[3] In climbing up to the Grande Chartreuse, he says he cannot "remember to have gone ten paces without an exclamation, that there was no restraining," and he added "There are certain scenes that would awe an atheist into belief." The horrid cliffs and crags, the hanging forests of pine, the fuming, thundering torrent made the "most solemn, the

---

[1] Piozzi, *Observations and Reflections*, I, 36.
[2] *Ibid.*, I, 42.
[3] Gray, *Correspondence*, I, 128.
[4] *Ibid.*, I, 122.

most romantic"[4] scenes he ever beheld. About two generations
later Wordsworth, describing his passage through the Simplon
wrote with much the same enthusiasm of

> *Torrents shooting from the clear blue sky.*
> *The rocks that muttered close upon our ears.*
> *Black drizzling crags that spake by the wayside*
> *As if a voice were in them, the sick sight*
> *And giddy prospect of the raving stream . . .*[5]

John Dennis passed over Mt. Cenis about a decade before
Addison went into Italy, and wrote of a "delightful horror,
a terrible joy."

> I wish I had force to do right to this renowned passage of
> the Alps . . . If these hills were first made with the world as
> has been a long time thought, and Nature designed them only
> as a mound to enclose the garden of Italy; then we may well
> say . . . that her careless and irregular and boldest strokes are
> most admirable. For the Alps are works which she seems to have
> designed and executed too in fury . . . Transporting pleasures
> followed the sight of the Alps, and what transports think you
> were those, that were mingled with horrors, and sometimes al-
> most with despair?[6]

Most travellers today would think no more of going through
the Swiss Alps by rail or of taking a plush seat for a flight
above them, than they would think of sitting down by their
lamps at home, to read a stirring tale of adventure. The notion of fear — real fear seems faintly ridiculous. And so when
we read Adam Walker's account of his journey from Inns-
bruck to Trento "stunned by the mountain passes," along
roads so frightful, "that my head turned giddy whenever I
ventured to look over our protecting parapet," our sympathy is
not touched. Nevertheless he "dismounted, and run [sic] on
foot on the opposite side of the road, to avoid seeing the vast
profundity below."[7]

II

If a traveller went by water from the South of France into
Genoa or Leghorn, his imagination might also be surprised.
Smollett, passing Capo di Noli, "a very high perpendicular

---

[5] Wordsworth, *Prelude,* Book VI.
[6] Dennis, *Miscellanies in Prose and Verse.* London, 1692, pp. 132-140.
[7] Walker, *Ideas suggested on the Spot . . . in Italy,* p. 106.

rock or mountain washed by the sea," found that "waves dashing against the rocks and caverns make such an awful noise," that one cannot hear, "without a secret horror."[8] Addison had also written of the mountains, the olive trees, the beautiful gardens, the "wild thyme, Lavender, Rosemary, Balm, and Myrtle."[9] He said, "It is so romantic a scene that it has always probably given occasion to" myths and fables. And then he thought of Homer.

Sailing eastward into Italy under the marvellous coast, with the sea purple as the skin of unrubbed grapes — so ruffled with the powdery white caps blown about by gusts and spreading a silky surface beneath the sun, one will suddenly think of wine, and understand perhaps for the first time Homer's phrase "the wine-dark sea." And as one scans the water seething like fields of grain blowing and blowing for miles before him, he may see the meaning of another figure — one of the most beautiful in literature — "Phorcys, Lord of the unharvested seas."

Addison concluded that it was not possible to know where Ulysses sailed, though that place where he was then sailing himself was like a "world of the poet's own making." Yet it is

> *Uncertain whether, by the winds conveyed*
> *On real seas to real shores he strayed;*
> *Or by the fable driv'n from coast to coast,*
> *In new imaginary worlds was lost.*[10]

III

How many thousand gouty old English gentlemen, nodding by an English fire, have been followed by the azure sea into that iridescent Halcyon world, where eyes lift up again to the

---

8 Smollett, *Travels through France and Italy*, p. 36. Speaking of this route Smollett says, "Rome is betwixt four and five hundred miles distant from Nice, and one half of the way I was resolved to travel by water. Indeed there is no other way of going from Nice to Genoa, unless you take a mule, and clamber along the mountains at the rate of two miles an hour, and at the risque of breaking your neck every minute. . . . Certainly no person who travels to Italy, from England, Holland, France or Spain, would make a troublesome circuit to pass the Alps by the way of Savoy and Piedmont, if he could have the convenience of going post by the way of Aix, Antibes ,and Nice, along the side of the Mediterranean, and through the Riviera of Genoa, which from the sea affords the most agreeable and amazing prospect I ever beheld." p. 27.

9 Addison, *Remarks on the Several Parts of Italy*, p. [13].

10 *Ibid.*, p. 14.

Apennines and places that stirred the younger heart. "Italiam! Italiam! Rev. Martin Sherlock exclaimed in 1778, "I never knew a being who saw it without being enchanted; or who could speak of it without enthusiasm."[11] (He didn't know Mundungus then). Italy is "the country of the imagination," he continued. "If the landscapes of Claude Lorrain are justly preferred to all others, what is the reason of it? His landscapes are Italian landscapes."

> But when should I finish, if I should speak of the pictures of Italy? The most beautiful of the universe is that of Italy itself. Nature formed it in a happy moment, drew it in her grand style, and finished its parts with a perfection that it is impossible to describe. She seems to have made an effort to unite all her beauties in a single work; and, to give to her favourite master-piece all the advantages of which a picture is capable, she has contrasted its parts with a happiness that doubles their effects. Smiling ascents and fertile plains, majestic rivers and delightful lakes, rich hills and richer valleys, are disposed almost with art.
>
> But a continued profusion of beauties, though varied, would have satiated at length . . . Here is a chain of barren mountains, and there a vast and dreary marsh. Nor are the terrible beauties wanting; a burning volcano . . . frightful precipices . . . That is the picture; and this its frame; the Mediterranean and the Alps.[12]

Some eighteenth century descriptions are curious, such as Walpole's "millions of little hills tipt with villas,"[13] written of Tuscany between Florence and Siena. Another writer climbed the Asinelli tower in Bologna and saw as far as Milan, the Alps, the Apennines — in other words the whole pano-rama of the Po Valley — "gently swelling hills crowned with castles and monasteries; the roads and rivers looking like long ropes." [!][14]

There was something else obviously that fascinated old travellers to Italy — its classic history which they had learned at school. Thomas Watkins said that when he entered into

---

[11] Sherlock, *Letters from an English Traveller,* p. 156. This author was suitably equipped with Virgil in one pocket and Horace in the other. His en-thusiasm for Italy knew no bounds. "Of all the countries of the world," he wrote, "Italy is the most adorned by the arts. Of all the countries of the world she had the least need of them." And he quoted Rousseau as saying, "Run, fly to Naples!" to the musician, and "Run, fly to Italy, painter, poet, sculptor and architect; men of genius of every class." See p. 141.

[12] *Ibid.,* pp. 132-133.

[13] Walpole, *Letters,* ed. Cunningham. London, Bentley, 1857, I, 40.

[14] Walker, *op. cit.,* p. 193.

"this charming country," he gazed on "every object with affection." And "how should it be otherwise?" he asked.

> Almost from my infancy I have been taught to admire it, for who can read the Roman authors, without acquiring the strongest partiality for Italy? To the lover of antiquity it is not the mere face of a country that makes it interesting, but the people who have possessed, or the authors who have described it; for believe me, I would sooner dwell a month in a cottage on the naked plain where Troy stood, than inhabit the most picturesque part of Switzerland, or view the falls of Niagara.[15]

One of the Englishman's favorite jaunts out of Florence was to mountains, where he sometimes called to mind Milton's

> *Angel Forms, who lay intrans't*
> *Thick as Autumnal Leaves that strow the Brooks*
> *In Vallombrosa, where th' Etrurian shades*
> *High overarch't imbowr. . . .*

Peter Beckford wrote a clear account of a climb to the convent.[16]

> The distance, which they call eighteen miles, may be somewhat more, and is a journey of at least five hours. Send on saddle horses to Pont a Sieve, and go thither in your carriage. You procure a guide at Pont a Sieve, who attends on foot; let him carry oats for your horses; the Convent providing only hay; and it may be necessary to inform you, that they keep early hours, dine at twelve, and shut their gates soon after sunset. Travellers of all ranks, known or unknown, are received with hospitality. If you are unable to ride, or too lazy to walk, you must not undertake a journey that admits not of a carriage of any kind; and, at any rate, must provide yourself with that patience and resignation which bad roads usually require . . . Every step requires caution, and is literally up-hill work; — it will repay your labour. At Paterna, a territory belonging to the convent, rough as the rest, but polished by industry, you may take repose, should you require it. Here you will see a barren soil rendered fertile by dint of cultivation; and sloping vineyards, that gratefully produce better wine than richer land can boast. Farm-houses scattered here and there, as if placed by art to embellish a savage scene, — and inhabitants, whose ruddy looks bespeak the pure air they breathe. You will be astonished, the whole way, at the boldness of the scenery and the grandeur of the objects: — the woods — the

---

[15] Watkins, *Travels in 1787, 1789 Through Switzerland, Italy, Siciliy . . . in a Series of Letters*, pp. 197-198.
[16] Beckford, *Familiar Letters from Italy in 1787*, I, 293-302.

cascades the rocks — the precipices, — and not least, at the mountain itself, which looks proudly down on all that surrounds it! A forest of chestnuts leads you to a forest of firs, and you at length arrive at the Convent of Vallombrosa, situated on a delightful lawn, inclosed in an amphitheatre of wood.

San Giovanni Gualberto, born at Florence in the year 985 of the noble family of Bisdomini, founded the Convent of Vallombrosa. His only brother Ugone had been assassinated. Giovanni accidentally meeting the murderer shortly after, and drawing his sword to revenge the death of the relation he dearly loved, the repentant sinner, embracing his knees, begged for mercy in the name of him who suffered for us on the Cross. It was good Friday. Giovanni struck with the circumstance, stopped his hand, and considering for a moment his prostrate enemy, suppliant and defenceless, raised him from the earth, embraced him, and forgave him . . . Greatly agitated by so affecting a scene, he entered the church of San Miniato, belonging to the Cluniacenzi Friars, and while he prayed, the crucifix at which he kneeled, seemed to assume a pleasing aspect, and gave signs of approbation. He sought retirement, and founded a Convent of the Benedictines in the midst of the woods, on top of the Apennines, inhabited by wolves and bears. Such was the state of Vallombrosa when San Giovanni Gualberto founded it. . . .

Without the wall of the Convent are the lawns of an English park, fed with sheep, and surrounded by woods, cascades, and mountains, that set art at defiance! The convent itself is enclosed in a forest of firs, the background of which is covered with beech to the mountain's top . . . Whichever way you turn your eyes, the view will both please and astonish you; If you like a distant view, you have Alvernia, Camaldoli, and Florence: the mountains to the Romagna, Radicofani, and Modena; and, if the day is clear, the sea at Leghorn. The nearer view is delightful. The Val d'Arno is beautifully variegated; and a savage scene on one side is finely contrasted on the other by lawns in the midst of woods, and an outline formed by nature with the beech, feathered to the ground, extending as far as the eye can reach.

IV

The Grand Tour routes leads southward from Lombardy along the coast of the Adriatic to Ancona and over the mountains to Rome. The passage of the Apennines delighted Addison.

The fatigue of our crossing was very agreeably relived by the Variety of Scenes we passed through. For not to mention the rude Prospect of Rocks rising one above the other, of deeper Gutters

42

worn in the Sides of them by Torrents of Rain and Snow-water, of the long Channels of Sand winding about their Bottoms, that are sometimes filled with so many Rivers: we saw, in six Days travelling, the several Seasons of the Year, shivering on the Top of a bleak Mountain, and a little while after, basking in a warm Valley, covered with Violets and almond Trees in blossom, the Bees already swarming over them, through Groves of Olives, or by Gardens of Oranges, or into several hollow Apartments among the Rocks and Mountains.[17]

In the midst of the high mountains is the famous cascade of Terni, which made deep impressions on the minds of both Addison and Smollett not to mention thousands of nameless travellers. Addison wrote:

I went out of my way to see the famous *Cascade* about three miles from *Terni*. It is form'd by the Fall of the River *Velino,* which Virgil mentions in the Seventh *Aeneid . . . Rosea rura Velini.*

The Channel of this River lies very high, and is shaded on all sides by a green Forest, made of the several kinds of Trees that preserve their Verdure all the Year . . . The Neighboring Mountains are cover'd with them, and by reason of their Height are more expos'd to the Dews and drizzling Rains than any of the adjacent Parts, which gives occasion to Virgil's *Rosea rura* (Dewy Countries). The River runs extremely rapid before its Fall, and rushes down a Precipice of a hundred Yards high. It throws itself into the Hollow of a Rock, which has probably been worn by such a constant Fall of water . . . It is impossible to see the Bottom on which it breaks for the thickness of the Mist that rises from it, which looks at a distance like Clouds of Smoke ascending from some vast Furnace, and distills in perpetual Rains on all the Places that lie near it. I think there is something more astonishing in this *Cascade,* than in all the Water-works of *Versailles,* and could not but wonder when I first saw it, that I had never met with it in any of the old Poets, especially in *Claudian,* who makes his Emperor Honorius go out of his way to see the River *Nar* which runs just below it, and yet does not mention what would have been so great an Embellishment to his poem. But at present I don't in the least question, notwithstanding the Opinion of some learned Men to the contrary, that this is the Gulf tho' which *Virgil's Alecto* shoots herself into Hell: for the very Place, the great Reputation of it, the Fall of Waters, the Woods that encompass it, with the Smoke and noise that arise from it, are all Pointed at in the Description . . . It was indeed the most proper place in the World for a Fury to make her *Exit,* after she had fill'd a Nation with Distractions and

17 Addison, *op. cit.,* p. 103.

Alarms; and I believe every Reader's Imagination is pleased when he sees the angry Goddess thus sinking, as it were, in a Tempest, and plunging herself into Hell, amidst such a Scene of Horror and Confusion.

The River *Velino,* after having found its Way out from among the Rocks where it falls, runs into the *Nera.* The Channel of this last River is white with Rocks, and the Surface of it, for a long Space, covered with Froth and Bubbles; for it runs all along upon the Fret, and is still breaking against the Stones that oppose its Passage: So that for these Reasons, as well as for the Mixture of Sulphur in its Waters, it is very well described by Virgil.

Sulfurea Nar albus acqua, fontesque Velini. Aen. 7.[18]

Smollett was even more impetuous:

Passing Utricoli, near the ancient Ocricoli, and the romantic town of Narni, situated on the top of a mountain, in the neighborhood of which is still seen standing one arch of the stupendous bridge built by Augustus Caesar, we arrived at Terni, and hiring a couple of chaises, before dinner, went to see the famous Cascata delle Marmore, which is at the distance of three miles. We ascended a steep mountain by a narrow road formed for a considerable way along the brink of a precipice, at the bottom of which brawls the furious river Nera, after having received the Velino. This last is the stream which, running from the Lago della Marmore, forms the cascade by falling over a precipice about one hundred and sixty feet high. Such a body of water rushing down the mountain; the smoak, vapour and thick white mist which it raises; the double rainbow which these particles continually exhibit while the sun shines; the deafening sound of the cataract; the vicinity of a great number of other stupendous rocks and precipices, with the dashing, boiling, and foaming of the two rivers below, produce altogether an object of tremendous sublimity.[19]

V

The situation of Rome in featureless, vacant, and even desert plains was disappointing. The desolate undulations of this zone were cursed with noxious airs, the *mal aria,*[20] the cause of which was not understood, of course in those years.

---

[18] *Ibid.,* pp. 99-101; see Smith, *A Sketch of a Tour on the Continent,* II, 303.

[19] Smollett, *op. cit.,* p. 139.

[20] See Piozzi, *op. cit.,* I, 378, concerning malaria and the melancholy Campagna.

It was believed by almost all travellers that sleeping outside of Rome would be fatal. Even a Roman would not dare to fall asleep in the country round about: on the other hand it was sheer suicide for a *contadino* of the Roman campagna to fall asleep at night inside the city walls.

The thistle-grown barren around Rome, became a metaphor of Catholic blight to all Protestant strangers. Though the violence of the schism had greatly abated in the eighteenth century, and though travellers were no longer in great physical danger on account of their religion, and though tutors from England might no longer be seized and imprisoned by the police of Catholic reaction, still an honest Protestant could tell he was drawing near to the abode of the Pope by the singed appearance of the earth.

Now, however, such is the change of taste, that to many who visit Rome this strange emptiness that invests it expresses a division of some sort — a separation of the world's most famous city from more common ground, and it is a feature of the approach to the ancient capital that gives a traveller a sense of immensity as though the plains rolled on and on. There is a severity in this isolation that we respect. But as Mrs. Piozzi said, "Italy is only a fine well-known academy figure, from which we all sit down to make drawings, according as the light falls."[21]

Light falls in different ways on other details of the land-scape too. Some of the old travellers for instance, even those who were particularly enthusiastic about the Italian country-side, did not like olive trees and cypresses. "How came it," asked Peter Beckford, "that the cypress, that hated tree, dedicated by the ancients to Pluto and Proserpine, and a constant attendant at their funerals, should be chosen to adorn the modern villas? Is it a *memento mori?*"[22] And the olive he remarked "is the most profitable tree in Tuscany," but it is "no beauty either in shape or complexion."[23] And even Mrs. Piozzi, who loved everything in Italy, thought the olive not a "happily coloured plant: straggling and dusky, one is forced

21 *Ibid.*, I, 288.
22 Beckford, *op. cit.*, I, 288.
23 *Ibid.*, II, 74.

to think of its produce . . . as in a deformed and ugly friend
or companion."[24]

VI

When a traveller had established himself at Rome, he almost always visited hill towns in the neighborhood, such as
Tivoli, Frascati, Palestrina, and Albano.[25] For several days he
would ramble among the gardens of Renaissance villas, or the
wrecks of the palaces of Mæcenus and Hadrian, which cover
prodigious tracts of ground, in situations high above wide
plains below. Only great rooms, and vaults, and mouldering
walls remained, and these were infested with lizards and
vagabonds.[26]

From Rome the way to Naples lies along the famous Via
Appia over mountains and lowlands into the Campania Felice.
"Naples," Addison said simply, has the "pleasantest situation
in the world," on a bay "the most delightful"[27] he ever saw.
Gray wrote to his mother, June 14, 1740, from Naples,

> Our journey hither was through the most beautiful part of the
> finest country in the world; and every spot of it, on some account
> or other, famous for these three thousand years past . . . The
> people call it a backward year, and are in pain about their corn,
> wine, and oil; but we, who are neither corn, wine, nor oil, find
> it very agreeable. The minute one leaves his Holiness's dominions,
> the face of things begins to change from wide uncultivated plains
> to olive groves and well-tilled fields of corn, intermixed with
> ranks of elms, every one of which has its vine twining about it,
> and hanging in festoons between the rows from one tree to an-
> other. The great old fig trees, the oranges in full bloom, and
> myrtles in every hedge, make one of the delightfullest scenes you
> can conceive; besides that the roads are wide, well-kept, and full
> of passengers. . . . Your map will show you the situation of
> Naples; it is on the most lovely bay in the world. . . . We have
> spent two days in visiting the remarkable places in the country
> round it, such as the bay of Baiae, and its remains of antiquity;
> the lake Avernus, and the Solfatara, Charon's grotto, etc. . . . We

---

[24] Piozzi, *op. cit.*, I, 350.

[25] A Mecca of the landscape painters. See Moore, *A View of Society and
Manners in Italy*, p. 340; Smith, *op. cit.*, II, 226, observed that Orizonte
achieved his fame with landscapes of the Campagna taken from these hill towns.

[26] Addison, *op. cit.*, p. 214. In his guide, p. 224, Martyn speaks of many
of the finest ancient sculptures lying among imperial ruins deep buried in
thickets of thorns.

[27] Gray, *op. cit.*, I. 162-163.

have but a few days longer to stay here; too little in conscience for such a place.[28]

Mrs. Piozzi says she had always been reading "summer descriptions" of the metropolis, and was familiar with the ideas of "an Hesperian garden, an earthly paradise"[29] before she arrived there; and everyone who saw it seems to have written with an idea of conveying these notions. Everyone wrote of Capri across the bay, of the Solfatara, *Grotta del Cane,* Phlæagrean Fields and of the astonishing mountain. Many Englishmen and even ladies wallowed up through smoking cinders to the edge of the crater, peered down through the fumes at the color-stained sides, and the steaming bottom, flung in stones, and escaped from the perilous zones with relief.

Capri was the southernmost point of the tour. And it pleased the eighteenth century traveller quite as much as the traveller of today.[30] The arrival from Naples was the same then as now. One debarked at a mole, below the slip of land between the eastern and western mountains, and ascended to the town through vines, figs, fruit-trees, and myrtles. One hired small boats to go around the island, marvelled at the burning blue sea, and the rocks rising straight up a thousand feet into the sky, peered into the grottoes,[31] and skirted rocks where the Sirens are reputed to have sung (and where they still sing if we are to believe certain people of our own time).[32] One climbed up to the ruins of Tiberius' villa, wondered what his sins had been, and envied him. One gazed across at the promontory of Sorrento, and the Bay of Naples, and at the bright wide sea, inscrutable expanding southward towards the sun.

The traveller had come to the edge of another world — for

---

28 Addison, *op. cit.,* p. 123.
29 Piozzi, *op. cit.,* II, 3.
30 Havens, "The Romantic Aspects of the Age of Pope," PMLA, XVII, 1912, pp. 297-324. Professor Havens suggests that classicism was merely a London fad or cult in England and that the genuine spirit of English poetry was always romantic; he quotes Addison on Capri in support of this view.
31 John Dryden, Jr., *A Voyage to Sicily and Malta,* p. 6. "On Friday [October 29, 1700] we took a felucca, and rowed quite around the island, whose high rocks make a terrible, yet pleasing, prospect . . . so romantique, that we cou'd not but fancy it belong'd to some sea god, as his court or palace."
32 See Axel Mundt, *Story of San Michele,* passim.

at Naples and Capri he had entered into the sphere of something more remote and even more splendid — Greece! Perhaps then, if not before, the Englishman felt an excess of the sun, and would fain wrap himself in an English fog or an English forest and disappear.

Brunelleschi's cupola, Santa Maria in Fiore, Florence: apotheosis in stone of haystacks that appear at the end of every Tuscan summer.

CHAPTER V

LOMBARDS AND VENETIANS

. . . benchè dalla proda veggia il fondo
in pelago nol vede, e non di meno
e lì, ma cela lui l'esser profondo.

PARADISO, Canto XIX

I

Genoa astonished Englishmen even after they had seen Versailles. *Palazzi* along the Strada Nuova forming "perhaps the most beautiful line of buildings in the world,"[1] terraces spilling out gay colored flowers, housetop gardens, frescoes painted on the outside of villas[2] — something quite unexpected — miles of marble balustrades, groves of oranges breathing perfumes into the glorious sun and throughout starry nights — all this "exhibited a degree of luxury unthought-on in colder climates," and gave one "new ideas of human life."[3]

And beggars showing their repulsive sores and horrible deformities, calling for help, falling in the dirt, grovelling at the traveller's feet, blocking his way, flinging their arms about his knees — they also gave "new ideas of human life." Some Englishmen supposed that there were similar wretches at home in some parts of London. But they had never seen them. And they were sorry to see those of Genoa.

There many travellers first saw *cicisbei.*

---

[1] Lady Mary Wortley Montagu, *Letters, written during her Travels in Europe, Asia, and Africa,* (Fourth Edition, New York, 1766), p. 185.

[2] Addison, *Remarks on the Several Parts of Italy,* p. 18.

[3] Piozzi, *Observations and Reflections,* I, 59; Gray wrote to West, November 21, 1739, "singing the praises of Italy," although he had as yet seen very little of it. "We are in a place so very fine, that we are in fear of finding nothing finer. We are fallen in love with the Mediterranean sea, and hold your lakes and rivers in vast contempt. This is

"The happy country where huge lemons grow, as Waller says; and I am sorry to think of leaving it in a week for Parma, although it be

The happy country where huge cheeses grow. (See Edmund Waller's *The Battle of the Summer Islands, Canto* I.)

The *cicisbeo,* who took his name from the Italian verb *cicisbeare* — "to whisper," (presumably into the delicate ear of the one he served) was a variety of knight errant, always bearing in mind the welfare of his lady, and worshipping her with a platonic ever-yearning love, like that of Dante for Beatrice, or of Petrarca for Laura.[4] The wife of a nobleman or gentleman was permitted, and often encouraged to accept the attention of one of these *cicisbei,* thus breaching even the appearance (which is worth something) of morality.

Such arrangements were very stimulating to the skepticism and curiosity of Englishmen, who sometimes discovered that the duties of a *cavaliere* were more arduous than those of a husband. And it was often seen that when a husband could not attend his wife to masquerades, operas, balls, and feasts, it was simply because he was *cavaliere* to another lady and his duties were very pressing. Peter Beckford suggests that the Genoese were quite philosophical about all this. They had put away jealousy of course. The best a man could do, if he happend to love his wife, was to pray for her honesty, and if that were too much to pray for, he would pray not to know of her dishonesty, and if that were too much, his prayer would then be "che non me n'importi un corno!"[5]

Genoa had no classic ruins — except the rotten iron beak of what might have been an ancient vessel. Only a person with special interests would stay long enough there to be able to speak of the inhabitants from personal experience.

One such, Sir James Edward Smith, the biologist, knew the noble family of Durazzo — and through them many of the leading citizens. He was a sensible judge and believed that the aristocracy of Genoa was much less proud and trifling than in other countries, and to illustrate he told of going to the Durazzo villa of Cornigliano,[6] where there was a large library of rare books, and a museum of natural history. Mornings were spent in this museum, which consisted of three

spacious apartments, surrounded with glass cases, containing minerals, quadrupeds, birds, fishes, corals, and a fine collection of shells. In the first room are good marble busts of Aristotle,

4 Baretti, *An Account of the Manners and Customs of Italy*; II, 101-105; cf. P. Beckford, *Familiar Letters from Italy in 1787*, I, 98.
5 P. Beckford, *op. cit.,* I, 102.
6 Smith, *A Sketch of a Tour on the Continent*, III, 90.

Pliny, Linnaeus, and Bergman. The minerals are disposed according to the Sciagraphia of the latter; the rest after the Linnaean system. Dr. Caneferi, Professor of Natural History, was of our party, and everyone had their department assigned; some labouring at the determination of the shells, others at the birds. The jaspers from Sicily in this collection are extremely fine, and are set in the window-shutters; a good method enough, as they thus take no room, and their hardness secures them from injury.[7]

II

Turin, clean and regular, was famous as the seat of the Savoys, whose court was much respected. Boyle in his letters from Italy described the Royal palace as fitted up "so elegantly, and so properly adorned," that, to one passing from room to room, the whole "appears a fairy castle. Amidst all those exquisite decorations, not one effeminte toy, not one Chinese dragon, nor India monster to be seen. I mention this," he said, "because many of our finest houses in England are disgraced by the fantastic figures with which they are crowded."[8]

The town being formal, one could not walk in the streets without an absolute loss of character as walking would indicate either an indecent poverty, or that a stranger had not received social instruction from the proper class of residents. Therefore one was reduced to the pleasure of wheeling up and down the *corso*, which was not very extensive, and when the king passed in his coach also wheeling up and down the *corso*, one might have the satisfaction of nodding gravely and touching one's hat; and he might have that pleasure fifteen times in an afternoon, as Gibbon discovered.[9]

Readers of Gibbon's letters will recall that in 1764 when the young historian was going down into Italy, he just missed Pitt at Turin.[10] A pleasing incident of Pitt's visit there is recorded by Louis Dutens, who introduced five British gentlemen to the court. "Les noms baroques formoient une cacophonie singuliere en les prononçant tous ensemble: c'etoient M. Dutton, Kendrick, Melikan, Kellikan, et Carmichael. Cette presentation fit une sensation d'un moment, parce que

7 *Ibid,* III, 91.
8 Boyle, *Letters from Italy,* pp. 53-54.
9 Gibbon, *Private Letters,* ed. Prothero, (London, Murray, 1897), p. 58.
10 *Ibid.,* p. 58.

quelquesunes des plus jeunes dames du palais s'aviserent d'en rire."[11] This incident has a sequel. When Dutens was in England several years later, he attended a dinner party where Pitt told this story as though he himself had introduced Dutton, Kendrick, Melikan, Kellikan and Carmichael. The cacophony was so successful that it became one of Pitt's favorite stories.

Thomas Watkins left a circumstantial account of one of these presentations. He arrived in Turin during September 1787 with the Autumnal migration of English into Italy. Two days later he and his friend Pocock, the oriental traveller, delivered letters from Lord Caermarthen to the Chargé d'Affaires. Then after visiting the prime minister and leaving their cards with the entire *corps diplomatique,* they were presented to the king and royal family by M. de Choiseul Praslin, the French Ambassador (as it was permissible only to a plenipotentiary to perform this ceremony). The court was then at the immense fortress castle of Moncalieri high on the banks of the Po, about four miles from the city. Watkins and his party was received by every member of the royal family, each in a separate apartment: the king's brother, the Duke of Chablais; the two young princes, the dukes of Aosta and Montferrat; the Princess of Piedmont; her consort; and finally His Majesty. All asked a few general questions, then signalled for departure with a bow. The king observed among other things, "that the English, like birds of passage, appeared in Italy all at a certain season."[12] It was at just such a presentation that young Gibbon with an air of bravado pulled out his snuff box "rapped it, took snuff twice" as he chatted with the royal princesses.[13]

Watkins and Pocock were presented on the Princess of Piedmont's birthday, "and in consequence of it the Court was full and brilliant. All military officers, as in England, appear at it in their uniforms; at Versailles it is quite the reverse."[14] After the formal introductions had ended, there was a levee, "at which the king and princes conversed, I think, with every individual in the circle; an act of no small difficulty, as the majority were foreigners." Having witnessed all the cere-

---

[11] Dutens, *Memoires d'un Voyageur qui se repose,* I, 201.
[12] Watkins, *Travels in 1787, 1789 through Switzerland, Italy, Sicily . . . in a series of Letters,* p. 208.
[13] Gibbon, *op. cit.,* p. 58.
[14] Watkins, *op. cit.,* pp. 208-209.

monies of the court, long "esteemed one of the politest in the world," they returned to Turin, dined with the French Ambassador, a gentleman every way qualified for his high situation, "and finished the evening in a *conversazione* at the Spanish Ambassador's."[15]

III

It was at Turin that Boswell was seized with the whim of having an intrigue with an Italian countess.[16] He bought a black dress suit.[17] He visited a hair-dresser. He found a motto in Ariosto to the effect that all the disdains, the repulses, the sufferings of love add flavor to a pleasure when it comes.[18] He determined to give himself the most exquisite pains of martyrdom, and he did.

As he expected his stay in Turin to be a short one, an older woman seemed proper as an easier mark. La Comtesse de St. Gilles was just past fifty, had a fine reputation for debauchery, and looked strong enough.[19] He was introduced to her box at the opera, moved a chair close to her, sat down *vis à vis,* talked a rhapsody of passion, and rubbed her legs with his, which she took graciously.[20]

Boswell wrote letters, lost sleep, called, and old Madame St. Gilles, though she did not turn him off completely, never gave him the least expectation of success; but she finally gave him a lecture. She said that she thought he had studied a good deal. She thought he should continue to study, and that he should take care of his health and his money, and she told him point-blank that he knew nothing of the polite world. And Boswell had to admit, though he abominated the old witch, that what she had said was true.

About ten days after his arrival, he began to eye a younger Comtesse, the Madame Skarnavis, who had the reputation of being even more debauched than Madame St. Gilles. He flattered her, but with no results except that Madame St. Gilles became his enemy and circulated a story of his violent attack

15 *Ibid.,* p. 210.
16 Boswell, *Private Papers . . . from Malahide Castle,* V, 115.
17 *Ibid.,* V, 116.
18 *Ibid.,* V, 9.
19 *Ibid.,* V, 111.
20 *Ibid.,* V, 116.

upon her.[21] Then he attempted a third Comtesse, Madame Bourgaretta, and as she was really bright and attractive, Boswell considered extending his stay in Turin. But one morning he went to call, and found two other young fops already in her boudoir. This was something of an irritant in itself, and when the Comtesse dressed before them all, his passion for her was quenched completely.[22]

By Monday, January 21, Boswell's spirits were very low. He thought of writing to his father saying it was so rare for a man of his hypochondriac nature to find happiness, that surely he would be pardoned for staying longer in Turin, where he was detained by an Italian countess. Then he called on the name of Rousseau and lamented his own moral decline since visiting the great man in his paradise of philosophy.[23] But Boswell was not one to sink in sadness long. He picked up his pen and wrote Madame Skarnavis a warm entreaty begging mercy and love. He was rejected; his letter was even flung into the fire by the lady.[24]

What could he do but see a learned and religious acquaintance named Needham who took occasion to discourse on the Trappists[25] — an appropriate subject! Lady Mary Wortley Montagu has written a very picturesque account of the founding of this order.

Bouthillier de Rance, a man of pleasure and gallantry [was] . . . converted to the deepest gloom and devotion by the following incident. His affairs obliged him to absent himself for some time from a lady with whom he had lived in the most intimate and tender connexions . . . At his return to Paris he proposed to surprise her agreeably, and, at the same time, to satisfy his own impatient desire of seeing her, by going directly . . . to her apartment by a back stair, which he was well acquainted with — but think of the spectacle that presented itself to him at his entrance into the chamber that had so often been the scene of love's highest raptures! his mistress dead — dead of the small-pox — disfigured beyond expression — a loathsome mass of putrifying matter — and the surgeon separating the head from the body, because the coffin had been made too short! He stood for a

21 *Ibid.*, V, 125.
22 *Ibid.*, V, 124.
23 *Ibid.*, V, 126-127.
24 *Ibid.*, V, 10.
25 *Ibid.*, V, 127.

moment . . . filled with horror . . . and then retired from the world.[26]

When their discussion was ended Needham advised Boswell to lay in a large store of learning.

Later as he was driving through the streets of Turin, Boswell happened to see a hanging. He jumped from his coach and ran up close to the ladder hoping that the emotions of shock would banish his depression, but it had quite another effect. A cross was held before the victim's eyes, and he was pushed from the ladder, without a cover to his face. The executioner stood upon the man's head and choked him in a minute. The spectacle was so horrible that Boswell was nauseated, and in an access of torment rushed into a nearby church and fell on his knees before a lighted altar.[27] Two days later he was on the road to Milan.

IV

Eighteenth century Milan was an important commercial center and one of the richest cities of Italy. It was a business city something like London, and like London it had its coffeehouse journal, *Il Caffè*,[28] counterpart of the *Tatler,* the *Spectator,* the *Bee,* etc. But as it possessed relatively few classical associations, it was not the kind of city Englishmen had crossed the Alps to see, and consequently was not a favorite travellers' resort, which was true generally of all the towns of *Alt'Italia.*

Mrs. Piozzi lived at Milan during her first winter in Italy. She wrote very little of the sights and a great deal about the people, whom she could hardly praise enough. She was delighted to see that the noble daughter of a Marquis could dance gaily with an apothecary's apprentice at a Christmas party without the least show of empty pride. She was happy when Milanese gentlemen complimented her, for she was sure they meant what they said, and were not merely overlaying indifference with foppery as sometimes happened in London.[29]

---

26 Lady Mary Wortley Montague, *Letters and Works,* pp. 76-77.

27 Boswell, *op. cit.,* V, 128.

28 P. Beckford, *op. cit.,* p. 84.

29 Piozzi, *op. cit.,* I, 73-83; also I, 100 on sincerity.

Mrs. Piozzi has been considered partial in her observations.[30] How could one have had her experience, she might have asked, and remained impartial? Because of her Italian husband, and certainly because of her own distinction, and her willingness to reciprocate, she did have uncommon opportunities of seeing behind the scenes into the everyday truth of Italian life; so that if her account is partial, it may still be true. Probably an unfortunate traveller could point to the works of Dr. Sharp, Sterne's Mundungus, and vouch for their accuracy. There is a great deal in them, as Dr. Johnson said himself after reading them over again;[31] but it all concerns the outside of people, and the outside of houses, but the inside of some of the vilest inns available — for which one had to hunt as you might say.

V

Travellers usually sped through other northern cities seeing next to nothing of the people. I have only been able to salvage one vignette of those parts outside the letters of Lady Mary Wortley Montagu, which I consider worth reading. And it would not discredit even the pen of Sterne. It is by Arthur Young, the agricultural economist, who had travelled across France on a mare — most undignified in the 1780's. But Young by his own admission was not a fashionable traveller; he was very uncomfortable, he said, in the presence of fashionable men. Nevertheless the presence of fashionable women, particularly if they were bewitching, as sometimes happened, did not trouble him at all. Just after his arrival in Milan, he was introduced to one of the prettiest ladies of the city, "Signora Lambertini, a young, lively, and beautiful woman, who conversed with an easy and unaffected gaiety, that would make even a farmer wish to be her *cicisbeo*."[32] But she had one already, and Young moved on to Bergamo to study crops and animals.

One evening as he was walking about the streets of that town in search of a certain agricultural scientist, and as the purple shades of dusk were thickening, the sweet voice of a

---

30 See above, p. 9 of the text.
31 Boswell, *The Life of Samuel Johnson*.
32 Young, *Travels during the Years 1787, 1788, and 1789* . . . p. 239.

lady called to him from a window to enquire the cause of his aimless movements. This introduced an unexpected note, and unexpected pleasures are oft the best-remembered and are stored up among the most precious secret treasures of our experience. Young told the voice that he was seeking Dr. Maironi. It replied that Dr. Maironi was in the country, but was expected the next day. He expressed his gratitude and accordingly on the morrow he continued the search with double interest.

I repaired to the street where the lady gave me information the night before; she was luckily at her window, but the intelligence cross to my wishes, for both the brothers were in the country; I need not go to the door, she said, for there were no servants in the house. The dusk of the evening in the dark town had last night veiled the fair *incognita,* but looking a second time, now I found her extremely pretty, with a pair of eyes that shone in unison with something better than a street of Bergamo. She asked me kindly after my business. *Spero che non è un grande mancamento?* words of no import, but uttered with a sweetness of voice that rendered the poorest monosyllable interesting. I told her that the bosom must be cold from which her presence did not banish all feeling of disappointment. It was impossible not to say something a little beyond common thanks. She bowed in return; and I thought I read in her expressive eyes that I had not offended: I was encouraged to ask the favor of Signore Mairone's address in the country — *Con grande piacere vi lo darò.* —I took a card from my pocket; but her window was rather too high to hand it. I looked at the door: *Forzi è aperta.* — *Credo che si,* she replied. If the reader is an electrician, and has flown a kite in a thunderstorm, he will know that when the atmosphere around him becomes highly electric, there is a cobweb sensation in the air as if he were enclosed in an invisible net of the filmiest gossamer. My atmosphere at this moment, had some resemblance to it; I had taken two steps to the door, when a gentleman passing opened it before me and stood upon the threshold. It was the lady's husband; she was in the passage behind, and I was in the street before him. She said, *Ecco un Signore Inglese che ha bisogno d'una dirizione a Signore Maironi.* The husband answered politely that he would give it, and taking paper and pencil from his pocket, wrote and gave it me. Nothing was over done so concisely . . . Certain it is, one now and then meets with terrible eyes in Italy; in the north of Europe they had attractive powers, here they have every sort of power.[33]

---

[33] *Ibid.,* pp. 243-244.

As travellers passed towards Venice, their comment on Padua was merely that the wild students no longer prowled along arcades of the streets at night to cry out *"Qui va la?"* and take pot-shots at strangers who failed to answer.[34] At Modena, where the famous *Secchia rapita* was conserved, most remarked only on the poor condition of the city and on the folly of starting a war over a bucket.. (See Tassoni's *La Secchia Rapita*.) At Brescia there was not much to stop a tourist either and the most interesting story I have come across concerning the place is one of sudden death related by staunch old Peter Beckford. "Dining at the Table d'Hote," he said.

> An ill-looking fellow, muffled up in a Ferraiolo, (kind of cloak) came into the middle of the room, and placing himself opposite to a person he had singled out, said — "Con permesso" (by your leave), and instantly, without further ceremony, discharged the contents of a loaded blunderbuss into his body; the wounded man sprang up, staggered a few paces, and fell dead in the passage. — Rare confusion at the Table d'Hote! — Those who were nearest the door left their dinner, and ran away; some got into the corner of the room, while others remained in their chairs without the power to move. The assassin without speaking another word, drew a long knife, held it between his teeth, and then loaded his blunderbuss with all the coolness imaginable. That done, he stuck his knife into the dead body as he passed, and walked away unconcerned.[35]

The explanation of this rather interesting episode was that the dead gentleman had engaged a bravo to rid him of an enemy; but as the quarrel had been made up, he sent for him to say he had no use for his services any more and added that he might keep the money. "I am a man of honor," replied the bravo. "I will keep your money, but I must kill your man"[36] This provoked a discussion. "You may take your choice, Sire," the bravo informed him, "whether it shall be you or him; for, to gain your money *honestly,* it is necessary that I should kill *one of you.*"[37]

---

[34] Drummond in *Travels Through different Cities of Germany, Italy . . .* (1754) tells (p. 80) of seeing the grave of Mr. Wauchop of Niddrie alleged to have been shot January 29, 1726, aet. 20, by the playful students at Padua.

[35] P. Beckford, *op. cit.,* II, 446.

[36] *Ibid.,* II, 446.

[37] *Ibid.,* II, 446-447.

VII

It was only towards the end of the century that Englishmen began to know Garda well, and Iseo, Como, Maggiore, and to write of "venusta Sirmio . . . Catullus's all-but-island, olive-silvery Sirmio!"[38]

Lady Mary was the first of the literate English to live there. A century before the *Risorgimento,* she was filling her letters with characteristic tales of Italian life, one of which must be included among our vignettes.

On a summer's day in 1749 as Lady Mary sat reading in her fairy-tale palace, the chambermaid of Signora Laura Bono burst in upon her, and flung herself at her feet, and weeping distractedly, besought her for the love of the sacred Madonna to go instantly to her master's house to prevent murder if she could.

I was soon there (the house touching my garden wall), and was directed to the bed-chamber by the noise of oaths and execrations; but, on opening the door, was astonished to a degree . . . by seeing the Signora Laura prostrate on the ground, melting in tears, and her husband standing with a drawn stiletto in his hand swearing she should never see tomorrow's sun, I was soon let into the secret. The good man, having business of consequence at Brescia, went thither early in the morning; but as he expected his chief tenant to pay his rent that day, he left orders with his wife, that if the farmer, who lived two miles off, came himself, or sent any of his sons, she should take care to make him very welcome. She obeyed him with great punctuality, the money coming in the hand of a handsome lad of eighteen: she did not only admit him to her own table, and produce the best wine in the cellar, but resolved to give him *chere entiere.* While she was exercising this generous hospitality, the husband met midway the gentleman he intended to visit, who was posting to another side of the country; they agreed on another appointment, and he returned to his own house, where, giving his horse to be led round to the stable by the servant that accompanied him, he opened his door with the *passe-partout* key, and proceeded to his chamber, without meeting anybody, where he found his beloved spouse asleep on the bed with her gallant. The opening of the door waked them; the young fellow immediately leapt out of the window, which looked into the garden, and was open, and escaped over the fields, leaving his breeches on a chair by the bedside — a very striking circumstance. In short, the case was such, I do not

38 Tennyson, "Frater Ave Atque Vale.'

59

think the queen of fairies, herself could have found an excuse, though Chaucer tells us she has made a solemn promise to leave none of her sex unfurnished with one to all eternity . . . The first word I spoke was to desire Signor Carlo to sheathe his poniard, not being pleased with its glittering.

Then Lady Mary proceeded to adjust everything, a task of no small difficulty. She talked to them for five hours, and, as a result, even two years later the family still seemed as though nothing had happened, the Lady Laura retaining the "satisfaction of insulting all her acquaintance on the foundation of a spotless character, that only she can boast in the parish," where she was heartily hated for her virtue, and for another important reason, being the best dressed woman about, "though one of the plainest in her figure."[39]

Perhaps it is pleasanter to remember Lady Mary in her beloved garden playing chess with old Cardinal Querini, or trying to persuade a country priest that the letters she wrote to her daughter were not the secret reports of an English spy, or reading through the latest novels sent from England, or haply walking by her fountain to throw bread upon its clear water, and to hear the bubbling of its marble Tritons.

VIII

The wonders of Venice have been described in poetry and prose by the writers of all nations, and they have been painted by her own artists — and with fine exactitude by Canaletto during the late eighteenth century. His paintings, therefore are particularly valuable as illustrations of the Grand Tour, for one may now see in them not only the gorgeous ceremonies that the English flocked to see; one may observe the English lords themselves, standing on the stone quays, hands on their hilts, and chatting with each other among the baskets of eel-vendors. One may look about and see in the sun of those days the maze of cordage in the rigging of wooden ships, the groups of multi-colored, turbaned Moors, the aloof Venetian noble garbed in sober black, gay shawls of the pretty women, and in the middle distance under a clear Mediterranean sky, the

---

[39] Lady Mary Wortley Montague, *The Letters and Works,* ed. Lord Wharncliff, (London, Bohn's Standard Library, 1887), II, 197-199.

weather-rusted towers and domes of San Marco and Santa Maria della Salute.

"This wonderful city realizes the most romantic ideas ever formed of it,"[40] wrote Mrs. Piozzi. It was quite like being wafted into some noble scene from Shakespeare. If there was color and movement, and if there were princely looking personages, ("I saw the handsomest, the most sightly, the most proper and grave men that ever I saw anywhere else![41] Lassels had said), if the squares and canals were as full of shapes as fancy, so was the very air swelling with delights. As Mrs. Piozzi sat in her hotel writing down her first impressions of "this wonderful city," she heard a strange and lovely harmony. In a rapture she ran to her window. The gondoliers were singing! Just as hundreds and thousands of travellers had reported for centuries — the gondoliers were singing. They were singing stanzas from Tasso. Some were on the shores. Others were on the lagoons. Some sang one verse. Others answered across the water with the next, and on and on until they might by singing by thousands, with the vast antiphony flooding the whole city· Then if never before, the travellers knew the glory of the human voice, and why Italians worshipped it. And so they sang until the light fell. If there is no really good account in English of this unique phenomenon, if one must look to the pages of Goethe[42] for it, it may be because the English hastened through Venice, which was not one of their favorite cities, and hastened through it pursuing other matters.

Venice was always the Mecca of men of pleasure. Courtesans were everywhere like tulips in red and yellow, with pretty faces, flowers in their hair, and bare breasts or nearly so. The loveliness of these bright beings often overheated the

---

[40] Piozzi, *op. cit.*, I, 175, 239; Bernhard Berenson, *Italian Painters of the Renaissance*, (London, Oxford University Press, 1938), p. 54. In the eighteenth century "Venice was still the most splendid, and the most luxurious city in the world."

[41] Lassels, *Voyage of Italy*, part II, p. 378. Arthur Young, *op. cit.*, p. 266, was much impressed by the antiquity of some of the Venetian noble families, particularly Contarini, Michieli, Morosini, and Tiepolo, who participated in the election of the first Doge in A.D. 697, and who had taken refuge in Venice when Attila invaded Italy in A.D. 452. About twenty families of Venice could trace their descent for 1300 years (now 1500), and there were from forty to fifty families which, "in point of antiquity well-ascertained, exceed all that are to be found in the rest of Europe."

[42] Goethe, *Italianische Reise*, ed. Friedrich, Leipsig, 1921, pp. 77-78, *i,e,* Oct. 7, 1786.

youthful imagination. Lassels hints that he had known young Englishmen who travelled two weeks across France without a good night's sleep, because they were Venice-bound.[43]

And what could one think of the wives in their masks, in their private gondolas, with their secret rooms near the Piazza? One English lady looked upon Venice as a place little calculated to restrain a woman's desires to be wild. She made it plain however that she had no such inclinations herself.[44]

In Venice one was free. "It is so much the fashion for everybody to live in their own way," wrote Lady Mary Wortley Montague, "that nothing is more ridiculous than censuring the actions of another. This would be terrible in London where we have little other diversion."[45]

There were *conversazioni*. They seemed to float from palace to palace all through the night. The city was a place where actual existence outshone the brilliance of dreams, and where one forgot the use of sleep,[46] as Mrs. Piozzi said. There was much card playing at these parties, and yet there were places where groups met to discuss everything, where everything might be learned by the talk of the company, as Dr. Johnson had boasted of his literary club, the only difference being that women were admitted.[47]

Ascension Day was the gala day for English travellers to Venice. Then the Venetian waters flowered with the most brilliant pageant in Christendom. The ancient Bucentaur, which had been afloat since the year 1171, "a heavy ill built, ugly guilded monster,"[48] according to Arthur Young, and a vessel equal to the ship of Theseus, in the opinion of others, was brought out and rowed into the lagoons where the Doge cast a golden ring into the waves and said, *"Disponsamus te, mare, in signum, perpetui dominii."*[49]

The deck of this old ship would be crowded with distinguished foreigners (Lady Mary had been on it), and with a select party of the Venetian nobility hooded in black and white so as to resemble great gaunt eagles. In the wake of the Bucen-

43 Lassels, *op. cit.*, preface, p. [1].
44 Hull, *Select Letters,* II, 238; see also II, 341.
45 Lady Mary Wortley Montagu, *Letters and Works,* Bohn's Library, II, 54.
46 Piozzi, *op. cit.*, I, 202-203.
47 *Ibid.*, I, 205.
48 Young, *op. cit.*, p. 257; cf. Piozzi, *op. cit.*, I, 186.
49 Piozzi, *op. cit.*, p. 190.

taur rode a fleet of smaller vessels and gondolas, plated with silver and gold, with fine glass windows, revealing red plush upholstery inside. Costumed oarsmen balanced on the golden decks among clusters of cupids and mermaids. Many of the sights of Venice were still seen in the nineteenth century, and are even now; but this of the ancient Bucentaur passed into history with the extinction of the Venetian Republic, though she still floats, "a painted ship upon a painted ocean," in the works of Canaletto.

Lady Mary described some of the lesser vessels, *bichonis* and *piotes,* as they were called, all decorated allegorically. One represented the chariot of Night, showing the rising of the moon, accompanied with stars; another showed the Liberal Arts; "Apollo was seated on the stern upon Mount Parnassus, Pegasus behind, and the Muses seated round him": This float also represented Painting, "with fame blowing her trumpet; and on each side, Sculpture and Music in their proper dresses."[50] Then there was a chariot of Flora, "guided by cupids, and adorned with all sort of flowers, rose-trees &c." Another showed the Garden of Hesperides, another the Chariot of Venus drawn by doves, "so well done, they seemed ready to fly upon the water." A most elaborate one represented Diana "hunting in a large wood: the trees, hounds, stag, and nymphs, all done naturally: the gondoliers dressed like peasants attending the chase: and Endymion, lying under a large tree, gazing on the goddess."[51]

And there was opera. There were private musicales. William Beckford was present at one of these near Venice up the peaceful river Brenta, within the halls of the forest-girdled palace of Cornaro at Fieso.

Galluzzi sang some songs her father had composed. She sang with surprising energy. "Her cheek was flushed, her eyes glistened, the whole tone of her countenance was that of a person rapt and inspired."[52] Young Beckford forgot both time and place while she sang. "The night stole imperceptibly away, before I woke from my trance." He never recollected another evening which every circumstance "conspired to render

[50] Lady Mary Wortley Montagu, *op. cit.,* II, 60-70. 69-70.
[51] *Ibid.,* II, 70.
[52] William Beckford, *Italy,* p. 106.

so full of charm." Usually his musical pleasures suffered from the "phlegm and stupidity," of the other listeners; but there "everyone seemed to catch the flame and to listen with reciprocal delight." What with the loveliness of the songs, the genius of the singer, and the glow of the assembled intellectual meteors, he "scarcely knew to what element" he was transported, and doubted for some time, whether he "was not fallen into a celestial dream." The splendor of the rising sun disturbed him from his reveries; he concludes "it was not without much lingering reluctance that I left those scenes of enchantment and fascination, repeating with melancholy earnestness that pathetic sonnet of Petrarch's —

> *O giorno, o ora, o ultimo momento,*
> *O stelle congiurate a' impoverirme!*
> *O fido sguardo, or che volei tu dirme,*
> *Partend' io, per non esser mai contento?*[53]

Not long after Ascension Day the English would have emptied out of Venice. Pleasure parties would pall. It would not take too long to see the pictures. The Venetian theatre with its Commedia dell'Arte was not much appreciated. Extemporaneous dialogue in Venetian dialect was too much for the tourist, and was as far as he could tell, quite insipid. On one occasion the Duke of Hamilton attended a play with Dr. Moore. A stutterer was going through his usual agonies trying to say a word, which of course would not come out on any account. Suddenly another actor backed off like a bull, and butted him in the paunch with his head. The word came out clearly enough and very loud. This so surprised both the Doctor and the Duke that they went into a fit of laughter, which amused the other spectators even more than what was happening on the stage.[54] But this kind of nonsense and puppets could hardly keep an Englishman in Venice long where a horse was "as great a curiosity as a camel, and a coach as great a rarity as a balloon."

---

53 *Ibid.*, p. 107.

54 Moore, *View of Society and Manners in Italy,* pp. 123-124; see also Hervey, Christopher, *Letters from Portugal, Spain, Italy and Germany in the Years 1759-61,* II, 499-505.

Hervey records the whole of a farce he had seen, in which the character of Englishmen is laughed at. Part of a scene will suffice. Lord Roastbeef is sitting in a Venetian inn with Don Alvaro, M. Le Blau, and the Count of Bosco

CHAPTER VI

ENTERING THE LAND OF ART

I

Thanks to our many excellent public galleries of art, our colored slides, our fine reproductions and photographs, no one need arrive in Italy without a fair knowledge of the wonders of art to be seen there. It is almost certain that a traveller will find himself walking into old familiar pictures. Even in the country he will be at home — absorbed, as it were, into that bright mirage, the land of music and marvellous bells, the land of far-off bliss, which all his life he has seen in the depths of Raphael, or beyond the columns and the crosses of Perugino, or over the hills in Ghirlandaio and Pinturicchio. But at the beginning of the eighteenth century Englishmen were just discovering that unknown country, the Land of Art, though it had lain waiting — nearly all of it — for two hundred years and more.

Anyone particularly curious about art then might have sought an introduction to the famous collector Dr. Mead, or to the Earl of Burlington, who travelled in Italy 1710-1713, and who had enthusiastically measured every structure known

---

Nero. The Englishman says not a word. The others talk of an enchanting widow. After listening in silence for a while, Milord rises abruptly from his chair.

Milord   Halloo! Halloo! (as though a-hunting; waiters rush in.)

Waiter   What commands have your noble honors?
       (Lord Roastbeef takes the waiter aside and asks if he knows the widow in question. He does.)

Milord   Take this ring. Carry it to her. Tell her that my Lord Roastbeef presents her with it, that it is the same she commended so much last night — (showing the Englishman had learned subtlety)

Waiter   But sir, you know —

Milord   Here are six zecchines for you!

Waiter   God bless your honor. I did not speak for this; but you know, Sir, Signor —

Milord   Fly this instant, or I knock you down!

Waiter   Oh! I beg your honor would not give yourself the trouble.

Milord   Halloo! Halloo! (enter four other waiters)
       A light! (turning to the foreign noblemen)
         Gentlemen, good night! (But the Englishman fails as utterly as Boswell.)

to have been created by Andrea Palladio, and who in 1715 brought out a translation of Palladio's *Quattro Libri dell'Architettura* (1570).

Or, some years later, in the thirties, a young nobleman, might, if he had already made the tour, become a member of the Dilettante Society, which met once a week and drank to "Grecian Taste and Roman spirit," paraded in robes of crimson taffeta, Hungarian hats, Spanish swords, and the dress of Machiavelli, and which selected promising artists, supported them in Rome, and gave them commissions on their return.[1] Most young lords would have learned something of painting and of Italy too from the landscapes of Poussin, Claude Lorrain, and Salvatore Rosa, which hung in the halls and corridors of great English country houses. As the years passed, collections grew in number and in size, taste improved by familiarity with the best, and many art books and sets of engravings were published; but at first the sources of information were few.

Lassels' *Voyage of Italy* (1670), though not specifically an art book, was extremely thorough in its discussion of galleries and churches, particularly in Rome.[2] Addison's *Remarks* (1705) was probably sufficient for the average tourist of the first half of the century.

There were some art books too, however. One of these, Edmund Warcupp's *Italy in its Original Glory, Ruin and Revival,* a folio of engravings, appeared almost symbolically in London in 1660. *The Painters Voyage of Italy* (1679) translated from Barri's *Viaggio Pittoresco* by William Lodge, gave a poor account of the chief pictures.[3] In 1685 William Aglionby published an important book, *Painting Illustrated in Three Dialogues . . . Together with the Lives of the most Eminent Painters* [translated out of Vasari] *from Cimabue, to the time of Raphael and Michael Angelo.* In this work two characters, one named *Traveller* and the other *Friend,* parley on painting. *Friend,* like many an other honest Englishman, regrets that he does not appreciate painting more than he does. He believes

[1] *Johnson's England,* ed. A. S. Turberville, Clarendon Press, Oxford 1933, II, 20-21.

[2] B. H. Blackwell's Catalogue 518, p. 18, quotes John Wilkes to the effect that Lassels' "is one of the best accounts of the curious things of Italy ever delivered to the world."

[3] Collison-Morley, *Italy after the Renaissance,* p. 15.

that it must be a very pleasant indoor sport, and he knows that it ''ought to be cherished by all those who do not place their felicity, as too many of us do, in a glass of claret.''[4] He wishes to clarify a few of the basic mysteries of the fine arts. It will be well, he suggests, if art, which is so much appreciated by "the most polite part of mankind," — meaning Italians,[5] should be preferred to the "sensual delights" of England that dull the mind.

One learns from *Traveller,* who seems to be Vasari *incognito,* that Titian has very fine flesh tints in his nudes,[6] and that Italians used to paint upon walls and on wood panels until painting on canvas was invented by John of Bruges and studied in Flanders by Antonio da Messina, who took the secret with him to Venice.[7] One learns how fine a painter was Giulio Romano, Raphael's beloved pupil,[8] that Michael Angelo was a sculptor in his painting, and disagreeable for his "musculous contortions," and an indifferent colorist, "for all Vasari commends him above the skies."[9] One learns that Guido Reni derived much from Lodovico Carraccio, uncle of Hannibale and Augustine. One learns that the Bologna school consisted of Reni, Sisto Rosa called Badalocchio, Albano, Dominichino, and that Pietro di Cortona[10] was contemporary of this school and independent of it, and that Veronese was a disciple of Titian.[11] One is told how to recognize good nudes, and the secrets of drapery design, appropriateness of coloring, and the beauties of light, which ought usually to fall into the center of a picture.[12] And finally one could read Vasari's *Lives,* a work which supplied Englishmen with most of their æsthetic principles.

In 1720 when it was seen that Englishmen were very eager to improve their taste, which was bad, the Jonathan Richardsons, father and son, published their well-known *Account of some of the Statues, Bas-Reliefs, Drawings and Pictures in*

4 Aglionby, *Painting Illustrated in Three Dialogues,* p. 3.
5 *Ibid.,* pp. 34-35.
6 *Ibid.,* p. 18.
7 *Ibid.,* p. 29.
8 *Ibid.,* p. 78.
9 *Ibid.,* p. 82.
10 *Ibid.,* p. 85.
11 *Ibid.,* p. 91.
12 *Ibid.,* p. 97.

Italy, a work of no great value, but which, as it came out in a near void, was in sufficient demand to warrant a second printing two years later. It was composed, according to Richardson senior, from jottings made on the spot during the tour of Richardson junior, who had to travel very fast (he finished Italy in six weeks) and did not have time to admire Titian, Veronese, and Tintoretto.[13] Every other page was left blank for the use of tourists who might have the fortune to stay more than six weeks.

On page twenty-one of the Avery Library copy at Columbia, for example, the author says of the Beheading of St. John, "a prodigious fine picture." The traveller writes "Not fine." On page fifty-two Richardson says "Fine," and the traveller gave his opinion, "Not so good." And on another page he remarks, "The author omits many capital pictures," which is very true.

About the same time Richardson was whisking through part of Italy, Edward Wright Esq. was looking it over very deliberately. From 1720 until 1722 he travelled. And in 1730 he published *Observations made in Travelling Through France, Italy &c.* He dedicated the work, which is considerable, (Lord Orrery called him "the best author who has traversed Italian ground"), to the Right Honorable George, Lord Park, Viscount of Ewelme, whom he had the honor of attending on his tour. He discusses agricultural practices, types of transportation a traveller uses on land and sea, and refers to other English travel-writers, notably Addison, who is often quoted, and whose quotations are often quoted. Wright's book has engravings on the culture of grapes, on circumcision instruments, on basilisks, on pavements of Roman roads, views of ancient buildings, views of cities. But the work is mostly devoted to the fine arts. The author admits that he may have "enlarged more upon the articles of painting and sculpture, than may possibly be agreeable to the taste of every reader." If so, those parts "are easily passed over."[14] He begins his text with a

---

13 Richardson, *An Account of some of the Statues, Bas-Reliefs, Drawings and Pictures in Italy . . . with Remarks,* see preface.

14 Wright, *Some Observations Made in Travelling through France, Italy . . . 1720-1722,* p. vi. Wright, to the best of my knowledge, is the first to record an expression still frequent among Romans, "Were our amphitheatre portable, the English would carry it off."

Temple of Bacchus — "see where that wretch is now strumming a mandolino."

short vocabulary of art words: *cameo, chiaro oscuro, distemper, façade, fresco, giesso* (error for *gesso*), *guazzo, intaglio, noli me tangere, terra cotta, ritratto,* etc.[15]

According to Wright, Englishmen required a high degree of verisimilitude in art. For example, Wotton, one of the Elizabethan predecessors of the eighteenth century picture-buying Milords had taken home a fine work, which he bought because it was so life-like an image of two dogs that it would anger other dogs.[16] Wright mentions (1725) the statue of a "bull and a cow, antique." And adds "Whether this may be taken as proof of their excellence, I know not; but a dog that was with us and was remarkable for his subtlety and cunnig . . . bark'd eagerly."[17]

He follows this with some pertinent translations from the Greek Anthology concerning Corinthean Myron's brass cow:

Why dost thou thump my sides, dear calf, why low?
Art on this udder could not milk bestow.

Leave pelting, herdsmen, put you stones away!
I'm Myro's statue of a cow, no stray.

Myro, himself deceiv'd, begins to swear,
I made the statue of this cow, not her.[18]

The author included these tid-bits because they were entertaining and elegant and not because they enunciated a principle of æsthetics. Nevertheless, a felicitous imitation of nature was greatly admired.[19]

Art books of the second part of the century belong really to the period of English enthusiasm for the galleries and palaces of Rome and Florence, and will be mentioned later. The north of Italy, excepting Venice, has much less of art in it than Tuscany and Rome, even now. And in the eighteenth century it appeared to be an artistic blank to most travellers. Passing through the Alps and *Alt'Italia* was, nevertheless, an experience of greatest æsthetic import — stimulating as it did an individual's response to physical values. The beauties or even the majesties of nature were forced upon him irresistibly.

---

[15] *Ibid.,* pp. [xi]-xvi.
[16] Collison-Morley, *op. cit.,* p. 15.
[17] Wright, *op. cit.,* p. 309.
[18] *Ibid.,* see addenda to p. 309.
[19] Moore, *A View of Society and Manners in Italy,* p. 267.

He discovered, perhaps for the first time, the full significant use of his eyes. This almost ecstatic seeing of things, is at the bottom of all artistic creation and æsthetic appreciation. So, although northern Italy did not have pictures that impressed a traveller then, it performed a very valuable service. It gave a new sense of sight, the golden key without which one never enters the Land of Art.

II

The "noble phrensy"[20] of Alpine scenery — "horrid" pines and rocks, cataracts, peaks, trembling bridges, lone hermitages by the road — inevitably caused attempts to paint in words; and this failing as it always must, a writer often spoke with deeper appreciation of that wild and colorful Neapolitan, Salvatore Rosa. Some were moved to praise Nicholas Poussin or Claude Lorraine; and one Englishman, an artist on his way to study at Rome, actually attempted to make a picture himself on Mt. Cenis — and *at night!* He saw the mountains and the Mediterranean so clearly (the moon appeared five times as big as usual and more distinct than he had seen it through a telescope) and he was so filled with awe at the spectacle of nocturnal grandeur that he stopped, unpacked his things, and prepared to draw.[21] At that moment a troop of Savoyards came along the pass, and discretion told him that drawing at night might by the military be interpreted as an unfriendly act. So he continued on to Turin with the picture in his head.

Turin was not much of an art center. One traveller mentions seeing a Rape of Helen, a fine head of Rembrandt by himself, a Lucretia by Guido Reni, a Prince of Piedmont on horseback by Vandyck, the Dropsical Woman by Gerard Dou, which everyone noted with admiration, and some cattle by Potter.[22]

Leonardo Da Vinci's Cenacolo, much spoiled by damp, was frequently visited at Milan partly because of the fame of the artist, and partly because one of the hands in it had six fin-

---

20 Barry, *The Works* (London: Cadell, 1809), p. 59.
21 *Ibid.,* p. 58.
22 Walker, *Ideas Suggested on the Spot . . . in Italy,* p. 388.

gers,[23] which was very difficult to understand. The great cathedral, being Gothic, had little interest for the tourist during most of the century. Addison, for example, had been disappointed by the gloomy interior — marble, silver, and brass smutted and dusty. He walked around the outside counting the marble statues and found more dust and smut driven by Tramontane winds against the north side. As for the forest of stone pinnacles, and the vastness of the structure itself he wrote, that though this profusion of marble was astonishing to strangers, "it it not very wonderful" in a "Country that has so many veins of it in its bowels." Englishmen often agreed with Addison that the most valuable thing at the cathedral was a statue of St. Bartholomew "new-flead with his skin hanging over his shoulder."[24]

Padua, Vicenza (excepting its Palladian buildings much admired by the Earl of Burlington and copied in England by several noble lords) Verona, Ravenna, Forlì, Rimini, none of these cities were known for art works. It is something of a surprise that Sir James Smith at Padua noted a Giotto Virgin which he liked less than a Titian.[25] Bologna, of course, was the great exception. There hosts of ordinary people and even those as intelligent as Gibbon could "sincerely admire" the painting of the Caracci and Guercino.[26] Guercino was such a "divine" painter that Mrs. Piozzi always thought of him on fine days and compared him to Mr. Pope.[27] Peter Beckford said boldly that there was only one picture there worth seeing. It was Guido's St. Peter and St. Paul, which Sir James Smith, whose opinion was always worth something, called the "masterpiece" of the Bologna school.[28] Mr. William Robinson preferred the paintings at Bologna because they were in a high state of preservation "which is but seldom the case at Rome."[29] The most famous painting there was Raphael's St. Cecilia. And

[23] Peter Beckford, *Familiar Letters from Italy,* I, 80.

[24] Addison, *Remarks on the Several Parts of Italy,* p. 27.

[25] Smith, *A Sketch of a Tour on the Continent,* III, 7.

[26] Gibbon, *Autobiography,* pp. 159-160.

[27] Piozzi, *Observations and Reflections,* I, 414.

[28] Smith, *op. cit.,* II, 346.

[29] William Powell Jones, "The William Robinsons in Italy," *Huntington Library Quarterly,* V, 1941, p. 353.

sometimes (though rarely) seeing it, produced a curious inner conflict. One traveller wrote:

> The curtain drawing I must confess I expected to have fell on my knees with admiration, but I find it is an education of some time and application to learn to see. I stood a quarter of an hour between doubt of my own, or other people's taste. My own is certainly defective: for I must honestly confess, at the end of the said quarter of an hour, I found my refractory opinion as obstinate as at first. Can that have no excellence which all the world admires, and has admired for this 250 years?
>
> For the future I shall be doubtful what I say of pictures, when in *this* I can find nothing but a vulgar wench looking as if she was selling the organ she holds in her hand to three insipid bystanders, and was abusing them for not bidding her enough for it. St. Peter looks as if he was considering whether the instrument was worth the money.[30]

III

At first glance it is not easy to understand why Englishmen admired the Bologna school as much as they did. Perhaps sentimentalism had something to do with it, and the English saw what Sterne professed to see in the face of the monk at Calais. "It was one of those heads which Guido has often painted — mild, pale — penetrating, free from all commonplace ideas of fat contented ignorance looking downwards upon the earth — it look'd forward; but look'd, as if it look'd at something beyond this world." Perhaps the reverence for Raphael had something to do with it, the eclectics being descended from him. It may be that the taste for the Bologna school was a facet of the taste for Greek purity with which it was contemporary. "For what reason," exclaims Martin Sherlock, "is the voice of Europe unanimous in favor of Raphael? Because Raphael formed himself on the Greeks." Just as Pope refined himself by study and translation of Homer, so had Raphael purified himself by studying Greek statues and medals. And the Bologna school had etherialised itself still more by studying Raphael. Perhaps is was idealisation in Greek art, which had appealed to Winckelmann, and, as a consequence,

30 Owen, *Travels into different Parts of Europe,* I, 387; see Moore, *A View of Society and Manners in Italy,* p. 152.

to most of cultivated Europe; and possibly it was this same idealisation in the Bologna school that pleased so many Englishmen. Richardson, for example, praises "Divine" Guercino, who on one occasion "called his colour grinder, a great greasy fellow with a brutal look like the devil and bade him sit down . . . then taking his chalk, drew a Magdalen after him exactly in the same view and attitude and same lights and shadows but handsome as an angel."[31]

But apart from Bologna in northern Italy, not even Venice, the city of many of our best loved painters, was much noticed. The coloring of Tiepolo, for example, seemed "too gay" to Sir James Edward Smith.[32] No one noticed, or at least wrote about, the paintings of Giorgione. No one appears to have felt the bright May morning spirit of the early Renaissance, when human life was so full of the promise of youth. No one was impressed by the towering visions of the poet painters, whose marble columns soar through the very clouds, and whose human figures soar with them. The art-seekers were Rome-bound, Naples-bound, Florence-bound, eager to set eyes upon the art and the ruins of ancient Italy.

[31] *Johnson's England*, II, 26.
[32] Smith, *op. cit.*, III, 5.

CHAPTER VII

EIGHTEENTH CENTURY SOCIETY AT ROME

The Goth, the Christian, time, war, flood, and fire,
Have dealt upon the seven-hill'd city's pride;
She saw her glories star by star expire,
And up the steep, barbarian monarchs ride.

"Childe Harold's Pilgrimage,"
Canto IV

I

For what must have seemed an interminable time (it is long enough even now by automobile) the eighteenth century traveller rumbled across naked plains and the wide basins of extinct volcanoes. Behind him lay green-tufted hills honeycombed with Etruscan caves. Behind him lay sea-crossings, dust, mud, snow, fogs, hunger, cold, scores of early risings and wan departures from strange starlit cortiles — all trifles. He was near the end of all roads. And then at last before his own two eyes lay Rome sombre beneath the level haze of Latium!

It was a city of decadence. "Rome had her reign," wrote an English divine. "Britain once her vassal, looks down with proud contempt upon her ruins." It was true. "See where that wretch is now strumming his *mandolino*," one exclaimed. "It is perhaps the place where a virtuous father killed his child rather than see her handmaid of an Emperor's lust."[1] The "drover and the vagabond" occupied ground "formerly possessed by Gods and heroes." And temples "once consecrated to religion and eloquence became the haunts for beggars and stalls for cattle."[2] Goldsmith expressed this "proud contempt" in his *Traveller*.

. . . in those domes where Caesars once bore sway,
Defac'd by the time and tottering in decay,
There in the ruin, heedless of the dead,

---

[1] Walker, *Ideas Suggested on the Spot . . . in Italy*, p. 318.
[2] Owen, *Travels into different Parts of Europe in the Years 1791-1792*, II, 5.

The shelter seeking peasant builds his shed,
And wondering man could want the larger pile,
Exults and owns his cottage with a smile.[3]

Ancient buildings had been plundered by Renaissance nobility. The old Pasquinade, *Quid non fecere barbari, fecere Barbarini* is quoted in almost every book of travels together with caustic remarks concerning Roman princely families who plucked down parts of the Colosseum to build palaces, or Popes who would strip bronze from the Pantheon to make the *baldacchino* at St. Peter's.

So shrunken was the city that only part of the area enclosed by ancient walls was inhabited. The rest was grazed by sheep that wandered among the outcroppings of ivy-covered brick and cracked pieces of marble. Faithful shepherds made music in the fields. Rome seemed to be sinking back into a primitive bucolic age. The Colosseum was choked with dirt and so grown over with shrubs, grasses, flowers, ferns, and little trees that from the south it resembled a small hill. Fountains bubbled in their mossy beards, and murmuring dreamily of old years almost gave up being fountains at all.[4]

Nevertheless the ancient mistress of the world still raised

---

[3] Gray, in a letter dated Rome, April 2, 1740, wrote to his mother, "As high as my expectation was raised, I confess, the magnificence of this city infinitely surpasses it. You cannot pass along a street but you have views of some palace, or church, or square, or fountain, the most picturesque and noble one can imagine." *Correspondence,* ed. Toynbee and Whibley, I, 146. But Walpole wrote, "I am very glad that I see Rome while it yet exists; before a great number of years are elapsed, I question whether it will be worth seeing . . . Everything is falling to decay; the villas are entirely out of repair, and the palaces so ill kept, that half the pictures are spoiled by damp." And then he speaks of the poverty of the richest Romans. *The Correspondence of Thomas Gray,* ed. Toynbee and Whibley, I, 148-149.

During the first half of the century comparatively few English went to Rome and fewer still stayed there. There were student painters and art sharpers; but the aristocrat could not be completely at ease in the city because of the Stuarts. Some even avoided it like Lady Mary Wortley Montague because of a "certain person," — the Pretender. Sir Horace Mann, the English resident at Florence, had his observers, who kept track of the movements of the exiled Royal family and of all North Britons and English who clustered around him. See Gray, *op. cit.,* I, 158, and Lady Mary Montague, *The Letters and Works* (London, Bohn's Library, 1887) II, 51-52.

[4] Shelley described Rome in his lines to the "Pardlike spirit, beautiful and swift,"

"Go thou to Rome," the poet says,
"The grove, the city, and the wilderness;
And where its wrecks like shattered mountains rise,
And flowering weeds, and fragrant copses dress
The bones of Desolation's nakedness." etc.

her head in melancholy dignity. There were still suggestions of majesty in her dark arches. A young Englishman's arrival among the ruins of ancient Rome was, after years of classic education, a grand climax, in a way a kind of spiritual home-coming, a realization — and often a surpassing — of all his loftiest imaginings. Probably everyone remembers Gibbon's account of it. He wrote:

> My temper is not very susceptible of enthusiasm, and the enthu-siasm which I do not feel I have ever scorned to effect. But, at the distance of twenty-five years, I can neither forget nor express the strong emotions which agitated my mind as I first approached and entered the *eternal city*. After a sleepless night, I trod, with a lofty step, the ruins of the Forum; each memorable spot where Romulus stood, or Tully spoke, or Caesar fell, was at once present to my eye; and several days of intoxication were lost or enjoyed before I could descend to a cool and minute investigation.[5]

No intelligent traveller could possibly feel the contrast between ancient Roman might and her eighteenth century rot without endeavoring to explain it. According to Addison:

> Desolation appears no where greater than in the Pope's Terri-tories, and yet there are several Reasons would make a Man expect to see these Dominions the best regulated, and most flourishing of any other in *Europe*. Their Prince is generally a Man of Learning and Virtue, mature in Years and Experience, who has seldom any Vanity or Pleasure to gratify at his People's Expense, and is neither encumber'd with Wife, Children or Mis-tress; not to mention the supposed Sanctity of his Character, which obliges him in a more particular manner to consult the Good and Happiness of Mankind. The Direction of Church and State are lodg'd entirely in his own Hands, so that his Government is naturally free from those Principles of Faction and Division which are mix'd in the very Composition of most others. His Subjects are always ready to fall in with his Designs, and are more at his Disposal than any others of the most absolute Govern-ment, as they have a greater Veneration for his Person, and not only court his Favour but his Blessing. His Country is extremely fruitful, and has good Havens both on the Adriatic and Medi-terranean which is an Advantage, peculiar to himself and the *Neapolitans* above the rest of the *Italians*. There is still a Benefit the Pope enjoys above all other Sovereigns, in drawing great Sums out of *Spain, Germany,* and other Countries that belong to Foreign Princes, which one would fansy might be no small Ease to his own Subjects. We may here add, that there is no Place in

---

[5] Gibbon, *Autobiography,* pp. 156 ff.

Europe so much frequented by Strangers, whether they are such as come out of Curiosity, or such who are obliged to attend the Court of *Rome* on several Occasions, as are many of the Cardinals and Prelates, that bring considerable Sums into the Pope's Dominions. But Notwithstanding all these promising Circumstances, and the long Peace that has reigned so many years in *Italy,* there is not a more miserable People in Europe than the Pope's Subjects. His State is thin of Inhabitants, and a great Part of his Soil uncultivated. His Subjects are wretchedly poor and idle, and have neither sufficient Manufactures nor Traffick to employ them. These ill Effects may arise in great measure, out of the Arbitrariness of the Government, but I think they are chiefly to be ascrib'd to the very Genius of the *Roman* Catholic Religion, which here shews itself in its Perfection. It is not Strange to find a Country half unpeopled, where so great a Proportion of the Inhabitants of both Sexes is ty'd under such Vows of Chastity, and where at the same time an Inquisition forbids all Recruits out of any other Religion. Nor is it less easy to account for the great Poverty and Want that are to be met with in a Country which invites into it such Swarms of Vagabonds, under the Title of Pilgrims, and shuts up in Cloisters such an incredible Multitude of young and lusty Beggars, who, instead of increasing the common Stock by their Labour and Industry, lie like a dead Weight on their Fellow-Subjects, and consume the Charity that ought to support the Sickly, Old and Decrepid. The many Hospitals, that are everywhere erected serve rather to encourage Idleness in the People, than to set them at Work; not to mention the great Riches which lie useless in Churches and Religious Houses, with the Multitude of Festivals that must never be violated by Trade or Business. To speak truly, they are here so wholly taken up with Mens Souls, that they neglect the good of their Bodies; and when, to these natural Evils in the Government and Religion, there arises among them an averitious Pope, who is for making a Family, it is no wonder if the People sink under such a Complication of Distempers. Yet it is to this Humour of Nepotism that *Rome* owes its present Splendor and Magnificence, for it would have been impossible to have furnish'd out so many glorious Palaces with such a Profusion of Pictures, Statues, and the like Ornaments, had not the Riches of the People at several times fallen into the Hands of many different Families, and of particular Persons.[6]

---

[6] Addison, *Remarks on the Several Parts of Italy,* pp. 111-114. Baretti explains the value of church government in a land so crowded as Italy. He defends the ignorance of mendicant friars by saying their function is to confess sots, listen to complaints of the sick, sweep churches, and march in processions — all things not pleasing to poets and philosophers, but very useful to keep people happy. He refers travellers to the moderation of the Church of England prayer book preface, which says, "every country should use such ceremonies as they shall think best to the setting forth of God's honour and glory." And as

Three generations later Smollett was asking why the Cardinals and Princes did not encourage "industrious people to cultivate the Campania of Rome," and why "they did not drain the marshes in the neighborhood of the city," and why they did not introduce commerce and manufactures, and give "some consequence to their state, which was no more than a mite in the political scale of Europe."[7]

Even His Holiness the Pope of Rome (1775-1799) during the height of the Grand Tour was of a character that harmonized with the spirit of the time.[8] The Braschi, Pius VI, in person handsome and elegant, in the performance of ceremonies as graceful and as supple as a dancing master, preserved all the customs of the church in their pristine rigour and purity, kneeling and praying by the clock both in private and in public, exceeding all hopes in the outward manifestations of piety, and reviving in full force the somewhat neglected Renaissance tradition of nepotism with the assistance of that inordinately covetous boor, Duke Braschi.

II

Noble society at Rome was dominated at this time by the able French Ambassador, Cardinal de Bernis, who being particularly attentive to English visitors, consequently enjoyed high repute as a man of good sense, taste, wit, and generous disposition. He was all of this.

---

for church services, Baretti declares incense is very fine in a sweaty congregation. And he asks, "is there any greater sanctity in an organ than in a clarinet or a fiddle? and is the air more holily shaken by the vibration?" As a Catholic, he asks proof that the Protestant nations are "more tenderhearted, more hospitable, more magnanimous," than they were in older times. Baretti suggests that the Church of Rome was the only example of a long-standing government perpetuated, not by force, but by a knowledge of character, of human needs and other political considerations. And of Rome's oft-mentioned degeneracy, he observes. "It still contains men like those who have by turns lorded it over a great part of the Pagan and Christian world." The Romans are not degenerate. But their "art of managing nations has at last been learned by the other people." See appendix 5.

[7] Smollett, *Travels through France and Italy,* p. 98.

[8] Starke, *Travels in Italy,* I, 179. His Holiness, says Mrs. Starke, "was a Man whom no Party could wish to elect," but as the Cardinals were sparring to gain time, they all concurred in voting for Braschi, much to their astonishment. Moore, in his *A View of Society and Manners in Italy,* p. 270, conjectures that the Conclave desired a simple-minded man who might become a zealous disciplinarian of the Church.

Originally he had gone to Paris to seek his fortune with only polished manners and polished verses to recommend him. His path had crossed that of a very famous woman — Madame de Pompadour, and rising swiftly through her favour and his keen judgment, he had achieved the honorable posts of Ambassador to Venice and of Prime Minister under Louis XV. And under Louis XVI he had been sent as a Cardinal to be ambassador to the Papal Court. In the middle of the seventies the de Bernis household was controlled by a charming, dignified lady, the Marquise du Puy Montbrun. At that time the family circle included Vicomtesse de Bernis with her daughter of sixteen, and her husband, and the Abbe de Bernis, who was nephew and secretary to the Cardinal. Lady Knight, widow of Admiral Sir Joseph Knight, and her daughter, who sketched and painted, were rather fixed guests. And each day an average of twenty-five fortunate people sat at the Cardinal's dinner table.[9]

When the Marquise du Puy Montbrun died, her place was taken by the beautiful and enchanting Princess of Santa Croce. De Bernis frequently lost sizeable sums to her at cards. Every day dinner guests would see four dishes uncovered by four servants. The major-domo stepped about the table explaining each dish as he pointed with his ivory-tipped ebony wand of office. The Cardinal then would examine each, ask questions, and order them covered again and sent hot in a coffer lined with crimson silk to the Princess.[9]

At the conclusion of this little ritual, the guests would be served the usual delicacies and fruits, sweet-meats, rich wines and ices. Music played all the while; and after finger-bowls had been carried about by the servants, and strong coffee poured, the Cardinal invited his friends to play billiards — or rather *boccetta* with little marble balls, or to see the Colosseum by moonlight.[10]

Perhaps it will not be amiss here to insert a note on the gay

---

[9] *Lady Knight's Letters from France and Italy* (1776-1795), ed. Lady Eliot-Drake, (London: 1905), p. 65.

[10] *Ibid.*, p. 60. "We went to see the Colosseum by moonlight . . . It's not possible to express the solemn grandeur of it. The moon entered the broken part and struck full upon that which is most perfect, and as by that light no small parts were seen, you could almost believe that it was whole and filled with spectators. There is a little altar and a hermit's chapel, at all of which were lights, but the moon made them appear quite faint."

abbes whose presence enlivened the society of Rome. The only thing priestly about them was their clothes, which consisted of a black coat, knee breeches, silk stockings, and a long black silk mantle. Like other gentlemen, they were expected to wear powdered hair and it was usually tied with a ribbon of black. This costume, though not expensive, gave the wearer a kind of station or rank in society, indicating he was of good family and breeding. Abbes might marry, though there was not great need to do so. If they did, their wives were not permitted to wear velvet or brocade, and their carriages must be plain black — without silver decoration or painted coats of arms.[11]

Another egregious personage of the time was Donna Costanza, heiress of the Falconieri family, wife to Duke Braschi, the favorite nephew of Pius VI. She was small, plump, dark, and piquant rather than beautiful. At great functions she was always splendidly dressed, and, at small cost to herself. Her embroidered satin dress would be sent by one cardinal, her gossamer turban with jewelled feathers by another. Her sable-lined cloak would be the present of an ambassador. Her neck and arms glittered with jewels, and all these adornments, down to the painted fan she carried and her diamond shoe-buckles, were tributes of appreciation heightened by expectations of favour in the future.[12]

At night the indigenous Roman society came to life, though the city after sunset was plunged in primeval blackness. Its narrow streets were palely lighted by the stars and the moon. Shutters were all closed against nocturnal exhalations creeping from the Tiber. In the squares flambeaux or wrought iron lanterns burned by the great palace walls. And at obscure corners there were little statues and glassed in paintings of the Virgin where sometimes candles glimmered. The dark holes of the streets (not to mention the caves of the Colosseum) were wonderful places for amorous assignations, and as a coach clattered along to *conversazioni,* frequent would be the cry to the coachman, *"Volti la lanterna!"*[13]

---

[11] *Ibid.,* p. 86. Abbe Winckelmann used to lie abed naked for hours with Margaret Guazzi, enchanting wife of Raphael Mengs, to vanquish his natural sensuality. He was also devoted to beautiful Baron Friederick Reinhold von Berg and to a handsome castrate, whose picture he had painted, much to the embarrassment of the Vatican.

[12] *Ibid.,* p. 97.

[13] Peter Beckford, *Familiar Letters from Italy in 1787,* II, 301.

Conversazioni were the staple entertainment of the Italians in all cities, and of course they were about the same in all cities — just talk and gossip. Sometimes it was good, and other times it seemed to Englishmen, who could not quite enter into the spirit of it, rather dull.

III

It was a source of amusement to the British, sometimes a cause of pity, that the Italians still persisted in the mummeries of an obsolete religion. Englishmen in times past had done what they could to persuade the Vatican of its error, but although some travellers in the eighteenth century were able to remark a decline of true religious feeling, it was generally conceded that the Church of Rome, would endure for some time to come. Not everyone acquiesced to this view. Several attempts were made to convert the Pope. At the end of the seventeenth century there had been

> two English Quakers, who (having been bred merchants in some part of Italy) and consequently speaking the language took a journey from London thither, on purpose to convert the Pope. On their arrival, they applied themselves to his chief domestics, for several days together, to get audience; but used so much of their ordinary cant, and were withal so very troublesome, that the officers, taking them for downright madmen, out of mere charity sent them to Bedlam. The keeper, taking their zeal and unusual flights of spirit for symptoms of a distempered brain, shut them up in a dungeon, and treated them with the utmost rigour. The physicians likewise took them in hand, and in short time purged them almost off their legs, repeating and strengthening their doses as they found the maggot work: but all proving ineffectual, they were at length left off for infatuated persons past all cure, and permitted to walk up and down the house amongst the harmless lunatics.[14]

Eventually they were recognized by a party of touring Englishmen, who got to the bottom of the matter, and sent them home.

Another attempt was made several generations afterward. A Scotch Presbyterian loved to read the *Book of Martyrs* and it excited his imagination. One night he dreamed of a "train of bonfires, with a tar-barrel and a Protestant in each, all the

---

[14] Veryard, *An Account of . . . a Journey through . . . Italy,* (1701), p. 187.

way from Smithfield to St. Andrews."[15] This worried him, and he talked about it with the result that all of his books, excepting only the Bible were removed from his library. He felt the good sense of this himself. Then he turned to studying the Bible — especially Revelations. Somehow he received the impression that "whore of Babylon" referred to the Pope, and that it was his solemn duty to go to Rome and talk the Pope over to Presbyterianism. This idea made him so happy and cheerful that his friends and relatives believed him to be cured of his troubles. And therefore they were greatly surprised when they found that he had gone to London and had taken ship for Leghorn. Not long after he arrived in fine health at Rome itself. As his overtures to the Vatican were unavailing, he appealed directly to the Pope as he was performing a ceremony in St. Peters. He approached and in a clear voice began

O thou beast of nature, with seven heads and ten horns! thou mother of harlots, arrayed in purple and scarlet, and decked with gold and precious stones and pearls! throw away the golden cup of abominations, and the filthiness of thy fornication![16]

The Swiss guard carried him away to prison and would have sent him to the galleys but for the intervention of Pope Clement XIV (1769-1774) himself, who said he had never heard of anybody "whose understanding, or politeness had been much improved by that school." He even added that he was "obliged to him for his good intentions, and for undertaking such a long journey with a view to do good."[17] Afterwards he defrayed the expense of shipping the Scotch divine from Civita Vecchia to England. English Protestants, although they could not be content with the Church of Rome, were always eager to see its ceremonies. A spectacle very much hoped for was the Pope's *possesso,* surpassing in worldly glory even a British coronation. In this ceremony a new Pope took formal possession of St. John's Lateran, the oldest church in Christendom. And, of course, the prerequisite, the funeral ceremonies of deceased Popes, provided a day's excitement as the following horrible doggerel shows.

---

15 Moore, *op. cit.,* p. 271.
16 *Ibid.,* p. 273.
17 *Ibid.,* p. 274.

Unwieldly, drag'd with creaking moan,
Cannon revers'd, behind move on.
Shrill trumpets and hoarse kettle-drums,
(Conjoin'd with sympathetic hums)
A military consort made,
Well suited to the sacred shade
Of him, that dy'd a glorious saint.
As General of Church Militant.

    Within St. Peter's spacious dome,
Erected stood a lofty tomb;
Near which some hours the body lay,
That all their last devoirs might pay.
Then I, amidst the gaping crowd,
As Roman catholic avow'd,
Curious of this most pompous show
The ceremonies all to know,
The holy toe, among the rest,
With lips in feign'd devotion prest:
When in that very point of time
The penance followed close the crime.
Half mounted on my back one rode;
Upon my heels another trod
Who from my foot an old shoe tore,
Which I could ne'er recover more.
For had I stoop'd to search it out,
I'd been demolished by the rout . . .
Each squeez'd, and push'd, and gor'd his brother;
All kick'd, and trampled one another;
'Til our own feet were hardly more
Alive, than those we would adore.

    But when the proper time was come
The sacred reliques to intomb:
With elbows force, and utmost strength
Of arms, I freed my-self at length;
And leaving soon the crowded dome,
Through darkness hopp'd and hobbled home,
One foot dry-shod, one wet with mire,
Half protestant, half bare-foot friar.[19]

IV

Nearly every English traveller had seen the Carnival at
Rome. The "Corso" during the festivities would glitter with
three rows of coaches in procession. The outer two rows moved

---

[18] Gray, *op. cit.*, I, 124-125.
[19] Russell, *Letters from a Young Painter abroad*, pp. 22-24.

Italian landscape with a mill by Claude Lorrain, a favorite artist of the eighteenth century and one of the greatest European landscape painters. In the collection of Prince Doria, Rome.

Photo Alinari

up one side and down the other, just as coaches did formerly in Hyde Park in London. The row in the center, as it was somewhat protected from the populace, was used chiefly by foreign princes and cardinals, and by his Royal Highness, the "exiled Majesty of England," who in 1786 was "lolling in his coach, the very image of a drunken Silenus, more asleep than awake . . . small remains of expression to be seen in his face."[20] The common people had nicknamed him "The King of the Twelve Apostles," because he lived in a Square so called.

At the Carneval at Rome Noblemen drive their own coaches, dressed like women . . . with their servants following them clothed like so many Harlequins or Scaramouches. The Lady apes the Cavalier; and the gentleman represents the grave matron, strumpet, or country wench. Some walk in the habit of a doctor, hung round with urinals and pisspots. Some in a lawyer's gown, with their books and papers; and others to play the prince, take their robes from Congo, Monotopa, and Prester John's dominions.[21]

Coaches were fantastically decorated. Tough footmen decked out as ladies fanned themselves with listless delicacy. Small women strutted in big breeches and coats. One of the commonest figures was that of Quaker, who ran about with a stupid expression blithering, buzzing with his lips. Those who burlesqued Englishmen shook hands with everyone.

At a given signal coaches and masks cleared the street and there followed a horse-race without riders. The horses set off furiously, spurred by little balls of metal spines that pricked their sides. Sometimes the best racer would stop short in the middle of the course, permitting a slow contestant to lumber on victorious.

On the last day of the Carnival excitement reached its climax. Sir James Smith wrote:

The crowd was prodigious: but although every body was full of tricks, and all distinctions of ranks and persons laid aside, the whole passed off without the least ill behaviour, or anything like a quarrel. It was the most good-humoured mob I ever saw. About dusk everybody took a small lighted taper in their hands, and most people held several; happy were they who could keep the greatest number lighted, for the amusement consisted in trying to

20 Smith, *A Sketch of a Tour on the Continent*, II, 47.
21 Veryard, *op. cit.*, p. 198.

extinguish each other's candles. Some people carried large flambeaux. All the windows, and even roofs, being crowded with
spectators, and scarcely anybody without lights, the street looked
like a starry firmament.[22]

During this excitement the tourist might glance about him and
see the windows of the whole corso hung with bright red and
gold embroidered tapestries, or he might become very much
absorbed in studying the faces of the individual Romans.
Dr. Moore wrote:

> I imagine I preceive a great resemblance between many of the
> living countenances I see daily, and the features of the ancient
> busts and statues; which leads me to believe that there are a
> greater number of the genuine descendants of the old Romans in
> Italy, than is generally imagined.
>
> I am often struck with the fine character of countenance to
> be seen in the streets of Rome. I never saw features more ex-
> pressive of reflection, sense, and genius; in the very lowest ranks
> there are countenances fit for the highest and most important
> situations; and we cannot help regretting, that those to whom they
> belong, have not received an education adequate to the natural
> abilities we are convinced they possess, and placed where these
> abilities would be brought into action . . . Here you have none
> of those fair fat glistening, unmeaning faces, so common in the
> more northern parts of Europe.[23]

And then he indulged in some interesting chit-chat about young
women. He believed that if one hundred Roman girls were
compared with one hundred English girls, ninety of the English
would be found prettier than ninety of the Romans, but that
two or three of the hundred from Italy "would have finer coun-

[22] Smith, *op. cit.*, II, 52.

[23] Moore, *op. cit.*, pp. 289-290; Sherlock, *Letters from an English Traveller,*
p. 57, says Roman women were so assured, firm-stepped, bold-souled and possessed such a natural depth of understanding and strength of character that he
often exclaimed to himself, "There goes a woman who might well be the
mother of a Gracchus." In her *Travels in Italy* ,II, 60-61, Mrs. Starke tells a
story of the Trasteverini, said to be descended from the ancient Romans, and
so proud of their ancestry that they seldom condescended to marry a person who
did not claim the same origin. "A gentleman told me," she writes, "he lodged
in the house with one of these Trasteverini, a barber by trade, and wretchedly
poor, when his daughter was addressed by a wealthy and respectable German;
but notwithstanding these advantages, the lover received a rude and positive
refusal from the mother of the girl. My acquaintance asked the mother why
she acted so imprudently? — 'Your daughter, (continued he) 'is wholly un-
provided for; surely, then, you ought of rejoice in an opportunity of uniting
her to a rich and worthy man.' 'Rejoice in uniting her to a . . . Barbarian!'
(exclaimed the woman). 'No sir; were my daughter capable of cherishing so
disgraceful an idea, I should not scruple to plunge a dagger in her heart.' "

tenances than any of the English." And he reported that in the opinion of the English artists at Rome there were many countenances even among the working people that were "highly interesting, and which they prefer to all the cherry cheeks of Lancashire"[24] — a highly treasonous opinion.

Until Italy was upset by Napoleon, the English circle at Rome grew steadily and it apparently lost little of its London flavor by being transplanted under Mediterranean skies. Smollett said he received cards immediately on his arrival from each English family. But when he went to call on them, they had left orders not to be at home, "a refinement of hospitality and politeness," he said, "which the English have invented by the strength of their own genius, without any assistance either from France, Italy or Lapland."[25]

Lady Knight, who lived for several years in Rome about the time of the American War of Independence, recorded an incident of English aristocratic society which might almost have come out of the pages of a Jane Austen novel. "I wish," she wrote, "I could give you a good account of H.R.H. Prince Augustus, but I cannot."

> At a ball at Lady Plymouth's, a man we knew not asked Cornelia to dance. After a dance we found he was one Fagan, a painter who had refused our seeing his paintings *because we were enemies to the Revolution.* He is an Irish Catholic who changed his faith in England, and changed again to marry the daughter of C. Ritson's *valet de chambre;* — a very worthless fellow Fagan is, but under the patronage of his Royal Highness. He asked Cornelia to dance a second time, she refused, and I believe said, 'No, no, not now we know you.' Cornelia did not dance with him, but the man went and told the Prince, and when my daughter was dancing a little while after, the Prince came and stood by a lady next to me and said very loud, 'I would have danced with Miss Knight, but perhaps she would not have taken me for a partner,' and went on. I stepped up. 'Sir,' said I, 'that man was impertinent to us, nor do I think he is a gentleman.' He then said it was rude to doubt of any of Lady's Plymouth's company. I said, "My daughter or I, if we had offended Lady Plymouth begged her pardon, but believed there were many present her Ladyship did not know.'
> After my child had danced I told her; she sought the Prince, and said, 'Sir, I am told you disapproved of my conduct.' He re-

---

24 Moore, *op. cit.,* p. 291.
25 Smollett, *op. cit.,* II, 89.

plied, 'Nobody could.' She added, 'Sir, that painter has been very rude to us, and of course when I knew who he was I would not dance with him.' He said he was a Prince of England and as such must defend the artists; she replied, 'I know no law to oblige me to dance with a man I do not choose. I would do no wrong to any, or if I did I would ask pardon were he a beggar.'

Since that time the Prince made a concert and left us un-asked . . .[26]

While the English were thus busily engaged at each other's parties, and at *conversazioni,* and with making the rounds of Rome's multitudinous wonders, while they strolled through ancient sun-drenched gardens admiring the water-works and mechanical birds, while they made love to Roman ladies, and scampered about in lacquered coaches, republicanism exploded in France, threatening to subvert the whole system of international dalliance. And when the smoke had blown away, lo! *deus ex machina* was spied among the bloodied wreckage. He was to make still another attempt to persuade the Pope of his error.

V

On the tenth of February 1797 everyone knew that Buona-parte was charioting in the direction of Rome with a large army of well seasoned victory-flushed veterans. And when it was evident that the Papal levies had practically all melted into the receiving earth, because lacking arms (the Pope pos-sessed fourteen old field pieces) they lacked the *dono di coraggio,* the English began to think of saving themselves.

Mr. Graves, a gentleman, "whose conduct was exemplary, as he neglected his own private interest to preserve the prop-erty and ensure the safety of his Fellow-Subjects,"[27] appears to have taken up the duties of a minister. He called upon the Vatican Secretary of State to request passports and horses, but

[26] *Lady Knight's Letters,* pp. 206-207. Augustus Frederick, Duke of Sussex, was married at Rome by a Protestant minister, April 4, 1793, and again at St. George's Hanover Square, December 5, 1793, both times to Lady Augusta Murray, daughter of the 4th Earl of Dunmore. These nuptials violated the Royal Marriage Act. Accordingly Prince Augustus and Lady Augusta were de-clared not to be man and wife on August, 1794, notwithstanding the fact that they, or at least she, had two children. In his *Queen Victoria,* Chapter I, Sec-tion 2, Lytton Strachey adds, "On Lady Augusta's death, he married Lady Cecilia Buggin; she changed her name to Underwood; but this marriage also was void."

[27] Starke, *op. cit.,* I, 139.

had the mortification to be told no beast of burden would leave Rome for twenty-four hours. Meanwhile there was nothing to do but wait, as often happens in war, and the English diverted themselves as well as possible. Mrs. Starke walked towards St. Peters, "wishing to see, perhaps for the last time, that beautiful and majestic edifice."[28] On her way she found droves of horses and mules moving toward the Castle of St. Angelo.

There she found a train of carriages guarded by cannon. When she inquired, she was told by the soldiers that she was looking at the immense treasure of Loreto, saved almost miraculously by General Colli, just before the arrival of French troops. The Pope was sending it south to Terracina.

She walked on across the Piazza of St. Peters and into the church. The altars were deserted. A few women were praying.

A little later the Piazza was filled with people. They had learned that His Holiness and the favorite nephew, Duke Braschi, were intent on fleeing Rome. They were already disgusted at the Pope's shilly-shallying. Their leader had not only refused to defend his Patrimony. He had now, so the word ran, determined to leave Rome altogether. They were shouting vengeance. Twelve thousand enraged people surged around the Vatican, and they were ready to "murder all the Sacred College, not sparing even the Pope himself,"[29] if any one of its members attempted to desert.

The Papal family decided to remain.

Meanwhile the convoy of treasure left the Castle of St. Angelo and set out on the Via Appia to Terracina. But it was not the treasure of Loreto. It was merely the personal savings, amounting to more than two million pounds sterling, of His Holiness and his nephew from Vatican revenues. When the convoy had departed, Mr. Graves had better luck obtaining transport for the English, and they also began streaming down the Naples road. During this confusion, Mr. Graves, who "neglected his own private interest to preserve the property" of his fellow-countrymen, may have been able to manage something that did not come to the attention of Mrs. Starke. On page 137 of the first volume of her *Travels in Italy*, a con-

28 *Ibid.*, I, 137.
29 *Ibid.*, I, 138.

temporary hand has pencilled the following note in the Columbia University copy. "Graves brought to England a collection of pictures for which he asked £10,000 — among them a fine Ecce Homo."

When he saw the game was up, the Holy Father sent a letter of apostolic greeting to his son, Buonaparte, bearing health and benedictions. In it he gave his sacred word that nothing had been sent out of Rome. He also hoped for an amicable termination of differences.

For almost a year Pope Pius VI was permitted to rule Rome so he could raise money for the French. Buonaparte was not ashamed to admit that the old master could squeeze the lemon better than he could. And when it appeared that the lemon was dry, His Holiness was permitted to depart with a few possessions in a covered wagon and go to Siena, where rooms had been prepared. He was escorted out of town by French Dragoons, to protect him from the farewells of the populace,[30] and thus at the end of centuries, on the twentieth of February, 1798 Rome was left without a Pope, and the wheel of fortune began to turn away from nadir towards *risorgimento*.

---

[30] *Ibid.*, 1, 175-176.

The Temple of Peace — "Rome had her reign."

CHAPTER VIII

Travellers and the Arts at Rome

> *Fine Arts have ever been the darling favorites
> of fine genius, and where they have been con-
> demned or neglected, it has been observable
> that there is no public spirit, but a savage
> barbarity predominates, and poverty of soul;
> or at best, private views and a wretched mind.*
>
> Robert Samber

I

An Englishman's chief morning occupation in Rome was
seeing the almost endless sights. Dr. Moore tells of a traveller
who, perceiving the truth of *ars longa est, vita brevis,* hired a
brisk *cicerone,* fast horses, a sound vehicle and swirled about
the city, ticking off objectives as he passed, thus in a hard two
days earning the privilege of saying truly that he had seen
everything in Rome.[1]

And although sightseeing for anyone was apt to be an
absorbing effort of considerable duration, with the English it
often became a kind of religious ceremony. It required the
faculty, possessed by many of them, of seeing not only what is
to be seen, but also what is not to be seen. Jonathan Russell,
a painter in Rome in the mid-century wrote:

Some I have known stand upon the same spot of ground for a
good while, as it were in deep contemplation, where there was no
appearance of anything very remarkable or uncommon. Tho' such
a one might be thought *non-compos,* he might probably, from
his knowledge in history, be then calling to mind some brave
action, performed upon that very spot; and enjoying a pleasure
not to be felt by anyone confined within the walls of a study
or a chamber.

Frenchmen, according to Russell were deficient in this kind
of sightseeing. He described one of them listening to the guide
tell at great length how the obelisk before St. Peter's had been

---

[1] Moore, *A View of Society and Manners in Italy,* pp. 243-244.

brought from Egypt with vast expense, erected at a cost of 79,000 crowns when Sixtus V was Pope, weighed 973,537 computed pounds itself, and with Domenico Fontana's casing of planks and iron and his cordage, 1,053,537 pounds &c. When the antiquary had displayed his learning a good while, "the Frenchman, turning on his red-heeled shoe, said, with a briskness peculiar to his nation, "Eh, bien Monsieur, ce n'est qu'une pierre." He had no notion that *"Dulce est desipere in loco*; to him all places are the same."[2]

II

Before describing what he had seen, the traveller often warned his fellow-countrymen to be on the lookout for sharpers, for although Rome was a great art center, where Allan Ramsay, son of "Gentle Shepherd" Ramsay, and Knapton, Nollekens, Cozens, Barry, Wilson, Reynolds, Stubbs, Romney, and Sir Henry Raeburn all learned painting,[3] it was also a place where fakirs from all Europe (including Britain) operated on the credulity of rich tourists whose enlightenment saved them from idolatry of St. Veronica's handkerchief, holy nails, sacred staircases, pieces of the cross, divine bits of bone, and the "raree-shows"[4] of the Pope, but offered no protection against the spell of any bit of cut stone reputed to be antique. Englishmen bought whatever they could afford to buy at Rome. One traveller was so impressed by the carrying off of artifacts that he declared in 1746 that all the best things had been sent away and could be seen in England.[5]

[2] Russell, *Letters from a Young Painter to his Friends in England*, II, 180.
[3] Borenius, Tancred, *English Painting in the Eighteenth Century*, pp. 17-32.
[4] Whately, *A Short Account of a late Journey to Tuscany, Rome, and other Parts of Italy*, (London: 1746), p. 84.
[5] *Ibid.*, p. 40. Stephen Whately's *Short Account* is not a very valuable work. Jonathan Russell expresses his feeling for it in *Letters from a Young Painter*, I, 182, by saying he will tear leaf from leaf, wipe his bum, and throw them down the Cloaca Maxima.
The moment English travellers set foot in Italy, according to Smollett, *op. cit.*, II, 88-89, they were "seized with the ambition of becoming connoisseurs in painting, music, statuary, and architecture." That is not all they were seized with; but for some it was enough. One would be "pillaged by an antiquated cantatrice," another "bled by a knavish antiquarian," and yet another robbed by dealers in "masterpieces." Some would "turn fiddlers and pretend to compose." Everyone began to parley familiarly of the arts. Even old men caught the rage. Smollett knew "a boy of seventy-two, . . . actually travelling through Italy, for improvement, under the auspices of another boy of twenty-two." Peter Beckford knew an old Irish boy, "turned of eighty," who lodged in Rome in 1788 to "finish his education."

Year by year through the Renaissance and the seventeenth century as ancient statues were found, only the most perfectly preserved of them were admitted into palaces of Cardinals and Popes. The battered bodies were heaved into secluded corners of gardens and dump heaps, to be exhumed later by needy artists, who grafted on missing legs, arms, noses, ears, or heads (no one liked a statue without a head) and disposed of them to English lords. Sir Osbert Sitwell tells the story of a bodiless head of Minerva, which "even an Englishman would not purchase." The artist Nollekens matched this head with a trunk of "the same, or another, goddess," which cost him 50 guineas and sold the whole combination for 1000 guineas.[6] Such an achievement still falls under the category of creative work. But the business did not stop there. It was evident that if an old head, for example, might bring in a given sum, then two half heads carefully sawed from front to back and mounted on two slabs of marble as small *alto rilievos* might bring almost double. And conversely good figures might be liberated from a genuine relief and be sold by the dozen at good prices while the unwieldy relief itself would have been passed over.[7] When an English gentleman reached home, if he had no statues, he often had a crate of hacked off fragments of the Roman Forum and other chunks of classic marble, which he would have made into a polished table top bound around in bronze.[8]

III

In the matter of paintings the ordinary tourist was not much more particular. Originals by the best Renaissance painters, or even by Carlo Dolce, the Carracci, Guido Romano, or Guercino would usually be out of the question. They were not often for sale, even though the cash was often ready. And many lords were satisfied with rich glowing copies, as paintings were more to be felt — as one gazed into the eyes of a friend or the delicacy of a china teacup[9]—than studied directly.

When a rare painting did reach England in the eighteenth

---

6 Sitwell, "Taste," in *Johnson's England* (Oxford: Clarendon Press, 1933), II, 17.

7 *Ibid.*, II, 17.

8 *Ibid.*, II, 12.

9 Whitley, *Artists and their Friends in England, 1700-1799*, 1928, II, 33.

century, it was apt to create a sensation. In 1785, for example, the American painter Benjamin West suddenly discovered he had acquired a Titian. It had been painted originally for the Emperor Charles the Fifth, and was given to the Duke of Buckingham as a present in Spain, then found its way into the collection of Charles I, who smutted it to conceal its value during Puritan days. West had bought it[10] in this condition.

At the very end of the eighteenth century Napoleon's invasions made it advisable for Italian Princes and nobles to dispose of their pictures and Englishmen were happy to assist. Two of the best known picture brokers in Rome were Charles Grignion, and James Fagan, that "worthless fellow," whom we have met molesting Lady Knight's young daughter at one of Lady Plymouth's balls.[11] One recorded transaction of 1799 was the purchase by these two dealers of the Altieri collection (Altieri was blind!) of Claude Lorrain. These pieces were sent in a wagon to Naples, then put aboard a small boat and carried to Palermo, almost being lost in a storm on the way. At Palermo Grignion sought an introduction to Nelson and told of his problem with the paintings. Nelson exclaimed, "This is a national concern," and called for pen and paper and wrote to the Governor of Gibraltar requesting a convoy to the Tigre, a small armed vessel; and thus the Claudes reached England, where William Beckford bought them for the enormous sum of 7,000 guineas.[12]

IV

Obviously such adventures have little to do with the average genteel young man whose chief privilege and duty at Rome was merely to look at masterpieces. St. Peters seems to have been the usual place to begin. The piazza with its double semi-circular colonnade, its gushing fountains, the mighty obelisk, and the grand façade of the church never failed to produce an effect. "Sublime," was the word commonly employed to describe this as well as other wonders of the very first order in art and nature. The interior of Saint Peters struck everyone

---

10 *Ibid.*, II, 224-225.
11 See Chapter 7, note 26.
12 Whitley, *op. cit.*, II, 224-225.

as small at first, an illusion explained by the excellence of proportion.[13] The vast airy bubble of the dome was what pleased Addison most, and having looked upward into it with astonishment he went over to the Rotunda, which was known to be its original.[14] The Rotunda he thought filled the eye better at first glance than Saint Peters. Smollett's remark became classic. "I was much disappointed," he said, "at sight of the Pantheon, which . . . looks like a huge cockpit open at the top."[15] Then he gave it a full blast with a bit of anti-catholic salt mixed in.

> It has much the air of a mausoleum. It was this appearance which, in all probability, suggested the thought to Boniface IV to transport hither eight and twenty cart-loads of old rotten bones, dug from different burying-places, and then dedicate it as a church to the blessed Virgin and all the holy martyrs. I am not one of those who think it is well lighted at the top . . . It must be very disagreeable to those who go to church below, to be exposed to the rain in wet weather, which must also render it very damp and unwholesome. I visited it several times, and each time it looked more gloomy and sepulchral.[16]

This provoked Smollett's rival wit, Sterne, to write "Every object he pass'd by was discolored or distorted . . . I met Smelfungus in the grand portico of the pantheon — he was just coming out of it — 'Tis nothing but a huge cockpit," said he — I wish you had said nothing worse of the Venus of Medici replied I."[17] Smollett was one of the few travellers to notice art objects in an original way.

For example, no one beside Smollett made critical observations on the mosaic work in St. Peters. He thought the finish too glassy; and yet he was curious enough to go to the nearby house where the pieces of stone were cut and was "not a little surprised at the great number of colours and tints . . . kept in separate drawers, marked with numbers as far as seventeen thousand."[18] One of the mosaics reproduced a Michael the Archangel by Guido Reni. Smollett admitted that he was

---

[13] Addison, *Remarks on the Several Parts of Italy*, p. 108; Smollett, *Travels through France and Italy*, II, 105-109.
[14] Addison, *op. cit.*, p. 108.
[15] Smollett, *op. cit.*, II, 109.
[16] *Ibid.*, II, 126.
[17] Sterne, *Sentimental Journey*, "In the Street: Calais." (The third chapter of the same title.)
[18] Smollett, *op. cit.*, II, 106.

fond of Guido Reni for his tenderness and delicacy" though his expression is often erroneous, and his attitudes are always affected and unnatural."[19] Of Raphael's Transfiguration he said "if it were mine, I would cut it in two parts."[20] The figures in the air made one picture and those below on the mountain made another. He was charmed by Salvatore Rosa's and Claude Lorrain's landscapes; he enjoyed the colors of Guido Reni's famous Aurora; but pictures that had the cross in them, he disliked — together with those depicting gruesome subjects of religious history.

> The nauseous repetition of the figure of the cross, which is in itself a very mean and disagreeable object, only fit for the prisons of condemned criminals, have contributed to introduce a vitious taste into the external architecture, as well as in the internal ornaments of our temples. All churches are built in the figure of a cross, which effectually prevents the eye from taking in the scope of the building, either withoutside or within; consequently robs the edifice of its proper effect. The palace of the Escurial in Spain is laid out in the form of a gridiron, because the convent was built in consequence of a vow to St. Laurence, who was broiled to death like a barbecued pig. What pity it is that the labours of painting should have been so much employed on the shocking subjects of martyrology. Besides numberless pictures of the flagellation, crucifixion, and descent from the cross, we have Judith with the head of Holofernes, Herodias with the head of John the Baptist, Jael assassinating Sisera in his sleep, Peter writhing on the cross, Stephen battered with stones, Bartholomew flayed alive, and a hundred other pictures equally frightful, which can only serve to fill the mind with gloomy ideas, and encourage a spirit of religious fanaticism, which has always been attended with mischievous consequences to the community where it reigned.[21]

Smollett studied Raphael's School of Athens in the Vatican, commended the attitudes and gestures, but concluded that Raphael "had too much phlegm to strike off the grand passions . . . He has the serenity of Virgil, but wants the fire of Homer."[22]

Michael Angelo's works in the Sistine Chapel were admired by most tourists. In a letter to James Barry Sir Joshua

---

[19] *Ibid.*, II, 134.
[20] *Ibid.*, II, 126.
[21] *Ibid.*, II, 128.
[22] *Ibid.*, II, 126.

Reynolds advised not to waste time copying late Italian trivialities (*i.e.,* Bologna school) for cavaliers' houses, the common occupation of poor artists, but to study Michaelangelo. "The Cappella Sistina is the production of the greatest genius that ever was employed in the arts."[23] But Smollett, on the other hand, felt that Michaelangelo's Last Judgment produced the effect of a mere mob "without subordination, keeping, or repose. A painter ought to avoid all subjects that require a multiplicity of groups and figures; because it is not in the power of that art to unite a great number in one point of view."[24]

V

Experts have told us that many of the statues so much admired in the eighteenth century are not Greek at all, but merely copies of Greek originals. The famous Venus de Medici, for example, is no longer a wonder, and we have abandoned the Laocoon group, and the Torso of Hercules and even the gracious Apollo Belvedere for the broken figures of the Parthenon pediment.

But Smollett, along with almost all other travellers believed this Apollo to be "the most beautiful statue that ever was formed." Peter Beckford wrote that it was "so delightfully formed that the eye is never satisfied."[25] Lady Millar wrote a soliloquy which included the question, "Is it but marble that I see?"[26] Sir James Smith wrote, "All description is needless; nor can I add anything to the praise which all persons of judgment . . . have bestowed up on this inimitable production."[27] Although there is dignity in this figure and although the God possesses a fine intelligent countenance, there were a number of statues that might have seemed more wonderful had not Abbe Winckelmann singled this one out to shine so brightly that spectators lost both their eyes and their reason when they looked upon him.

Winckelmann's famous "hymn" to Apollo is quoted *in toto*

---

23 Barry, *The Works,* p. 85.
24 Smollett, *op. cit.,* II, 126.
25 Peter Beckford, *Familiar Letters from Italy,* II, 272.
26 Smith, *A Sketch of a Tour on the Continent,* II, 182, quoting from Lady Millar.
27 *Ibid.,* II, 182.

for three and a half pages by Sir James Smith. Among other things he says, "We must endeavor to penetrate into the empire of incorporate beauty; seek to become creators of a celestial Nature, in order to elevate the soul to the contemplation of such supernatural perfection . . . This body is neither warmed by veins, nor agitated by nerves." Then he imagines that the God has just shot his tremendous bow and given a mortal stroke to a tremendous Python, and that his sublime satisfaction passes into infinity. "Peace is seated on his forehead, and his eye is all sweetness . . . His locks seem perfumed with etherial essence . . . From admiration I pass into extacy."[28]

Martin Sherlock is typical of the late century admiration of Greek art. "Marble and bronze," he writes, "breath only coming from the hands of the Greeks." One day he went walking through the Vatican and the Villa Borghese not permitting the guide to say a word, and he discovered that all the statues that struck him most were done by the Greeks. "I consider the Greek nation not only as the best source of a perfect taste, but as the only one." Later he asks, "For what reason is the voice of Europe unanimous in favor of Raphael?" And the answer is, "Because Raphael formed himself on the Greeks." And not only Raphael — "Racine and Guido have viewed nature with the eyes of the Greeks."[29] The blindness of common culture-seekers is, of course, proverbial. A little anecdote of Sir Joshua Reynolds has a very familiar ring. He says that it is a tendency of tourists not to look for themselves at a picture.

> Instead of examining the beauties of the works of fame, and why they are esteemed, they only enquire the subject of a picture, and the name of the painter, the history of a statue, and where it is found, and write that down. Some Englishmen, while I was in the Vatican, came there and spent above six hours in writing down whatever the antiquary dictated to them. They scarcely ever looked at the paintings the whole time.[30]

Before Abbe Winckelmann appeared as the valiant defender of Greek taste, there had been a scattering of books about the arts at Rome, most of which had made no great stir

---

[28] *Ibid.*, II, 182-186.
[29] Sherlock, *Letters from an English Traveller*, pp. 158-169.
[30] Leslie and Taylor, *Life and Times of Sir Joshua Reynolds*, I, 2.

in the world. Lassels in 1670 had devoted 258 pages to the villas, palaces and churches of Rome. Robert Samber's *Roma Illustrata, or a Description of the most beautiful Pieces of Painting, Sculpture, and Architecture at and near Rome,* first came out in folio at London in 1676, and a second time in 1721, when it was dedicated to the Earl of Burlington.

Addison had written much about coins and medals, and had showed how the actions and expressions of statues could be understood better by bringing to bear information culled from the old writers (and how the old sculptures could illustrate the old writers). He had even recommended taking off wood models of ancient musical instruments in order to sweeten English music. Interpreting one art from the others he suggested would be a most fruitful study.[31] And a generation after Addison when Spence went to Rome, he too found that writings of the poets began to take on a new reality as he discovered visible parts of ancient Mediterranean civilization. Suddenly the light of the deathless Gods shone around about him. He determined to cross-fertilize poetry with statues, bas-reliefs, coins, and medals, and the result of his long labor of love was the publication in 1747 of *Polymetis* in ten books. In 1739 Chevaliere de Brosses wrote his *Lettres Familieres* on the excavations at Portici, and his Greek taste was a standard until Winckelmann began tussling with the stone serpents of æsthetics.

Abbe Winckelmann who reached Rome 1755 and was Librarian of the Vatican until his death in 1768, did more than any other individual to assure a general taste for Greek art. His first work, *Imitation of Greek Works of Art in Painting and Sculpture* appeared in 1755. One of his ideas was very simple. "Truth springs from the feelings of the heart."[32] He looked at classic art directly and intently as he felt the ancients would have done; from his own experience he derived the canon of beauty accepted by most Europeans for several generations.

His *Reflections on the Painting and Sculpture of the Greeks* (1760) translated by Henry Fuseli, and published at

31 Addison, *op. cit.,* pp. 29, 176, 187, 201.
32 Winckelmann, *Reflections on the Painting and Sculpture of the Greeks,* translated by Henry Fuseli. London, 1767, p. 10.

London in 1767 reminds one of Pope's critical dictum "nature methodised." In art there are rules, which happen to have been discovered by the Greeks. Greek statuary was finer than any, and Greek cut gems and intaglios, in the opinion of Winckelmann were more beautiful than any. Raphael was superior to other modern artists because his students collected Greek material for his use as models. Living persons were sometimes lovelier even than Raphael's beauty — but the Greeks threw out beauty higher than any which nature affords. The explanation lay in their familiarity with physical perfection in a variety of motions. Praxiteles used his exquisite concubine as a model, and Phidias visited the gymnasium every day were he saw youth in the glow of many exercises. Winckelmann's conclusion was, "Let no man, who has not formed his taste upon antiquity, take it into his head to act as the connoisseur of beauty; his ideas must be a parcel of whimsies."[33]

But even without Winckelmann a cult of Greek taste would have developed. In 1749 Lord Charlemont, a member of the Dilettanti Society, and one of the first to distinguish between Greek and Roman art, travelled to Greece with a draughtsman. On his return he published the first engravings of the Parthenon and Erectheion. And in 1753 Robert Wood's *The Ruins of Palmyra* appeared, and was soon followed by James "Athenian" Stuart's and Nicholas Revett's *Antiquities of Athens,* the result of a four year (1751-1755) expedition to Pola, Istria, Zante, Corinth and Athens. In 1764 Lord Charlemont produced another important work *Ionian Antiquities,* for which he had gathered information in an expedition to Smyrna. The Adam brothers were travelling in southern Italy, Sicily and Dalmatia at considerable expense. Robert Adam returned to England in 1758 after four years in the Mediterranean, and his brother Robert in 1763 after three years.

Nowadays perhaps the most admired artist of eighteenth

---

[33] *Ibid.,* p. 265. Sherlock, *op. cit.,* p. 63, quotes a saying of Poussin. "Raphael compared with the moderns is an angel; compared with the ancients, he is an ass," and he adds, "Taste and the arts have been carried by them [the Greeks] to such a height, that to think to surpass them will be always not to know them." Sherlock, as the reader must have gathered, is a very emotional, rhapsodic author. Benedetto Croce has an article on him, "Un viaggiatore in Italia nel settecento apostolo dello Shakespeare," *Critica,* 1928. The Italian reaction to this kind of travel-writing is discussed in Chapter VII of G. Natali, *Il Settecento,* Milano, 1929.

century Rome is that inveterate enemy of Greek taste, Winckelmann's great rival, Giambattista Piranesi, who believed in, and illustrated the universal supremacy of classic Roman genius, with engravings of wild, colossal ruins, that foreshadow the mood of Byron's

> Arches on arches! . . . There is given
> Unto the things of earth, which Time has bent,
> A spirit's feeling, and where he hath leant
> His hand, but broke his scythe, there is a power
> And magic in the ruined battlement,
> For which the palace of the present hour
> Must yield its pomp, and wait till ages are its dower.

Piranesi's engravings *Le Antiquità Romane* appeared at Rome in 1748 and such was the demand for them that they were issued again in 1756. In 1750 the series *Carceri* was published. But the admirers of Greek art gave him little rest. In 1751 le Comte de Caylus issued his *Recueil d'Antiquité's Egyptiennes, Etrusques, Grecques et Romains,* in which he hinted at the superiority of Greek over Roman ruins. The French were never loath to tread upon the Italians' pride in their antiquity. In 1758 J. D. Le Roy published *Les Ruines des plus beaux monuments de la Grece.* This provoked Piranesi's *Della Magnificenza ed Architettura de' Romani,* in which he declared that Greek art had too much ornament. And for some tastes this is true at least of the Ionic and Corinthian orders. In 1764 Pierre Jean Mariette replied to Piranesi in a letter to the *Gazette Litteraire* saying that Greek art was not ornate at all. Piranesi retaliated in 1765 with the famous *Parere su l'Architettura*; but in 1769, principally because of Winckelmann, he thought it wise to modify his assertions in *Diverse Maniere.*[34]

---

[34] A lucid account of the rise of Greek taste and of the Winckelmann vs. Piranesi aesthetic dispute is given in James Lees-Milne, *The Age of Adam,* London, Batsford, 1947, pp. 1-50. He says, p. 48, that the interest in Greece "coincided with that reaction, culminating in the French Revolution against the pictorial and the baroque, which had come to be associated with a tyrannous and decadent aristocracy." See also John Stegman, *The Rule of Taste,* London, MacMillan, 1936. Concerning baroque he says, p. 22, that it requires the hard clear atmosphere of the Mediterranean for contrasts of light and shade, and an accompanying splendor and extravagance, and that the style is almost incompatible with Protestantism, which explains its never taking root in England, and never becoming a popular style with the English tourists. B. Sprague Allen, *Tides in English Taste,* and Sir Osbert Sitwell's "Taste" in *Johnson's England,* Oxford, Clarendon Press, 1933, are both very

As this Winckelmann-Piranesi controversy died down, volumes of prints appeared, such as Marquis de Venuti's *Collection of some of the Finest Prospects in Italy,* 1762; Stephen's *Views in Italy, etcher . . . on the Spot,* 1767; Sandby's *Sixteen Views in Naples and other parts of Italy,* 1777.

Just before Napoleon descended on Rome John Smith brought out his romanticized or idealized *Select Views in Italy;* Merigot published *Views and Ruins in Rome*; and Andrew Lumisden published *Remarks of the Antiquities of Rome and its Environs.* In 1800 J. Salmon, Antiquary, after long residence in the capital of art, published two illustrated volumes densely packed with minutiæ, *An Historical Description of Ancient and Modern Rome, also the Works of Art, Particularly Architecture, Sculpture and Painting.* Also in 1800 Mariana Starke's *Travels in Italy* appeared with long lists of pictures and statues that must be seen, and each piece graded for value as in Baedeker — *e.g.,* Venus de Medici!!!! — four exclamations being the maximum. But such works were only the humble companions of travel, for the most part, and not important contributions to art or to art criticism and history.

VI

Among the other wonders of Rome are its fountains and its gardens. Sir James Smith wrote, "Rome is the only place to see really fine fountains: how different from the impertinent squirts of Versailles!"[35] Concerning gardens in Rome and in all Italy opinions differed. In general, although eighteenth century travellers enjoyed Italian gardens, they no longer admired the idea of them enough to plant them in England, as their noble ancestors had done in the time of Queen Elizabeth. It has been said that the English in their later eighteenth

---

illuminating. Capt. John Northall, *Travels through Italy,* London, 1766, pp. 9-10 divides painting into several schools: the Florentine, scrupulous in point of anatomy; the Roman for strength of expression nursed among the Greeks; Venetian, strong in coloring, but weak in design because it did not follow the Greeks; Lombard or Bologna, flowing mellow design, life-like colors laid on with a slight pencil (i.e., brush); German, commonly called Gothic gout, reproducing nature as we generally see her, i.e., with her defects and irregularities — not in her purity; Flemish, like German, excepting better colors and "claro obscuro"; French, "always so divided that no just idea can be given of it."

[35] Smith, *op. cit.,* I, 345.

century gardens were trying to use all nature to reproduce the romantic vistas of Salvatore Rosa,[36] although baroque serpentine still crept across many an English park.

It was natural that the old formal geometrical gardens should seem obsolete and that in them "Art [had] . . . most cruelly disfigured Nature, by endeavoring to embellish her."[37]

Smollett, as usual, has some delightful remarks on the subject.

In a fine extensive garden or park, an Englishman expects to see a number of groves and glades, intermixed with an agreeable negligence, which seems to be the effect of nature and accident. He looks for shady walks encrusted with gravel; for open lawns covered with verdure as smooth as velvet, but much more lively and agreeable; for ponds, canals, basins, cascades, and running streams of water; for clumps of trees, woods, and wildernesses, cut into delightful alleys, perfumed with honey-suckle and sweet briar, and resounding with the mingled melody of all the singing birds of heaven; he looks for plats of flowers in different parts to refresh the sense, and please the fancy; for arbours, grottos, hermitages, temples, and alcoves, to shelter him from the sun, and afford him means of contemplation and repose; and he expects to find the hedges, groves, and walks, and lawns kept with the utmost order and propriety. He who loves the beauties of simple nature, and the charms of neatness, will seek for them in vain amidst the groves of Italy. In the garden in the Villa Pinciana, there is a plantation of four hundred pines, or rather firs, which the Italians view with rapture and admiration; there is likewise a long walk of trees extending from the garden-gate to the palace; and plenty of shade, with alleys and hedges in different parts of the ground; but the groves are neglected; the walks are laid with nothing but common mould or sand, black and dusty; the hedges are tall, thin and shabby; the trees stunted; the open ground, brown and parched, has scarce any appearance of verdure. The flat, regular alleys of evergreens are cut into fantastic figures; the flower gardens embellished with thin cyphers and flourished figures in box, while the flowers grow in rows of earthenpots, and the ground appears as dusky as if it was covered with the cinders of a blacksmith's forge. The water, of which there is great plenty, instead of being collected in large pieces, or conveyed in little rivulets and streams to refresh the thirsty soil, or managed so as to form agreeable cascades, is squirted from fountains in different parts of the garden, through tubes little bigger than common glyster-pipes. It must be owned

---

[36] Sitwell, *loc. cit.*, see also Myra Reynolds, *Italian Landscape*.
[37] Peter Beckford, *op. cit.*, I, 283.

indeed that the fountains have their merit in the way of sculpture and architecture; and that here is a great number of statues that merit attention: but they serve only to encumber the ground, and destroy that effect of rural simplicity, which our gardens are designed to produce. In a word, here we see a variety of walks and groves and fountains, a wood of four hundred pines, a paddock with a few meagre deer, a flower-garden, an aviary, a grotto, and a fish-pond; and in spite of all these particulars, it is, my opinion, a very contemptible garden, when compared to that of Stowe in Buckinghamshire, or even to those of Kensington and Richmond. The Italians understand, because they study, the excellencies of art; but they have no idea of the beauties of nature.[38]

Nevertheless, observed Mrs. Piozzi, "An English nobleman clumps his trees, and twists his river to comply with his neighbor's taste, when perhaps he has none of his own," and then when he is thoroughly "disgusted with all he has done, . . . runs away to live in Italy."[39]

VII

The average traveller had little to say concerning music. There were books by experts devoted to a study of that art in Italy. But the tourist might write a hundred pages about statues, buildings and pictures to every one in which he discussed music. Sometimes one runs across references to famous singers, such as Senesino (Gray and Walpole met him as they were descending from the heights of Radicofani)[40] or the gifted and capricious Gabrielli.[41] There are remarks at random. Walker thought Italian taste in music "debauched" by listening to opera, like "snuff-takers who are first pleased with the gentle *Rapee,* after that with *Strasburgh,* then *Scotch,* and at last with *Irish Blackguard and Ground Glass."* And he felt that the Italians had been so long used to simple melody and unlearned harmony, that "except the ear is harrowed up with dissonance, discord, out-of-the-way sounds, they consider it vulgar, common, unworthy attention . . . Few think for

---

38 Smollett, *op. cit.,* II, 102-104.

39 Piozzi, *op. cit.,* II, 192.

40 Gray, *Correspondence,* ed. Toynbee and Whibley, I, 145. Francesco Bernardi ("Senesino") famous soprano engaged by Handel, 1720-1735, at London; see Peter Beckford, *op. cit.,* II, 382 ff.

41 Brydone, Patrick, *A Tour through Sicily and Malta, in a Series of Letters.* 2 vols., London, Strahan and Cadell, 1778. See last pages of vol. II.

Temple of Romulus and Remus at the foot of the ruins of the Palace of the Caesars

themselves," he concludes. "Fashion, that universal peda-gogue, draws us all into the great whirlpool; and we must think as other people do, not as we do ourselves."[42]

The painter, Russell, used to go to the Cappella Sistina to hear the choir perform music "so solemn, and so affecting"[43] that it was beyond believing, music no one could have a copy of, he said.

The music of the Cappella Sistina was mentioned years later by Sir James Smith.

> The performance is entirely vocal, yet sounds of instruments frequently seemed intermixed. Nothing can be sweeter, more plaintive, nor more harmonious . . . Well might Lady Miller . . . own "she never heard music before," and that "she had now heard enough to make her dissatisfied with the finest opera, and the most perfect performance to be found elsewhere." It is said that Emperor Joseph II, was so delighted with this music, he procured an accurate copy of the notes, and had it performed at Vienna; but the effect was not the same. German execution would not do; Italian taste was requisite.[44]

The next day Smith went again to hear the Miserere of another composer and wished that the impression might remain for-ever. Sir James was evidently more responsive than most tourists. He tells of visiting the church of Santa Maria in Vallicella at Rome. He was admiring a cupola painted by Pietro da Cortona, and some works of Guido and Caravaggio when the light began to fail and he prepared reluctantly to take his leave. Every one had gone from the church. Some-where rose "the most heavenly strains surely that ever came

---

[42] Walker, *Ideas suggested on the Spot . . . in Italy,* p. 302.

[43] Russell, *Letters from a Young Painter,* p. 52. Brydone, *op. cit.,* speaks of the native Sicilian music, heard as he went over to Malta.

"There was a profound silence, except the noise of the waves breaking on the distant shore, which served to render it more solemn. It was dead calm and the moon shone bright on the waters: The waves followed one another with a slow and equal pace. The scene had naturally sunk us into meditation; we had remained near an hour without speaking a word, when our sailors began their midnight hymn to the Virgin. The music was simple, solemn, and melancholy, and in perfect harmony with our feelings. They beat exact time with their oars, and observed the harmony and cadence with the utmost precision. We listened with infinite pleasure to this melancholy concert, and felt the vanity of operas and oratorios. There is often a solemnity and a pathetic [sic] in the modula-tions of these simple productions that causes a much stronger effect, than the compositions of the great masters, assisted by all the boasted rules of coun-terpoint."

[44] Smith, *op. cit.,* II, 264-266.

from mortal voice." It was a simple evening hymn. The singer was in a gallery above. The music was soon ended. "Its impression will never be erased from my mind."[45]

VIII

Nor did the traveller go to Italy to read Italian literature. During the Renaissance gentlemen from England often studied Italian and conversed with learned men. Milton wrote back to Florence that he would always love the banks of the Arno and the Faesulan hills, which had become as dear to him as Ilissus, because of the kindred spirits he discovered there.[46] In the eighteenth century there appears to have been much less contact with literary and learned men for two reasons: They were rarer in Italy then than before or afterward, and the national pride of the English made them seem even rarer than they were.

There were exceptions. Arthur Young went to talk with Italian agriculturalists. Watt sent letters to be delivered personally into the hands of Volta.[47] There were Academies, where meetings could be attended by foreigners. Condamine describes one at Rome, "a numerous audience . . . I fancied myself at Elis in the Golden days of Greece."[48] The Academy of Cortona, one of the Etruscan mountain cities, was publishing volumes of antiquities, under the patronage of Marquis Venuti. There were academies in almost all the Italian cities with doors open to learned visitors. At Padua Cesarotti was translating Fingal's *Ossian* and was mentioned by Robert Gray, Arthur Young, and Mrs. Piozzi. William Beckford heard him read "affecting passages in his Fingal, with all the intensity

---

45 *Ibid.*, II, 29-30.
46 Milton in a letter to Benedetto Buonmattai wrote:
Ego certe istis utrisque linquis non extremis tantummodo labris madiclus; sed siquis alius, quantum per annos licuit, poculis marjoribus prolutus, possum tamen nonnumquam ad illum Dantem, et Petrarcham, aliosque vestros complusculos, libenter et cupide comessatum ire. Nec me tam ipsæ Athenæ Atticæ cum illo suo pellucido Ilisso, nec illa vetus Roma sua Tiberis ripa retinere valuerunt, quin sæpe Arnum vestrum, et Fæsulanos illos Colles invisere amem.
Quoted in Toynbee, *Dante in English Literature,* I, 124.
47 Walker, *op. cit.,* p. 384.
48 Condamine, *An Extract from Observations,* pp. 140-141. Moore, *op. cit.,* pp. 351-352, speaks of recitations of Ariosto before street crowds.

of a poet, . . . persuaded that into his own bosom the very soul of Ossian had been transfused,"[49] a serious affliction certainly.

Of the *Commedia dell'Arte,* which gave most Englishmen so little satisfaction, Addison writes a clear account.

> The Comedies I saw at *Venice,* or indeed in any other Part of *Italy,* are very indifferent, and more lewd than those of other Countries. Their Poets have no Notion of genteel Comedy, and fall into the most filthy double Meanings imaginable, when they have a mind to make their Audience merry . . . There are four standing Characters which enter into every Piece that comes on the Stage, the Doctor's Character comprehends the whole of a Pedant, that with a deep Voice, and a Magisterial Air breaks in upon Conversation, and drives down all before him: Everything he says is backed with Quotations out of Galen, Hippocrates, Plato, Virgil, or any Author that rises uppermost, and all Answers from his Companions are looked upon as Impertinencies or Interruptions. *Harlequin's* part is made up of Blunders and Absurdities: He is to mistake one Name for another, to forget his Errands, to stumble over Queens, and to run his Head against every Post that stands in his way. This all attended with something so comical in the Voice and Gestures, that a Man,, who is sensible of the Folly of the Part, can hardly forbear being pleased with it. *Pantalone* is generally an old Cully, and *Coviello* a Sharper.[50]

Peter Beckford says he saw in the Pergola at Florence a "bloody Ballet," in which all the principal characters were killed, and it reminded him of a famous Italian tragedy, where towards the end of the last act, everyone goes off stage for a battle. After a short skirmish and a pause of dead silence, the prompter appears and says —

> *Uditore, m'accorgo che aspettate*
> *che nuova della pugna alcun vi porti*
> *Ma l'aspettate in van', son'* TUTTI MORTI.[51]

The poor state of literature in Italy was explained in various ways: too many *improvisatori* who recited poetry in public, no copyright, no encouragement from nobility, too great smoothness of the language. But, as I say, most travellers were not much interested in reading Italian literature anyway.

[49] William Beckford, *op. cit.,* p. 205.
[50] Addison, *op. cit.,* 67-68; Drummond, *Travels through* . . . *Germany, Italy, Greece,* p. 88.
[51] Peter Beckford, *op. cit.,* I, 260.

To be sure, there was a revival of interest in Italian studies during the second half of the eighteenth century.[52] English ladies learned the language in preference to the *più duro Latino,* and some great lords prided themselves on their ability to write letters in Italian.[53] But travellers were so busy, and rightly, with other things that they had no time for literary studies. One can see many unique sights and look through a hundred pictures in the time it would take to master an Italian work. Books could be perused in England later.

One of the controversies of taste at the time, concerned the relative merits of Tasso and Ariosto,[54] and though no traveller argued the point at length or with erudition, it was Tasso who received the preference, while some admitted the superior humor and wild fancy of the other.

Probably the most fascinating literary or quasi-literary phenomenon was that of *improvisatori.* The most accomplished of all the genuine bards was a Signora Corilla of Rome, whose extemporary poetry, which she sang and recited to the accompaniment of violins, was much admired by all the Romans and foreigners of the best taste. Mr. Ramsay told Dr. Moore that one night he had heard her sing for an entire hour, after a subject was given her, with only three or four pauses of about five minutes each, during which she recovered her breath and voice, the inspiration never flagging. "At her first setting out, her manner was sedate, or rather cold; but gradually becoming animated, her voice rose, her eyes sparkled, and the rapidity and beauty of her expression and ideas seemed supernatural."[55]

---

[52] See Roderick Marshall, *Italy in English Literature,* passim.

[53] Trevelyan, G. M., "Englishmen and Italians," *Proceedings of the British Academy,* 1919, p. 95.

[54] Peter Beckford, *op. cit.,* II, 409-410.

[55] Moore, *op. cit.,* pp. 356-357.

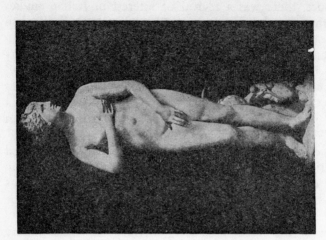

Venus dei Medici — Uffizi, Florence.

"This body is neither warmed by veins nor agitated by nerves . . His locks seem perfumed with etherial essence . . . From admiration I pass into extacy."

WINCKELMAN

"The softness of the flesh . . . inexpressible."

ADDISON

"I cannot help thinking that there is no beauty in the features of Venus; and that the attitude is awkward [sic] and out of character . . . Hercle! quanta dorsi concinitas! ut exuberantes lumbi amplexantes manus implent!"

SMOLLETT

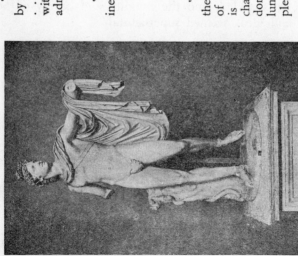

Apollo del Belvedere — Vaticano, Museo Pio Clementino.

CHAPTER IX

NAPLES: CITY OF THE SPANISH KINGS

*I own I have sometimes envied them their feelings;
and in my heart cursed the pride of reason and
philosophy, with all its cool and tasteless triumphs,
that lulls into a kind of stoical apathy these most
exquisite sensations of the soul.*

Patrick Brydone

I

"*Et in otia natam Parthenopen,*" Ovid wrote. "The people
free from cares, serene and gay,"[1] said Addison. "Whoever
wishes to lead a quiet and retired life, must not come to
Naples, the noise and bustle of which is inconceivable,"
warned Peter Beckford. "The inhabitants numerous; the
streets crowded with carriages; and the populace vociferous in
the extreme. When two Neapolitans converse together, an
Englishman would think they were quarreling: they gesticulate
even more than the French."[2] A Florentine nobleman once
told Mrs. Piozzi that he had asked a *lazzarone* to carry his
portmanteau for him and offered about a shilling. He had not
more than twenty yards to go with it. "Are you hungry,
master?" the fellow shouted. "No!" replied Count Manucci,
"but what of it?" — "Well then, I'm not either!" was the
answer, "and it's too hot to be carrying things."[3] So he rolled
over on the other side, and lay still. And there you have it!
Naples two thousand years ago, Naples two hundred years
ago, Naples at this very hour, and Naples at any given time
in the future.

There is a kind of clotted density of human life — a start-
ling confusion, unexpectedness, impropriety, indecency, and
cosmic comedy in Naples that absolutely defies definition or

---

1 Addison, *Remarks on the Several Parts of Italy,* p. 129.
2 Peter Beckford, *Familiar Letters from Italy in 1787,* II, 377.
3 Piozzi, *Observations and Reflections,* II, 18-19.

description. One either finds a richness of experience he never dreamed of there, or he shudders away from it with mingled apprehension and disgust. For example, crusty old schoolmaster Ascham wrote, "I was once in Italie myself, but thank God, my abode there was but nine days: and yet I sawe in that little tyme, in one citie [Naples] more liberty to sinne, than ever I heard of in our noble citie of London in nine years."[4]

Naples was in a very profound sense a foreign city. First of all, those who learned Tuscan Italian were no better off in the streets and shops than if they had never Italian at all. In February 1792 John Owen dropped down to Naples from Rome to see the end of the Carnival. He disguised himself in a long artificial nose and went to the San Carlo opera house, which was ablaze with lamps and candles. He hoped to enjoy the follies of the crowd, but found his entertainment "considerably abridged,"[5] by the extreme difficulty of "conversing with the natives." He said, "The monosyllable *mo* is used with a frequency and variety, for which I am entirely unable to account." As he was being rowed across the harbor, his boatman had "uttered with a loud emphatic tone of voice, to a fisherman at a distance *Mo!* The other, lifting up two fingers of his right hand, and inclining his head, replied, "Mo!"[6] It wasn't in the grammars. They seemed to speak with their bodies at Naples.

II

The great religious festival of Naples was of course, the feast of St. Januarius — San Gennaro, the patron of the city. Every tourist had something to say about it. It was an amazing affair, which occurred every Spring in Holy-Week. The Saint, to go back to the beginning of things, had been martyred in the third century. When he was decapitated a religious lady caught about an ounce of his blood which, having congealed, has been preserved carefully ever since in a small vial. The head also was kept and is enclosed in a large silver *busto* studded with gems of great price. Several times a year the

---

[4] Quoted by Baretti, *An Account of the Manners and Customs of Italy*, II, 139.
[5] Owen, *Travels into different Parts of Europe in the Years, 1791-1792*, II, 97.
[6] *Ibid.*, II, 97-98.

head and the vial are brought forth from the church. There are processions. Naples is crowded with orders of ecclesiastics all splendidly arrayed. Files of monks carry their varied banners. Crosses and heavy silver images are borne along the streets, and crowds surge from all quarters to come as near as possible to the place where the miracle will occur.

Perhaps it is better to let Dr. Moore describe it:

> A magnificent robe of velvet, richly embroidered was thrown over the shoulders of the bust; a mitre refulgent with jewels was placed on its head. The archbishop with a solemn pace, and a look of awe and veneration, approached, holding forth the sacred phial which contained the precious lump of blood. He addressed the Saint in the humblest manner, fervently praying that he would graciously condescend to manifest his regard to his faithful votaries of the people of Naples, by the usual token of ordering that lump of his sacred blood to assume its natural and original form.[7]

In most instances the blood would liquify without delay. It was very simple. Addison said that it was no miracle — only "one of the most bungling tricks"[8] that he ever saw; but he did not explain it.

Though the miracle or trick was successful when Dr. Moore saw it, the Archbishop first prayed earnestly for twenty minutes without results.

> An old monk stood near the archbishop, and was at the utmost pains to instruct him how to handle, chafe and rub the phial; he frequently took it into his own hands, but his manœuvres were as ineffectual as those of the archbishop. By this time the people had become exceedingly noisy; the women were quite hoarse with praying . . . the archbishop was all over in a profuse sweat . . . I never saw more evident marks of vexation and alarm than appeared in the countenance of the right reverend personage . . . I observed a gentleman come hastily through the crowd, and speak to the old monk, who, in a pretty loud voice, and with an accent and a grimace very expressive of chagrin, replied, "*Cospetto di bacco, è duro come una pietra!*" . . . An universal gloom had overspread all their countenances . . . One very beautiful young lady cried and sobbed as if her heart had been ready to break . . . [Others] were filled with rage and indignation at the Saint's obstinacy . . . and some went so far as to call him an old ungrateful yellow-faced rascal.[9]

---

[7] Moore, *A View of Society and Manners in Italy*, p. 400.
[8] Addison, *op. cit.*, p. 119.
[9] Moore, *op. cit.*, pp. 401-402.

The Neapolitans to this day, if they are teased enough by their patron, call him names and fling fruits and rocks. The Saint must understand that they have been faithful and loved him, and they still do love him; nevertheless they do not want bad luck for a year, and they are all ready to sing and drink wine and dance in his honor. He should cooperate. Dr. Moore goes on to say that when finally it was getting dark, a signal was given that the miracle had succeeded (though a Roman Catholic friend who was very close told him afterward it had utterly failed). Immediately there was an irruption of joy. A band began to play. Cymbals began to clash, couriers rode off to Portici to inform the royal family. The crowd began to move and wine began to flow. The pretty lady, who had wept so bitterly dried her tears. They were simple people, and they adored their saint.

III

The sights and sounds of crowded Naples were the same two hundred years ago. When you sat down in your *trattoria* for a coffee or a beer or a glass of *Lachrima Christi,* a mob of dirty boys and sly beggars would surge in among the tables. Waiters would drive them tumbling neck and heels into the street. But in a short time they would be back again like a wave breaking upon the shore.

When you walked along the sea-side (now Via Partenope) stepping carefully among the nets, you would be confronted with a man, a very poor looking man, who would, as a friend, sell you a Sygnathus Hippocampus, or sea-horse, for a *porta fortuna.*[10] He would carefully open his hand and the dried yellow little beast would lie exposed in his palm. It would certainly bring you good luck, though you might wonder why it had brought its finder so little, unless to live upon the bay of Naples is fortune enough in this world.

Then you would see the naked children brown as nuts. You would see beggar boys sleeping upon the bulks and benches, stretched out in parks, curled around the bases of lampposts in the middle of the street.

Hundreds of lazzaroni basked in the winter sun under the

---

[10] Smith, *A Sketch of a Tour on the Continent,* II, 91.

palace walls, and on hot days slept in the parks. Others pranced upon the rocks of the breakwater without so much as a flake of cloth to cover them in any part, while fine ladies twinked past on the *corso* in carriages that were "painted gilt, varnished, and lined in a rich and more beautiful manner" one traveller said, "than has as yet become fashionable either in England or France."[11] These vehicles would be drawn by six and sometimes by eight horses. As this last was the number allotted to his Britannic Majesty when he went to Parliament, some of the English were "offended that any individuals whatever should presume to drive with the same number."[12]

The real question in the minds of English visitors was this: how could the Neapolitans, obviously lazy, uncommercial, unindustrial, and uneducated according to English ideas of education, how could they support such finery in their equipages, so many servants, and so many expensive horses? They easily eclipsed the splendour of the richest English family.

It is still a question. The Kingdom of Naples was not capitalized. The only income was from the ground — and perhaps from the pockets of tourists. But this was a trifle confronted with the immense poverty of the city. Perhaps the answer is that thousands were desperately poor — though their innate wisdom gave them courage and happiness. Thousands were unemployed. And the thousands who worked as domestics were grievously underpaid. And yet it was amazing! When Dr. Moore went to dinner in one prince's palace, he saw an "infinite variety of dishes, and vast profusion of fruit, and the wines of every country in Europe." It was the most magnificent dinner he ever attended. At another prince's he walked through "twelve or thirteen large rooms" before reaching the dining hall, where "there were thirty-six persons at table."[13] There were servants in each of the rooms. There was one servant for each guest during dinner. The guests passed through another suite of rooms on the way out, and there they found still other servants. All this struck Dr. Moore as being rather Medieval, as indeed it might.

---

11 Moore, *op. cit.*, p. 325.
12 *Ibid.*, p. 324.
13 *Ibid.*, p. 325.

Unable generally to establish a free and easy social relationship with the Neapolitans, the English fell back upon their own resources, and amused each other. During the second part of the century Sir William Hamilton and Lady Hamilton held what amounted to a court for the tourists staying in the city. Sir William was one of those Englishmen who was "universally respected" and deserved to be so.

After the death of his wife Sir William's house was kept by the enchanting Emma Hart. Goethe has an account of an uncommon form of entertainment originated by Sir William and performed by Emma, which consisted of draping veils and posing in the characters of Bacchanals, muses, or whatever else become her. Such was the charm of this celebrated lady that George Romney painted at least twenty-four portraits, and made an untold number of sketches of her.[14]

IV

It was just as necessary for the tourist to see monarchs as it was to see pictures or any other works of art, and at Naples it was with the assistance of Sir William Hamilton that this was accomplished. William Beckford went one morning to watch the King of Spain eat breakfast in his palace.

I jostled along to the presence chamber, where his majesty was dining alone in a circular enclosure of fine clothes and smirking faces. The moment he had finished, twenty long necks were poked forth, and it was a glorious struggle amongst some of the most decorated who first should kiss his hand, the great business of the day. Every body pressed forward to the best of their abilities. His majesty seemed to eye nothing but the end of his nose, which is doubtless a capital object.

Though people have imagined him a weak monarch, I beg leave to differ in opinion, since he had the boldness to prolong his childhood and be happy, in spite of years and conviction. Give him a boar to stab, and a pigeon to shoot at, a battledore and an angling rod, and he is better contended than Solomon in all his glory, and will never discover, like that sapient sovereign, that all is vanity and vexation of spirit.

His courtiers in general have rather a barbaric appearance, and differ little in the character of their physiognomy from the

---

14 Borenius. Tancred, *English Painting in the Eighteenth Century*, p. 28.

118

most savage nations. I should have taken them for Calmucks, or Samoieds, had it not been for their dresses and European finery.

The King of Spain's Palace at Caserta was filled with paintings of stately huntsmen with their heaps of game.[15] Whenever Sir William Hamilton was unavailable to the English at Naples, it was a safe wager that the King had usurped him for a shoot. One of his favorite parks was the royal preserve near Pozzuoli — perhaps the surest place in the world for a successful slaughter.[16] The reader must imagine a small volcanic crater, a regular bowl about three quarters of a mile in diameter. The sides shelve steeply down to the floor about four hundred feet below the rim. All around the rim is a stout fortifying wall with little towers at regular intervals. There is one gate only on the south side. The *cacciatore* passed through and descended by rather steep road towards the bottom. The entire crater was densely grown with chestnuts and oaks. At the side opposite the entrance lay the royal hunting lodge, and in the woods around it lay hundreds of animals waiting to be shot.

The King's maximum efforts were directed against the wild denizens of the Apennines. On March 13, 1781 Sir William wrote that he had been "shooting for three weeks at Venafro . . . from morn to night without intermission persecuting boars, wolves, *chevreuil* and foxes, of which we have slain above 1000; 613 wild boars, some, most enormous and very fierce, which made it necessary for us to be entrenched." He continued the description of this bloody campaign saying, "We had two men wounded and numberless dogs killed." But the main thing was that the King told him *"senza adulazione avete sparato come un angelo."* There was nothing more important than being a good shot. "A good shot is a great man with us . . . Some days we had no less than 1000 men and 100 dogs in the woods, with drums, cow-horns, grenades etc. to drive the boars out of their impenetrable cover. But I have boar'd you enough!"[17]

---

15 Hill, *Observations and Remarks,* p. 67, was amused that the King of Naples had so many paintings of sea ports and of wild boar hunts hanging in the palace of Caserta. "The royal orders are that the colors must be all bright and glaring," which was a great strain for Mr. Hackert, who had the honor to be the King's first painter.

16 Martyn, *Guide,* p. 270.

17 Hamilton and Nelson Papers, from *The Collection of Autograph Letters formed by Alfred Morrison,* Vol. I, 1756-1797, p. 68.

In a kingdom ruled by a monarch like this, where there was so much confusion in the streets, so little contact with the nobility, comparatively few art objects, so much poverty and dirt, the Englishman could not wish to stay long. Most remained only a few days and then returned to Rome.

V

Not until the second half of the century did Naples come into its own as an art center. In 1738 excavations were begun in earnest at Herculaneum by the King of the two Sicilies.[18] And then Pompeii was discovered. In these sealed off chambers numerous bronzes were found, many of them of Greek workmanship.[19] From Naples a more intrepid tourist set out to see

[18] Gray, *Correspondence,* ed. Toynbee and Whibley, I, 163-164. "About a year ago, as they were digging, they discovered some parts of ancient buildings about thirty feet deep in the ground: Curiosity led them on, and they have been digging ever since; the passage they have made, with all its turnings and windings, is now more than a mile long. As you walk you see parts of an amphitheatre, many houses adorned with marble columns, and incrusted with the same; the front of a temple, several arched vaults of rooms painted in fresco. . . . Wood and beams remain so perfect that you may see the grain; but burnt to a coal, and dropping into dust at the least touch." In 1739 Chevalier De Brosses began describing the work at Herculaneum in his *Lettres Familieres.* His Greek taste was a standard until Winckelmann appeared.

[19] Martyn, *The Gentleman's Guide,* pp. 281 ff, tells of the superb museum of antiques at the royal country seat at Portici. To view this, it was necessary to have permission from the King of Naples himself; and this was obtained through the Ambassador, Sir William Hamilton, who was always very obliging. Only one party was admitted at a time and no one was permitted to make sketches or even to write notes while he was in the museum. Many statues were found, and 150 of them were engraved at the expense of his Sicilian Majesty. They were mostly bronze, the best one a Mercury sitting life size and a Jupiter larger than life. There were wrestlers, a drunken and a sleeping faun, and a multitude of small bronzes. Several rooms were full of *busts,* many of them of Greek workmanship. There were medals of gold, one struck in Sicily of Augustus in the 15th year of his reign. And there were intaglios, cameos, medals, altars, and inscriptions and even a vast collection of domestic utensils, such as tripods of elegant shape, and exquisite workmanship, lamps in endless variety, candelabras, silver strainers nicely worked, cases and basins of ample dimenions, scales for weighing, with a variety of weights, mirrors of polished metal, elegant cups and saucers in silver, shells and moulds for pastry, spoons, but nothing like forks; utensils for the bath, as brushes, strigils, phials for oils and perfumes; tesseræ or ivory tickets for the theatre, dice for playing, some of them loaded; all the apparatus for writing, as styles, tablets; a kitchen completely fitted with bronze pots and pans, some lined with silver, kettles, cisterns for heating water; a lady's toilet, fully furnished with combs, thimbles, rings, paint, ear-rings, bracelets, pins for the hair; surgical instruments; musical instruments, flutes, sistrums, lyres, cymbals; cratoli, altars, censers, pateras, and other appurtenances of sacrifice; a fine lectisternium, or couch, dedicated to the gods, a curule chair of bronze; helmets, shields and arms; screws, locks, keys,

the Dorian temples at Pæstum after their "discovery"[20] in 1755. Or one went to Sicily and the ruins of Greek colonies at Taormina, Syracuse, Girgenti and Segesta. Some few even went to the sites of Sybaris and Locri beyond the wilderness of Calabria.

The knowledge of these Greek places and things, and the tremendous enthusiasm for them coincide with the Greek predilections of Winckelmann and with the chaste classicism of the Adam brothers. As the decades passed Sir William Hamilton at Naples brought out his imposing folios of engraved Greek vases, designs and pictures.[21] Although there were expeditions to Greece itself, it is fair to say that most Greek dreams were assuaged in Italy. Even Winckelmann died without ever having seen Greece. But he had seen ancient relics from the shores of Naples, and he had seen the Temple of Poseidon at Pæstum, which shows the power and the glory of Greek genius as well as anything in the Mediterranean.

---

latches, bolts, hinges, and nails; various utensils in glass; and colored glass so hard and well colored as to appear like precious stone, which also were found in great numbers though no diamonds. Precious stones included amethists, emeralds, onyxes, cornelians clumsily set in gold. There were little crystal bottles, nets, balls of thread, gold lace, colours for painting, the measure of a Roman foot; bells to hang around the necks of cattle, letters in metal for marking. Eatables were recognizable though burnt to cinders: corn, bread loaves, pies, almonds, dates, beans, nuts, figs, grapes, eggs, fish, oil, and wine. The floors of these rooms preserved in the bowels of the earth, safe from the ravages of time and barbarians during seventeen centuries, were paved with most beautiful mosaics. There were many (800) volumes of mss. found, but they were very difficult to unroll. One of them was unrolled and was found to be a Greek treatise on the bad effects of music in a republic. The paintings, of which about 700 were collected, were usually small and represented single female figures, centaurs, etc., on dark grounds; cupids or winged genii in a variety of amusements or employments, arabesques, animals, fruits, vases, shells, whimsical buildings. Most of these pictures were not particular in any way. The coloring of course may have suffered. As far back as 1689 some inscriptions had hinted that Herculaneum was buried under Portici. The Prince d'Elbeuf in the year 1718 put the matter beyond all doubt. The first knowledge in England was in 1732, and the first real large scale excavations were made by his Sicilian Majesty in 1738. The city was seen to have been buried by ashes, not lava ,as had been supposed, though subsequent to its original first burial six layers of lava had flowed over it. The digging of Pompeii began in 1755. In 1753 Bellicard's *Observations on the Antiquities of Herculaneum* was published with 42 plates.

20 "Discovered" is Brydone's word, and it was appropriate as far as cultivated European society was concerned.

21 Sir William was also writing to Josiah Wedgewood recommending the forms of ancient vessels. See *Hamilton and Nelson Papers,* collected by Alfred Morrison, 1, 19. See list of works consulted for Sir William's publications.

St. George by Donatello who shared obscurity with Botticelli, the della Robbias, Masaccio and Piero della Francesca during the 18th century while blind aestheticians knowingly discussed the relative merits of Greeks and Romans. "Tis thus aspiring Dulness ever shines," as Pope says.

CHAPTER X

LIFE IN FLORENCE AND TUSCANY

I

At Florence under the shadow of the cupola and the campanile imagination reaches out through gardens, through
country-places, and lone profiles of cypresses to windy Apennines in the West and North, to Vallombrosa in the East,
through vistas of Chianti to Mt. Amiata, and down Valdarno
to melancholy Pisan shores where pines whisper forever to the
western strand. At Florence the spirit tranquillizes and ex-
pands to all the farthest corners of Tuscany's blue peace.
There an Englishman can open his eyes to the hills around
him, to the far-off mountains, and, overwhelmed by the
mystery of this land as all northerners have been, see the art
that inspired art, and is still beyond its utmost reach — nature
affable, humanized, punctuated by little cities that lift their
towers like cries of joy into the azure light. It is Tuscany,
after all, that is the Englishmen's second home — more than
Venice, more than Naples, and more even than Rome. In those
places, except rarely, the foreigner lives in the city. Venice is
cut off by water; the plains of Rome are a desert. Naples
seems to turn its back on the Campagna Felice, or at any rate,
the poverty of the country there, despite its apparent fruitful-
ness, has seldom invited Northerners to rustic life excepting
on the shores. But all of Tuscany's happy rural life invites.
It seems to have its heart in Florence just as little England
once had its heart in Elizabethan London. Old London has
lost itself; but Florence has remained the same. So that in the
city and in the country around it, Englishmen find something
of the past. They escape into the simplicity and the harmony
they once possessed at home, so that Tuscany has, since the
mid-eighteenth century, been their other England.

Florence, wrote Captain Northall, is "the Italy of Italy
itself."[1] It was the well of the Renaissance, and excepting the

---

[1] Northall, *Travels Through Italy*, p. 38.

classic collections in the Galleria degli Uffizi, what was to be seen in Florence was distinctively Italian. Lady Mary Wortley Montagu wrote

> The palaces, squares, fountains, statues, bridges, do not only carry an aspect full of elegance and greatness, but discover a taste quite different, in kind, from that which reigns in the public edifices in other countries. The more I see of Italy, the more I am persuaded that the Italians have a style (if I may use that expression) in everything, which distinguishes them almost essentially from all other Europeans. Where they have got it, whether from natural genius or ancient imitation and inheritance, I shall not examine; but the fact is certain.[2]

Thirty years after his visit there Horace Walpole still remembered Florence as "the loveliest town upon earth!"[3] Mrs. Piozzi said Florence was "so lovely, so neat that . . . she should be seen only on holidays."[4]

II

Englishmen were profoundly impressed by the capabilities of the Medici family. Arthur Young, the economist, wrote:

> How commerce could enrich it sufficiently to leave such a prodigious remains is a question not a little curious; for I may venture, without apprehension, to assert that all the collected magnificence of Bourbon governing for eight hundred years twenty millions of people is trivial when compared with what the Medici Family have left for the admiration of succeding ages — sovereigns only of the little mountainous region of Tuscany, and with not more than one million of subjects. And if we pass on to Spain, or England, or Germany, the same astonishing contrast will strike us.[5]

It is one of the curious coincidences of history that the English first began to live in Florence at the time the Medici became extinct. The last Medici Grand Duke, Giovanni Gastone, sunk into a coma in his pearl covered bed and breathed his last on July 9, 1737.[6] His sister, the Electress Anna Maria Ludovica, then seventy years old and a widow, was living in

---

[2] Lady Mary Wortley Montagu, *Letters and Works* (London: Bohn's Standard Library, 1887), pp. 77-78.

[3] Doran, *Mann and Manners at the Court of Florence*, II, 200.

[4] Piozzi, *Observations and Reflections*, I, 321.

[5] Young, Arthur, *Travels in France and Italy*, pp. 285-286.

[6] Col. C. F. Young, *The Medici*, p. 735.

Florence, and according to a decree of the city's Senate, she should have ascended the throne. Great powers outside of Tuscany, however, sent M. de Beauveu, later called Prince de Craon, with a collection of Lorrainers to the Palazzo Pitti, where he held a garish court soon famous for vulgarity.[7]

Anna Maria, "the last of the Medici," lived apart with quiet scorn in a retirement of the utmost splendour. Horace Walpole was presented to her in 1740. She stood "with much ceremony" dressed all in black under a pavillion of black. The strictness of her life did not appeal to him or to Thomas Gray. She never went out, "but to church, and then she has guards, and eight horses to her coach."[8] Three years later on the 18th of February she died.

Horace Mann, the English Resident, wrote that the instant the Electress expired, "the gates of the town were shut and not a creature permitted to go out."[9] Hundreds of people from the country were obliged to stay in Florence that night. "Even the French courier was not permitted to go. These precautions were interpreted that the Spaniards might not be appraised of it."[10] And these precautions also show the importance of the passing of the Medici in the minds of the Tuscans. It is said that the poor wept inconsolably and that the public demonstration of grief was something almost without parallel in history.

The funeral was a spectacle of dark grandeur. At night on the 22nd of February Mann saw the body "on a sort of coach, quite open, and with a canopy over the head,"[11] drawn slowly from the Palazzo Pitti, along the Via Maggio, across the Ponte Santa Trinità, and through the Via Tornabuoni to the mausoleum. The way was lighted by a "prodigious number of torches carried by different orders of priests."[12] The whole city was thus gloomily illumined to signal the end of the family that had guided it through the Renaissance.

---

[7] *Ibid.*, p. 737.

Also see Boyle, *Letters from Italy,* p. 234. He says the Prince de Craon lived far beyond his means in Florence, and when he went back to Lorrain he was compelled to sell his plate and other other household effects to pay his debts; see Gray, *Correspondence,* ed. Toynbee and Whibley, I, 135, note 7.

[8] Gray, *op. cit.,* I, 136.

[9] Doran, *op. cit.,* I, 145.

[10] *Ibid.,* I, 151.

[11] *Ibid.,* I, 30.

[12] *Ibid.,* I, 15.

III

Horace Mann's letters from the Court of Tuscany are for Florence in the eighteenth century what the letters of Walpole are for England of the same time. They cannot be compared to Walpole's for literary quality. They lack the poise and *elan vital* of Walpole. The author was quite as much as a gentleman. He possessed the same iridescent worldliness; but he was no writer. The matter of spelling for example never ceased to be a mystery to him. He had many amusing things to tell. Yet he was almost never witty, and if he makes the reader laugh, it is, or seems to be, rather by accident.

Mann went to Florence in 1740 about the same time Walpole and Thomas Gray went through Italy. Walpole returned home like most travellers. He was glad to get back to the "middling houses," of England "so snug."[13] But Mann replied, "If we could alter some things (many things), and totally change the climate, it (England) would be preferable to all other places."[14] As it was, he was happy to be in Florence. And he took great pains to stay there for the next forty-six years, and at last died there, at a time when Florence and the banks of the Arno and the hill of Fiesole had become almost as much a part of the English scene as Strawberry Hill, and the banks of the silver streaming Thames. It would be interesting to know how many thousands of English travellers had sat at his Florentine dinner table.

IV

Horace Mann's first duty in Tuscany was to report the Pretender's movements. In May 1741 Prince Kaunitz had been hired by England to spy at Rome,[15] and comparatively inconspicuous persons flitted about with speed and precision to gather the facts.

On August 22, 1741 Mann wrote:

the Eldest boy . . . going off at night, in company with Murray and one servant. It was in so private a manner that nobody knew

---

13 *Ibid.*, I, 33.
14 *Ibid.*, I, 35.
15 *Ibid.*, I, 229.

it. My Abbe got notice of it two days after . . . They went in a borrowed chaise 3 posts from Rome; and then they took post by Foligno, Fossombrone, so to Brescia, by the Grisons into France . . . The French King (but I can't believe it . . .) declares him Commander-in-Chief of all his troops by sea and land.[16]

And to make matters even more serious "202's (Mann's) friend at 77 (Rome)" informed him "that two of Miss North and Grey's tenants (Scotsmen) have been there to confer with 11 (The Old Chevalier)."[16] This was the beginning of something that materialized many months later. On August 6, 1743 Mann reported letters of the Pretender in code intercepted and sent to Hanover for study. The following January he was alarmed at the rumor that the Pretender's son was on a visit to "Miss North and Grey" with the French Fleet. On April 28, 1744 Skelton and Stafford left the Old Pretender at Rome to join his son somewhere. In August 1745 he wrote that everyone was talking of the Young Pretender's arrival in Scotland, and "none but villains are received at Rome."[17] His friend Chute was told by Murray there that "the King his Master," was highly offended at his "insolence in not going to court," since he must know "how things go now."[18] On May 31, 1746 Mann was finally at ease on account of the Pretender. "Well!" he exclaimed with a touch of sarcasm, "the Duke (Cumberland) is a glorious little hero. I am glad the nation is obliged to him."[19]

V

As Mann stayed on at Florence, he lost touch with the life of London. Pope's new *Dunciad* was to him "vastly obscure."[20] And he was not ashamed to admit it. "I so detest that abject creature that I am even prejudiced against all he can write."[21] His prejudice was not confined to Pope. It extended to the whole English spirit at the time, which he thought was tiresome and ridiculous. One day he heard of the suicide of a young Englishman at Leghorn. Why did he do it? "The young

16 *Ibid.*, I, 202.
17 *Ibid.*, I, 234.
18 *Ibid.*, I, 58-59.
19 *Ibid.*, I, 287.
20 *Ibid.*, I, 162.
21 *Ibid.*, I, 272.

fellow has been long enough in Italy to purge off the English spleen which made him cut his throat."[22]

Why didn't the English have better manners? "Most of our fashionable travellers bring us to shame; no language; no address, 'tis horrible."[23] And "Basta! We have no English here now; and so much the better."[24]

By 1751 his countrymen had become so thick in Florence that Mann was thinking of a villa outside the city. "But I am afraid of its becoming a cheesecake house for all the English. . . . We have a larger flight of Woodcocks than has been seen for many years past — near thirty stareing [sic] boys."[25]

Few English tourists "are ever worth mentioning, except for their absurdities."[26] He mentioned for this reason the ex-Lady Walpole or Orford, who had various lovers at Florence after her husband's death and returned to England, married, separated, went back to Florence again, where she became decorous, and lived on the hill of Fiesole for many years, remembering a youth of excessive frailties.[27] He mentioned Lord Plymouth, "the most sweet temper and fat body I ever knew . . . immovable before he is thirty." Florence was bad for the young English. "Lord F— losing his whole time by acting Cicisbeo to Marchese—. Then Sir B. B. nursing a dancing girl in an obscure villa . . . Lord Archibald Hamilton lives in the woods of Tuscany. He is a wild boy."[28]

There were exceptions. Mr. Conway and Lord Stourmont were the "two most perfect gentlemen that ever came from England into Italy." And another, a "roving genius," Lord Huntington, had acquired great knowledge of the world in his travels. "He has learnt Italian to a surprising degree . . . in a

---

22 *Ibid.*, I, 326.

23 *Ibid.*, I, 370.

24 *Ibid.*, I, 380.

25 *Ibid.*, I, 233.

26 *Ibid.*, II, 69.

27 *Ibid.*, I, 370. William Robinson at Florence April 1761 writes, "We dined the other day with Lady Orford at Sir Horace Mann's, who really behaves with so much freedom that she gives no small offense in this country which is so civil and forgiving to the frailties of your sex. She is at present engaged in nursing a young gallant to whom they say she gives £100 a month. If his illness proceeds from his too great attention to her, I hope you allow her Ladyship gratitude at least." See *The William Robinsons in Italy*, William Powell Jones, The Huntington Library Quarterly, April, 1941, letter #1.

28 *Ibid.*, I, 428.

month." He studied medals with Dr. Cocchi and statuary with the British sculptor Wilton. "With all his application he loves dress." He had that very easy politeness (*disinvoltura*) that distinguishes those who have kept select company, "so that in every article, he is made to shine with great gout."

Dr. Cocchi was Mann's best friend at Florence. He was described by the Earl of Corke as "a man of the most extensive learning, who understands, reads, and speaks all the European languages." He said that if he could converse often with Mann and Cocchi, he would "scarce desire to return to England for many years." And the Earl also after he had lived a little in Florence in 1755 noticed the defects of English manners. — "that shyness, that obstinate, silent, rude reserve which we practice towards ourselves and all the rest of the world."[29]

No account of Anglo-Florentine friendships in the eighteenth century would be complete without mention of Mrs. Piozzi and the "Della Cruscan" episode which resulted in the publication of the *Florence Miscellany,* 1785. Soon after her arrival at Florence during the previous year, Mrs. Piozzi and three young English travellers, Bertie Greatheed, Robert Merry, and William Parsons began diverting themselves as polite people have often done by writing compliments to each other and Italy in verse. In order to give the collection of poems a truly "Della Cruscan" flavor several Italians were induced to contribute: Pindemonte, Pignotti, the Count d'Elci, and D. M. L. The English verse was not only devoted to Italian subjects. The meters and rhymes of Italian poetry were imitated, and the whole work was supposed to contribute to the defense of the Tuscan poetic traditions.

There may be some question as to the value of the verse. It is not all bad. But it is a forced and academic collection at best, a pretty kind of run-down Milton. On page 159 appears the following ditty.

> *Hail Diana, Goddess fair!*
> *Jocund huntress ever hail!*
> *Haste, and bind thy flowing hair;*
> *Let us seek the distant vale.*
> *Exercise shall there be near*
> *Cheerful sport shall shake his spear* [!]

---

[29] Boyle, *op. cit.,* p. 143.

And raise his merry voice,
Rejoice, rejoice, rejoice,
And search the grounds, around, around . . .

As the corks unnumber'd fly,
Mirth attend with wanton eye,
Quaint device, facetious story
And loud song of England's glory.

Other better pieces might be selected, but this will suffice.[30]

VI

Sporting Englishmen were much at home in Florence where great skill was shown in management of horses. "You who pique yourself on being a good whip, and . . . drive a set of horses almost as well as your coachman, what think you of a gentleman who drives sixteen horses, eight pair, without a postillion?" Beckford asked. Commendatore Pazzi had frequently done it in the narrow passages of Florence. There was one gentleman who drove four abreast standing up in a two wheeled chariot. "Low was the car and open behind; conveniently constructed to get up or down — to fight or fly.[31] This modern Paris" was the wonder of Florentine sportsmen. Still another showed his finesse by driving up and down the *corso* during the hullabaloo of the carnival in a coach the body of which was all porcelain![32]

Even without the sporting part of it life was very pleasant in Tuscany — one of the cleanest, most prosperous and refined parts of Italy. "What a delightful thing is a nobleman's seat near Florence! How cheerful the society!"[33] exclaimed Mrs. Piozzi. The peasants were happy. They were rich enough to

30 Marshall, Roderick, *Italy in English Literature*, (1755-1815) New York, Columbia University Press, 1934, gives a thorough discussion of the "Della Cruscans," and of the *Florence Miscellany*, pp. 173-195. He says "It was based on affection for Italian poetry, liberty, history, and scenery. It has been hailed by the few persons who have read it as a definite prelude to many of the poetic forms, themes, and emotions which reached their height in Byron, Keats and Shelley. In no way was it more romantic or more prelusive than in its turning to Italy for inspiration." p. 180. In this last Prof. Marshall has hit the nail on the head, for actually the poetry itself is unispired, weak, ultra-conventional. Perhaps it should be respected for what its authors wished it to be. Mrs. Piozzi did not have much to do with the miscellany.

31 *Ibid.*, I, 272. Peter Beckford, *Familiar Letters from Italy*, I, 272.

32 *Ibid.*, I, 263.

33 Piozzi, *op. cit.*, I, 305.

wear jewels, "and those of no small value." The *contadinella Toscana* arranged her ornaments with such natural elegance as to deserve a woman's attention. On holidays she wore an exceedingly rich white silk skirt full and not too long so that her slipper and pretty ankle might be appreciated. Her hair might be drawn away from the face a bit too tight for English taste, and yet this gave her a perking air "infinitely nymphish and smart."[34]

VII

Other Tuscan towns were of considerable interest. Pisa was depopulated and grass grew in the streets. Smollett wrote that if he were to fix anywhere, it would be in this quiet city by the Arno, and though[35] he rushed ahead with his tour, still he had his wish, for he came back to Italy, and lived at Pisa working on his masterpiece. It was there that he was stricken with mortal illness. Eager to live a little longer he removed nearby to the slopes behind Leghorn, where he could look at the sea from which he derived deep solace. There, chastened and calm, he sat in the spring sun (1770) and finished *Humphrey Clinker*.

The City of Leghorn itself with its bawling seamen, and rattling chains and carts was not the favorite resort of English tourists, though many of them saw it in their travels to and from Italy. As early as 1720 Edward Wright observed:

> There are so many English always there [Livorno] and so many of our merchant ships use that port, that our language is understood by many natives of that place; so that even in walking along the streets, one should not speak that in English, which he would not care to have a Livornine hear.[36]

It was a place of great tolerance and was worth considering at a time of mounting nationalisms. Mrs. Piozzi described it in an excellent figure of speech. "The geometricians tell us," she wrote, "that the figure which has most angles bears the nearest resemblance to that which has no angles at all; so here at Leghorn, where you can hardly find forty men of a mind,

---

34 *Ibid.*, I, 306.
35 Smollett, *Travels through France and Italy*, II, 52.
36 Wright, *Some Observations made in Travelling through France, Italy, ...* in *1720-1722*, p. 378.

dispute and contention grows vain, and comfortable though temporary union takes place while nature and opinion bends to interest and necessity."[37] The English Protestants had chaplains[38] and churches there, and what is even more remarkable the Moors were permitted to worship in a mosque in the port.[39]

Not far from Pisa Lucca lay lost in trees and grasses. She was much admired for her ancient and still extant liberty, though the pride of some Englishmen was piqued when guards at the gate took their pistols before permitting them to enter.[40] And Lucca was surrounded by lovely villas too, with views of a verdant, gardened valley, and jagged mountains in the sky around it.[41]

VIII

And now a word must be said of Siena, after Florence the Englishman's favorite Tuscan city. It most resembles some cloud-capped city of phantasy. Certainly after seeing Siena one can never look with patience on hackneyed artists' visions of the sweet land of fairy with golden roads winding up steep hills into swooning castles. And there is one thing at least, on which no artist of fairy-tale cities is likely to improve. This is, of course, the flying Torre del Mangia. And if Italian is the most expressive living language in the world, as some believe it is, Siena is the city where it has always been spoken in its

---

[37] Piozzi, *op. cit.*, I, 353.

[38] George Berkeley preached there.

[39] Drummond, Alexander, *Travels through different Cities of Germany, Italy, Greece*. London 1754, describes very minutely the King of Sardinia's admiral galley, commanded by an Englishman, Brigadier Paterson, whom he visited at Leghorn, July 20, 1744 O.S. "The cabin is sixteen feet in width, the length of the rising amounts to thirteen feet; the width of the galley, from plank to plank, extends to three and thirty feet; the length of the whole, two hundred and nine feet; the diameter of the main-mast is one foot and ten inches; the main yard with the spurs, is in length one hundred and thirty four feet, being in circumference nine feet and a half; the oars, being sixty three in number, are eight and forty feet long each. The crew consists of seventy-five sailors and three hundred and sixty three rowers; seven men to an oar abaft the mainmast, six to each forwards. . . . Three times a week the slaves are shifted, and wash each other every morning; so that every thing is so sweet and clean, that, notwithstanding the crowd of people who cannot move from their banks, and the heat of the sun in this climate, there was not the least offensive smell." pp. 33-34.

[40] Doran, *op. cit.*, I, 72. Mann settled a dispute between the city of Lucca and a hot tempered Englishman named Wright, June, 1742.

[41] Piozzi, *op. cit.*, I, 336.

greatest purity. Even the speech of her children is bell-clear. And her gentle courtesy is a by-word and has been among the travellers of many centuries. Cut in stone at Porta Camollìa you will see *Cor magis tibi Sena pandit*. And in the Piazza del Campo surrounded by rose-red walls of Gothic palaces you know you have indeed entered into a unique heart· "The Piazza of Siena is the finest of any city in the world," wrote Montaigne in the sixteenth century. And Maurice Hewlett in the twentieth century said simply, "I am very sure he is right."[42]

What did the Rome-seekers and ruin-hunters of the eighteenth century think of Siena? They did not admire its Gothic architecture, and many sped through like Smollett, stopping only long enough to sleep and eat a poor meal. A few lived in Siena for years. Mrs. Piozzi mentions a Mr. Greenfield who had formed himself a sweet retreat in the hills outside the walls,[43] and she says she would gladly fix there for life. Others were detained for a while like Boswell, by a combination of romance and a desire to perfect their language. "According to Peter Beckford, "You cannot pass a summer more pleasantly than at Siena . . .[44] Nor will you find so much courtesy, and so much cordiality in any other town in Italy."[45] He admired the air of freedom. "Liberty that mountain nymph, was ever dear to this lively people."[46] He enjoyed the fanciful traditions. Take care not to drink water of the Fonte Branda; it will make you extravagant like the Senese.[47] He loved to promenade in the Lizza on summer nights where there was a "freshness of air unknown in other parts of Italy."[48] He liked the women, who walked up and down the hills in the city so much that they looked "healthier and handsomer than in other places."[49]

---

[42] Hewlett, *The Road in Tuscany,* p. 192, note 1.

[43] Piozzi, *op. cit.,* I, 375. "I with half a word's persuasion would fix here for life."

[44] Peter Beckford, *op. cit.,* II, 44. Thomas Martyn in his guide writes that Siena, in the midst of hills, of the most pleasing shapes, excellently cultivated, is perhaps the most desirable place in Italy for a stranger to pass some time in. The climate being moderate, living reasonable, society good, and the language spoken in the greatest purity . . . about 16 or 17 thousand inhabitants. particularly agreeable because of its lofty situation.

[45] *Ibid.,* II, 44.

[46] *Ibid.,* I, 435.

[47] *Ibid.,* I, 441.

[48] *Ibid.,* I, 444.

[49] *Ibid.,* I, 448.

He enjoyed the Palio, which he described as the "best contrivance for breaking bones, the rack only excepted, that I ever beheld." It has "more the appearance of a battle than a race," and is surely "an invention of the surgeons."[50] Then he describes the festivities of the victorious Contrada after the Palio, its nightlong revels, its demi-deification of the successful horse and jockey, and all the rest that one can read of in a hundred books on the subject now that the Palio has become one of the favorite spectacles of Europe. Twice a year the noisy city is filled with those who come to see flag-flaunting processions, burnished armor, cloth of gold, frenzied horses and riders, to hear drums and clarions.

Siena gave Beckford ideas of what English life ought to be. He liked the *contadini*. "They plough with oxen. I am old enough to remember that custom in England, before farmers became gentlemen, and sent their daughters to a boarding-school."[51]

Of the people within the walls he wrote:

Their hearts are excellent, and their manners courteous. Society is on a pleasant footing. The women receive you at home. How is it in England? Your visits there nine times out of ten are to the porter. Madam is at her toilette, or is engaged in some domestic concern and does not chuse to be at home. Here the fair sex have literally nothing to do, and society is always welcome. Besides, though I esteem and respect the virtues of my countrywomen, there is a coldness and reserve in their manners totally unknown to the inhabitants of warmer climes.[52]

---

[50] *Ibid.*, II, 30.
[51] *Ibid.*, II, 73.
[52] *Ibid.*, II, 10. Peter Beckford is by nature a hard-boiled writer with no grace and a sharp, sometimes a blunt thrust which is supposed to penetrate or shock the risibles of his chauvinist reader. But he had lived in Italy for fifteen years, so that parts of his book shows an uncommon, and almost anti-English favor to the Italians.

CHAPTER XI

TUSCAN ARTS

I

The Uffizi Galleries according to Addison housed the "noblest collection of art in the whole world."[1] The behavior and the expressed feelings of Englishmen in this place are revealing to say the least. That cold reserve which masks the true sentiment of an English heart (a sentiment which has for centuries made Italy a second homeland) seemed to vanish. First they were disarmed by Florence and its visionary and Elysian landscape, the pale gray of olives, the hills wrapped in purple haze, their tops swimming in saffront light.

On a bright day of September 1780, having slept as well as his impatience would allow, William Beckford went to visit the Gallery "and worship the Venus de Medici."[2] He felt, upon entering, as though he could have taken up his abode there forever; and confused by so many objects, he could not give serious attention to any one. He ran by the ample ranks of sculptures, "like a butterfly in a parterre, that skims, before it fixes, over ten thousand flowers."[3] He fled past all the masterpieces of bronze and marble, pausing momentarily for sober reflection beneath the bust of Jupiter Olympus, moving on past Minerva, and Cybele, through the hall of self-portraits, and then past a file of ancient Cæsars, (a favorite part of the collection for most Englishmen) and cabinets of medals, of ancient talismans, of cut gems, perfumed cases of miniatures, and finally to the Tribuna. "Need I say I was spellbound the moment I set my feet within it, and saw full before me the Venus of Medici?" He marvelled at the "warm ivory hue of the original marble," and the "softness of the limbs."[4] Another traveller said he could tell immediately that Venus was con-

---

1 Addison, *Remarks on the Several Parts of Italy,* p. 235.
2 William Beckford, *Italy,* p. 126.
3 *Ibid.,* p. 126.
4 *Ibid.,* p. 129.

scious of being disrobed. "She looks on one side afraid that some eye may be near . . . and she has that enchanting doubt regarding the propriety of her situation, that one becomes afraid of looking at her." She stands on one leg, "which inflates one muscle in the thigh, and depresses another into a beautiful dimple."[5] Gibbon acknowledges at her feet "that the chisel may dispute the pre-eminence with the pencil, [*i.e.*, brush] a truth in the fine arts which cannot . . . be felt or understood"[6] north of the Alps.

It would be long work to collate all the encomiums of English travellers on "this statue which enchants the world," to read how spectators "kindled as they gazed," and how words could never describe. Lady Mary thought that the Venus and the nude Antinous should be placed together. Yet if marble could see and feel, which almost seemed credible, perhaps the separation was prudent.[7] Some measured her. Addison felt her wrist and found her the right size of woman, and "the softness of the flesh . . . inexpressible."[8] Lady Anna Millar, despairing of description, took a tape measure and found she was four feet nine and three quarters inches high.[9]

One noble and poetic lord early in the century wrote some verses on the goddess.

> *When approached, the marble dame*
> *Gives not astonishment, but flame;*
> *So just, so fine, so soft each part,*
> *Her beauties fire the lab'ring heart.*
> *The gentle risings of the skin*
> *Seem push'd by muscles mov'd within:*
> *The swelling breasts, with graces fill'd*
> *Seem easy to the touch to yield &c. &c.*[10]

I hardly think it incumbent on me to defend the beauty of these lines, but the things they say deserve a word. It is so much the custom now to be amused at the old admiration of this statue, generally believed to be a third century B.C. imita-

[5] Walker, *Ideas suggested on the Spot . . . in Italy*, p. 346.
[6] Gibbon, *Autobiography*, pp. 148-150.
[7] Lady Mary Wortley Montagu, *Letters and Works*, Bohn's Library, II, 78.
[8] Addison, *op. cit.*, p. 236.
[9] See Maugham. *The Book of Italian Travel*, p. 43.
[10] Wright, *Some Observations Made in Travelling Through France, Italy . . . in* 1720-1722, p. 407.

tion of an Aphrodite of Praxiteles, that one might easily think our English forebears had no eye for beauty at all. It is true that the western world has learned much more about art since, and that our taste, (we hope) is more enlightened and inclusive, thanks to a historical approach. Still the Venus of Medici is by no means a completely bad or dull statue. The hands are, as Peter Beckford said, *"maniere."*[11] But if one will look at the statue, not photographs of it, and imagine it without arms, one will see that there *is* a surprising and heartwarming feminity there — an exuberant allure of flesh.

Smollett's summary is quite appropriate, though Sterne remarked, "in passing through Florence, I had heard he had fallen foul upon the goddess, and used her worse than a common strumpet, without the least provocation in nature."[12] This last phrase is not strictly accurate. There is some provocation in the nature of Venus de Medici, and the innane stupidity of her face almost compels the eye to that provocation, as frequently happens with ill-favored women.

Smollett writes:

> With respect to the famous Venus . . . I believe I ought to be entirely silent, or at least conceal my real sentiments, which will otherwise appear equally absurd and presumptious. It must be want of taste that prevents my feeling that enthusiastic admiration with which others are inspired at sight of this statue: a statue which in reputation equals that of Cupid by Praxiteles, which brought such a concourse of strangers of old to the little town of Thespiæ. I cannot help thinking that there is no beauty in the features of Venus; and that the attitude is aukward and out of character. It is a bad plea to urge that the ancients and we differ in the ideas of beauty. We know the contrary, from their medals, busts, and historians. Without all doubt, the limbs and proportions of this statue are elegantly formed, and accurately designed, according to the nicest rules of symmetry and proportion; and the back parts especially are executed so happily, as to excite the admiration of the most indifferent spectator. One cannot help thinking it is the very Venus of Cnidos by Praxiteles, which Lucian describes, "hercle quanta dorsi concinitas! ut exuberantes lumbi amplexantes manus implent! quan — scite circumductae clunium pulpae in se rotundanture, neque

[11] Peter Beckford, *Familiar Letters from Italy,* I, 167.
[12] Sterne, *Sentimental Journey;* see "in the Street: Calais." Gray called it "a modern performance, and that a very indifferent one." I, 141.

tenues nimis ipsis ossibus adstrictae, neque in immensam effusae Pinguedinem![13]

To conclude with a moral, as art has to do with what man feels (not merely what he knows, for that is science) originals must be seen. And even when a traveller stands before an original, he may be unable to see it. As Berenson expresses it "the most difficult thing in the world is to see clearly and with one's own eyes, naively . . . So invincible is the business of learning to see for one's self, that all except the few men of genius — with a gift for seeing — have to be taught how to see."[14] Although Smollett has not ever been proposed as a great art critic, I would like to suggest that his gift of seeing, which is manifest in his novels, actually made him a most penetrating observer of the fine arts as far as he went. He discovered no neglected part of Italian painting. He contributed nothing to the scholarship of pictures, statuary, architecture. But again and again within the limits of art familiar then, he saw clearly and wrote frankly and with intelligence.

In the same room with the sculptured Venus was a painting of her by Titian, which charmed Smollett by its "sweetness of expression and tenderness of colouring."[15] Evidently Smollett had exhausted himself on the first Venus for the second is by no means deserving of such laconicism. Titian's goddess, whose succulence was better appreciated by Captain Northall,

is quite naked, lying at full length, and her body turned toward the spectator: one hand with flowers in it, hanging carelessly down, the other on the seat of love: one leg extended; and the other is a little crooked, with the foot under the leg. A most beautiful face, looking full at you with a soft alluring eye, and a mouth half smiling: so sweet a feature invites a kiss.[16]

As Peter Beckford said, "It is clear that Titian was a lover as well as a painter."[17]

Two other statues in the Uffizi claimed attention; *I Lotta-*

---

13 Smollett, *Travels through France and Italy*, II, 67-70. See Young, Arthur, *Travels in France and Italy*, p. 274.
14 Berenson, *Italian Painters of the Renaissance*, pp. 172-173.
15 Smollett, *op. cit.*, p. 73.
16 Northall, *Travels through Italy*, p. 62.
17 Peter Beckford, *op. cit.*, I, 146.

tori or wrestlers, which was not known then to be a patched up copy of a bronze original, and *Arrotino* or, *Whetter,* also a copy, which attracted much popular attention because of the "story" that explained it. It is always easier to argue about the meaning of a piece of art than it is to look at it. Some thought the crouching figure was sharpening a knife and listening to the plotting of a conspiracy — Cataline's perhaps.[18] Meanwhile travellers passed hundreds of Italian paintings quite unable to see what in later generations has provided so much of the wonder of poetry to imaginations de-humanized by science and ochlocracy.

Nevertheless the bewildering number of treasures that were seen — inlaid tables, medals, precious stones, military engines, statues, busts, sarcophagi, bas-reliefs, polished marble, gilt-work and fretted ceilings — was enough to make one "fancy himself in a palace of the fairies, raised and adorned by the power of enchantment."[19]

Before crossing the Arno to visit the Pitti, which was the other famous gallery of the time, tourists often went to see the Chapel of San Lorenzo. The work of Michaelangelo there was passed over lightly.[20] The Mausoleum of the Grand Dukes, as most people would expect, was felt to be oppressive — "a monument to ill taste and extravagance."[21] It had a gloomy effect. It seemed much too rich. Sir James Smith was one of the few who felt "Nothing can be richer, *nor more noble.*"[22] It is the custom now to disparage this room, and yet it has its beauty. As Lassels said, and he saw it more times than most travellers, "Indeed these stately tombs make almost death itself looke louely, and dead mens ashes grow proud againe."[23]

Within a few years of the time the Medici family was to be extinct, its significance began to be appreciated by travelling Englishmen. It had not always been. Addison, for example, was not in the least impressed by the suffocating

[18] Smollett, *op. cit.,* II, 70.
[19] *Ibid.,* II, 73. Edward Wright prepared a two-page plate, showing the floor plan and order of statues and busts.
[20] Lassels, *Voyage of Italy,* Part I, 160, says Michelangelo's Day, Night, Aurora and Evening were "hugely cried up by Sculptors."
[21] Smollett, *op. cit.,* II, 74.
[22] Smith, *A Sketch of a Tour on the Continent,* I, 304.
[23] Lassels, *op. cit.,* Part 1, 158.

splendour of the Grand Duke's Mausoleum. It was simply a room of great expense — too great expense by implication — and a work that would not be completed while the Medici lived.[24]

But in 1738 John Breval published two volumes of *Remarks on Several Parts of Europe,* dedicated to his Grace Charles, Duke of Richmond, a "great traveller" and virtuoso. This commentary is valuable for two things: it records an exploration of Sicily, which amounted to a Greek quest.[25] And it furnishes an enlightened essay on the Medici. Breval speaks of Lorenzo's invitation to the Greeks to live in Florence after the Turks overran their native country, of his unlimited commissions to buy from the Turks what could be recovered from the ruins of Constantinople, and of his fabulously expensive efforts to recover what lay concealed under famous old Italian towns, and of Pope Leo's uncovering an unbelievable number of exquisite pieces "from the rust and oblivion of ages."[26]

The Duomo of Firenze according to Peter Beckford was "a magnificent building of Gothic architecture."[27] Some tourists because of the whiteness within thought the architects had turned their cathedral wrong side out. Ghiberti's gates everyone admired by quoting Michael Angelo to the effect that such panels should adorn the gates of Paradise. Smollett was the only one who preferred the gates by Giambologna on the Duomo at Pisa, which shows at least that he looked at them both with great attention.[28]

II

At the Pitti, built to last with the world, the most famous picture was Raphael's *Madonna della Seggiola.* Englishmen thought it defective in dignity. As Smollett said, "It is a fine figure, gay, agreeable, and very expressive of maternal tenderness; and the *bambino* is extremely beautiful."[29] But he found

---

24 Addison, *Remarks on the Several Parts of Italy,* p. 244.
25 Breval, *Remarks on Several Parts of Europe,* I, 7-43, describes his Sicilian journey and quest for Pagan temples.
26 *Ibid.,* p. x.
27 Peter Beckford, *op. cit.,* I, 123.
28 Smollett, *op. cit.,* II, 73; also see p. 55 concerning Giambologna.
29 *Ibid.,* II, 75.

fault because it seemed a peasant woman with a peasant expression. Dr. Moore tells a story of his visit to the Pitti. He was listening to the lecture of a professional critic, while one of his friends, who had rather be in ignorance forever than listen to a connoisseur, walked ahead into another room.

Very soon he came posting back and said, "I know no more about painting than my dog, but there is a picture in the next room I wouldn't change for all those you seem to admire so much!"[30] The group followed him to the *Madonna della Seggiola*. The lecturer called out "Viva!" and complimented him as a man of true taste because he was able without any instruction to single out the best picture in Florence; but when the Cicerone had explained the picture, the tourist said that if it was intended to represent the Virgin Mary, then it was not as fine a picture as he had thought when it seemed only the representation "of a blooming country wench." But the connoisseur insisted, "The Virgin Mary was not of higher rank. She was only a poor woman from a little village of Galilee." This did not content the Englishman who felt her rank as Mother to the Son of the Highest was great enough that it ought to appear somehow in the picture. The look of love upon her face was not enough. It ought to be a look of divine love.

In general I believe the modern tourist in Florence would find an eighteenth century Englishman a rather queer bird. He would admire some of the same things. He would like Tuscan columns, and the Tuscan rustic of the Pitti, Strozzi, and Medici palaces. He would admire the cycloidal arches of Ponte Santa Trinita, but he had no interest in the primitive painters, rarely spoke of Fiesole, or of the sculptured work of Michaelangelo.[31] He rarely noticed Cellini's *Perseo*, and almost never seems to have heard of Verrocchio or Donatello, or Botticelli.[32]

If you had the pleasure of riding about the streets of Florence with the eminent British sportsman, Peter Beckford, you would doubtless hear much talk of horses, wine — "it is unpardonable not to talk of wine"[33] — and manuscripts in the

30 Moore, *A View of Society and Manners in Italy*, pp. 475ff.
31 See note 20 above.
32 Starke, *Travels in Italy*, I, 272-273.
33 Peter Beckford, *op. cit.*, I, 248.

Laurenziana. You might learn of the old squire's surprise on finding that the Egyptian mummy in the Pitti palace "is not a bit bigger than ourselves,"[34] as though you would expect it to be! If you wandered far enough from Meggot's *Locanda di Carlo* on the Lungarno and came to the Piazza della Santissima Annunziata and the hospital of Brunelleschi, Beckford would pass Giambologna's last work (Ferdinando I on horseback) without a glance. The fountains would not be noticed either, and the della Robbia medallions of children in swaddling clothes would seem a bit queer. "The art is lost, nor is it to be regretted."[35] But at this point, it is to be hoped you would descend to look at them.

III

The Leaning Tower of Pisa is one of the famous wonders of the world. Lord Chesterfield made jokes about Englishmen's eagerness to see it.[36] Gray and Walpole on their tour renounced "staring after crooked towers,"[37] because it was such a vulgar thing to do. And yet it is not the crookedness of the tower which is so wonderful, though that makes a curious sight across the green fields from roads around Pisa. The wonder is that this ponderous tube of marble with its columns and arches should convey an impression of such airy elegance, light as lace. A much greater marvel is the cathedral itself, which in its details, is more interesting for crookedness than the *campanile*. And again it is not crookedness which touches the imagination of a visitor. He can make curious discoveries of wit and humor in stone by the hour if he wishes, as William Beckford did, but what he must feel there is the power and the glory of the human spirit. And again at Pisa, if there seems to be a certainty of beauty in life, the matchless loveliness of the Campo Santo promises beauty in death.

The architecture of the Duomo of Pisa and of Lucca and Pistoia was not understood at all. They were built, according

---

[34] *Ibid.*, I, 176. A curious offshoot of the 18th century idea of a golden age in antiquity — or at least an age of superior men.

[35] *Ibid.*, I, 198-199.

[36] Piozzi, *Observations and Reflections*, I, 342.

[37] Walpole, Horace, *The Letters of . . .*, I, 31.

to Lassels, "after *la maniera Tedescha,* a fashion . . . much used in Italy four or five hundred years ago."[38] He gave Vasari as his authority.

Later in the century the church itself received some of the attention it deserves. Sir James Smith looked closely enough to discover that it was a "motley edifice."[39] Smollett said he could have wondered at the brass gates for many hours. And the paintings in the Campo Santo excited him curiously. "The manner is dry, the drawing incorrect, the design generally lame, and the colouring unnatural; yet there is merit in the expression; and the whole remains . . . a monument of the efforts made by this noble art immediately after her revival."[40]

William Beckford thought the Duomo, "insulated in a vast green area," was the strangest edifice he had ever beheld. "I have dreamed of such buildings, but little thought they existed."[41]

The place is neither sad nor solemn . . . There is so much caprice, such an exotic look in the whole scene . . . Every object is new, every ornament original . . . I think of returning, to hear visionary music and commune with spirits, for I shall never find in the whole universe besides so whimsical a theatre.[42]

At the very end of the century Miss Starke explained that Pisa was the true "cradle of the Arts," and that it was under the guidance of a Greek, Buschetto, the Duomo was erected, and that those who viewed Pisa first and then went on to Florence could have the pleasure of tracing the progress of Greco-Pisan taste.[43]

The rest of Tuscany had very little artistic interest for eighteenth century gentlemen. Robert Gray chanced to see at Pistoia some pictures "in an old style."[44] But they had no meaning. At Leghorn and Florence the Marquis Ginori, the Tuscan Wedgewood, was carrying on ceramic experiments,[45]

38 Lessels, *op. cit.,* I, 228.
39 Smith, *op. cit.,* I, 267.
40 Smollett, *op. cit.,* II, 56; Smith, *op. cit.,* I, 270.
41 William Beckford, *op. cit.,* p. 138.
42 *Ibid.,* p. 140.
43 Starke, *Travels in Italy,* p. 199.
44 Robert Gray, *Letters during a Journey through Germany, Switzerland and Italy,* p. 329.
45 Condamine, *An Extract from the Observations made in a Tour to Italy,* pp. 25-27.

preparatory to a fabrication that has supplied plate to princely and noble houses throughout Europe. Lucca, closed in a wall the color of old rose and set in the midst of an emerald plain, struck most travellers as a work of art in itself.

The Florence-Siena road passes through San Casciano in val di Pesa, through high Barberino, and then descends to Poggibonsi. From the road there one sees San Gemignano, with its blue-gray towers standing in a cluster atop a far off hill. In our time this is one of the favorite medieval places in Italy; to my knowledge it is not even mentioned by the old travellers. But the country was something they all saw as they came among the hills, with many miles of vineyards and olive groves, and fields of grain, and gleaming roads.

Peter Beckford Esq. wrote, "The face of the country is beautiful." He saw one of the reasons. "The white houses have a gay appearance on the sides of the green hills; and their flat roofs, peculiar elegance. Whatever may be our reason for adopting the opposite extreme, beauty most certainly is not one of them."[46]

Past Poggibonsi one skirts "the Gothic castle of Monteriggione," (Monteriggion di torri si corona),[47] which put Walker in mind of "the days of Knight-Errantry, when Damosels were imprisoned in lofty towers, in wilds, and deserts; among rocks, and precipices."[48]

In this very country Sir James Smith wrote of Claude Lorrain:

The more we saw of Italian landscape, the more reason we found to admire this excellent painter. The glowing refulgence of his evening, the clear brightness of his mid-day skies, which one is apt to think the exaggerations and improvements of nature, are the very tints of nature herself in this delightful climate, and all his variations of effect are strictly and exactly her own.[49]

---

[46] Peter Beckford, *op. cit.*, II, 50.
[47] "Inferno," XXXI, 41.
[48] Walker, *op. cit.*, p. 340.
[49] Smith, *op. cit.*, I, 323-324. Robert Gray, *Letters during the course of a Tour through Germany, Switzerland, and Italy,* 1791-1792, London, 1794, p. 296, makes a typical traveller's comment on Italian landscape painting. "I have frequently remarked the existence of that strength of coloring which painters have taught us to expect from an Italian sky. The distant blue hills have all the depth of shade that I have often thought unnatural in pictures; and I have seen the morning sun disperse the mists and scatter a tinge equal to any that Claude Lorraine has exhibited."

Then in a little while the voyager came to Siena, where the Duomo, "a solemn sort of zebra, black and white,"[50] as Walker described it, was the principal object of curiosity. Addison said it was a cathedral "a man may view with pleasure after St. Peter's, tho' tis quite of another make, and can only be looked upon as one of the masterpieces of gothic architecture."[51] His comment reveals the confusion of a sensitive spirit in the presence of a lovely and original creation with which, as a matter of principle, he is out of sympathy:

When a man sees the prodigious pains and expence that our forefathers have been at in these barbarous buildings, one cannot but fansy to himself what miracles of architecture they would have left us, had they only been instructed in the right way; for when the devotion of those ages was much warmer than it is at present and the riches of the people much more at the disposal of the priests, there was so much money consum'd on these Gothic cathedrals, as would have finish'd a greater variety of noble buildings, than have been raised either before or since that time.

One would wonder to see the vast labour that has been laid out on this single cathedral. The very spouts are loaden with ornaments, the windows are form'd like so many scenes of perspective, with a multitude of little pillars retiring one behind another, the great columns are finely engraven with fruits and foliage that run twisting about them from the very top to the bottoms . . . the front cover'd with such a variety of figure and over-run with so many little mazes and labyrinths of sculpture, that nothing in the world can make a prettier show to those who prefer false beauties, and affected ornament, to a noble and majestic simplicity.[51]

Seventy or eighty years later, when Gothic was beginning to be the mode, and competing with Greek purity to possess the northern imagination, the cathedral of Siena was still called Gothic, even though the most indifferent eye could see that it was quite unlike any Gothic of France, Germany, the Lowlands or England. It is still a puzzle, being Greco-Pisano-Orvietano-Gothic — in short Sienese. And there is

50 Walker, *op. cit.*, 334.

51 Addison, *op. cit.*, 224-225. Fines Moryson had said in 1580, "It seemd to me the fairest church in Italy." *An Itinerary*, reprinted by MacLehose, 4 vols., Glasgow, 1907-8, I, 349.

nothing like it. The floors of this cathedral, being a master-piece of a unique art detached from any obvious tradition, were admired in the eighteenth century as much as in the sixteenth or the twentieth by those few who took the trouble to have the boards raised up so they could see them.[52]

For the most part Sienese art being old and "Gothic" held little attraction for tourists of the time. And just as it is now not easy to understand how a century of tourists could have been blind to the paintings of Botticelli, it is also not easy to see how thousands of highly educated and sensitive English-men could have passed through Siena without taking note of the Torre del Mangia "incomparably the noblest tower in Italy," as William Heywood calls it,[53] or how they could have passed slowly in the coaches from San Quirico to Radicofani on the Rome road without appreciating the quasi-African mood of those reddish, sun-hammered, wind-gouged stretches that lead to Mt. Amiata. Perhaps discomfort and uneasiness were uppermost in their minds. Whatever the reason, this blasted southern part of Tuscany had to wait almost until the beginning of this century to find its English admirers, when at last it found them in Heywood and Hutton.

---

[52] Lassels, *op. cit.*, Part I, 237-238. "The pavement is the best in the world; and is indeed too good to be trod on; hence they cover a great part of it with boards handsomely layd together, yet easy to be taken up, to show strangers the beauty of it . . . I scarce saw anything in Italy that pleased me better than this pavement." For a good modern account see Cust, *The Pavement Masters of Siena* (London: George Bell & Sons, 1901); Peter Beckford, op. cit. I, 437.

[53] Heywood, *Guide to Siena, Siena,* Libreria Editrice Senese. 1924, p. 59.

CHAPTER XII

LANDS OF OBLIVION

Sicily, Corsica, and all of Italy south of Naples, though not parts of the usual classic tour of Italy, became, as time passed, very natural extensions of it. They appealed to the prevailing taste for grand scenery. Magna Graecia appealed to the love of Greek antiquity. And then in all of these places there hovered a golden aura of romantic adventure. They could not be reached by travelling coach and the post. Sometimes a horse, a mule, or a burro could be found; sometimes not. Sometimes one encountered brigands; sometimes not. These were challenges eagerly accepted by three of the best English travel writers of the century: James Boswell, Patrick Brydone, and Henry Swinburne. Boswell went to Corsica in the autumn of 1766 and published *Memoirs of Pascal Paoli* with great *eclat* two years later. Brydone travelled in 1770 and 1771 and published *A Tour through Sicily and Malta* in 1773. Henry Swinburne knocked about Calabria, Puglia, and Sicily for four years, 1777-1780, publishing his two volume classic, *Travels in the Two Sicilies,* 1783-85.

I

Boswell wrote, "I wished for something more than just the common course of what is called the tour of Europe; and Corsica occurred to me as a place which no body else had seen, and where I should find what was to be seen no where else, a people actually fighting for liberty . . ."[1]

At Leghorn he discovered with "astonishment how little the real state of Corsica was known, even by those that had good access to know it. An officer of rank in the British navy, who had been in several parts of the island, told me that I

---

[1] Boswell, *An Account of Corsica,* p. 263.

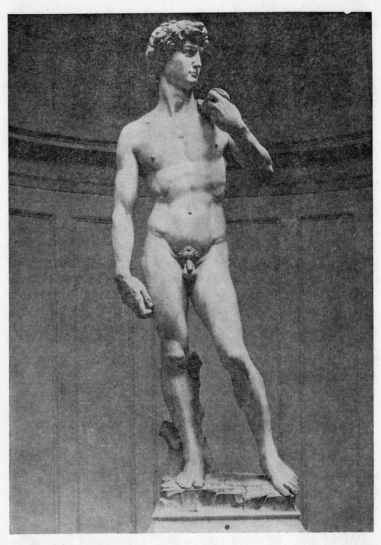

David by Michelangelo — Another work not noticed by antiquity-seeking travellers of the 18th century, who preferred, for example, the comparatively dead Apollo Belvedere in the Vatican.   *Photo Alinari*

run [sic] the risk of my life in going among those barbarians."[2] But he was "under no apprehension." He procured letters from Count Rivarola, then the Sardinian consul, the old friend both of the English and of General Paoli. "I had found that I was able to accommodate myself to my fellow-creatures of different languages and sentiments. I did not fear that it would be a difficult task for me to make myself easy with the plain and generous Corsicans."[3] The only danger, he felt, was of being taken by the Barbary Corsairs, though that of being shot as a spy was actually much greater.

Italian politicians with some reason suspected that Boswell might be going to Corsica on an official commission.

He sailed from Leghorn in a Tuscan vessel bound to Capo Corso for wine. On the way over to Bastia the sailors sang and prayed as the sun went down. "It was pleasing to enter into the spirit of their religion, and hear them offering up their evening orisons."[4] Leaving Bastia, he had "curious travelling, mostly on foot, and attended by a couple of stout women,"[5] who carried his baggage on their heads. Later, as he went on with other guides, they appeared "so hearty," that he often got down from his mount and walked along with them, doing just what he saw them do. "When we grew hungry, we threw stones among the thick branches of the chestnut trees which overshadowed us."[6]

Once he stopped at a little village to rest his mules.

The inhabitants came crowding about me as an ambassador going to their General. When they were informed of my country, a strong black fellow among them said, *"Inglese! sono barbari; non credono in Dio grande . . .* I told him, Excuse me, Sir. We do believe in God, and in Jesus Christ too. Um, said he, *e nel Papa? . . .* No. *E perchè? . . .* This was a puzzling question in these circumstances; for there was a great audience to the controversy. I thought I would try a method of my own, and very gravely replied, *Perchè siamo troppo lontani . . .* a very new argument against the universal infallibility of the Pope. But the opponent thought of Sicily — but we are ten times piu lontani che la Sicilia, "Aha!" said he; and seemed quite satisfied.[7]

---

[2] *Ibid.,* p. 268.
[3] *Ibid.,* p. 269.
[4] *Ibid.,* p. 271.
[5] *Ibid.,* p. 278.
[6] *Ibid.,* p. 288.
[7] *Ibid.,* p. 289.

The spirits of Boswell rose to such a pitch that he harangued the men of the town of Bastelica with great fluency in Italian praising their courage and telling them their bravery had spread the glory of Corsica all over Europe.

At last Boswell reached the plain little house where Paoli lived.

> I found him alone, and was struck by his appearance. He is tall, strong, and well made; of a fair complexion, a sensible, free, and open countenance, and a manly, and noble carriage. He was then in his fortieth year. He was dressed in green and gold. He used to wear the common Corsican habit, but on the arrival of the French he thought a little external elegance might be of use to make the government appear in a more respectable light . . .

> In consequence of his being in . . . danger from teachery . . . he has formed a habit of studiously observing every new face. For ten minutes we walked backwards and forwards through the room, hardly saying a word, while he looked at me, with a stedfast, keen and penetrating eye, as if he searched my very soul . . .

> This interview was for a while very severe upon me . . . I ventured to address him with a compliment. "I am come from seeing the ruins of one brave and free people (Rome) : I now see the rise of another.[8]

Paoli was gracious but corrected him saying that Corsicans could not be aptly compared to the Romans, whose power had engulfed the whole world.

> He smiled a good deal, when I told him that I was much surprised to find him so amiable, and polite; for although I knew him to be a great man, I expected to find a rude character, an Attila, king of the Goths, or a Luitprand, king of the Lombards.[9]

Boswell had much talk with Paoli altogether. In one of the most interesting discussions Paoli said

> Virtuous sentiments and habits . . . are beyond philosophical reasonings, which are not so strong and are continually varying. If all the professors in Europe were formed into one society, it would no doubt be a society very respectable, and we should there be entertained with the best moral lessons. Yet I believe I should find more real virtue in a society of good peasants in some little

---

[8] *Ibid.,* pp. 292-4.
[9] *Ibid.,* p. 302.

village. It might be said of these two societies, as was said of Demosthenes and Themistocles *Ilius dicta, hujus facta magis valebant.* [10]

After a few days Paoli directed some guides to take Boswell around the island. Among other things he climbed Mt. Cinto from which one can see France and Italy and many islands of the sea. One day the Corsicans wanted to hear him play upon his German flute. He did not refuse. To have said

> Really gentlemen, I play very ill, and put on such airs as we do in our genteel companies, would have been highly ridiculous. I therefore immediately complied with their request. I gave them one or two Italian airs, and then some of our beautiful old Scots tunes, Gilderoy, the Lass of Patie's Mill, Corn riggs are Bonny. The pathetic simplicity and pastoral gaiety of the Scots musick, will always please those who have the genuine feelings of nature. The Corsicans were charmed with the specimens I gave them, though I may now say that they were very indifferent performed . . . .
>
> My good friends insisted also to have an English song from me. I endeavored to please them in this too, and was very lucky in that which occurred to me. I sang them "Hearts of oak our ships, Hearts of oak our men." I translated it into Italian for them, and never did I see men so delighted with a song as the Corsicans were with Hearts of oak . . . "Cuore di quercia, cried they, bravo Inglese." It was quite a joyous riot. I fancied all my chorus of Corsicans above the British fleet.[11]

Finally he went off from Corsica with a cold he had caught in an old decayed draughty stone house in Sollacaio, where he lived a while. But he was happy as he made his way out of the mountains accompanied by a "great swarthy priest" — a bluff, hearty, roaring fellow, who rode before him "and sat in an attitude half turned around, with his hand clapped on the crupper . . . He would burst out with songs about the Devil and the Genoese, etc. In short he kept me laughing whether I would or no."[12]

Boswell was not finished with Corsica when he left it. In the first place he was a man of very genuine sympathy, and he loved the Corsicans for their heroism and their good

---

[10] *Ibid.,* pp. 328-9.
[11] *Ibid.,* p. 321.
[12] *Ibid.,* pp. 354-5.

151

humor. In the second place, where was another man like Paoli?

> The contemplation of such a character as Paoli's really existing, was of more service to me than all I had been able to draw from books, from conversation, or from the exertions of my own mind. I had often enough formed the idea of a man continually such as I could conceive in my best moments. But this idea appeared like the ideas we are taught in the schools to form of things which may exist, but do not; of seas of milk and ships of amber. But I saw my highest idea realized in Paoli. It was impossible for me, speculate as I pleased, to have a little opinion of human nature in him.[13]

Boswell had not been at all sure of his way when he entered the Mediterranean world, but now, going out, it was very clear. He would write a book about Corsica and Paoli. He would call the attention of Europe to an unknown place and brave men.

It is pretty generally accepted now that Boswell felt for Paoli "a reverence that he did not display even towards Johnson."[14] The affection of Paoli for Boswell is recorded in Fanny Burney's *Diary*. Harking back to their first meeting the General said:

> He came to my country, and he fetched me some letter recommending him; but I was of the belief he might be an imposter and an espy; for I look away from him, and in a moment I look to him again, and I behold his tablets; Oh! he was to the work of writing down all I have to say! Indeed I was angry. But I soon discover he was no imposter and no espy; and I only find I was myself the monster he had come to discern. Oh! is a very good man; I love him indeed; so cheerful! so gay! so pleasant![15]

That part of the *Account* which relates to Paoli is a fine free-spirited work and one of the most interesting pieces of biographical writing in the literature of the century, which is now no more than we would expect, of one "who excelled all mankind in writing the lives of others."[16] Even Horace Walpole, who had no use for Boswell, wrote to Thomas Gray,

---

[13] Quoted by Tinker, *Young Boswell*, p. 94.
[14] *Ibid.*, p. 108.
[15] *Ibid.*, p. 111.
[16] See the first paragraph of Boswell's *Life of Johnson*.

that the part pertaining to General Paoli would "amuse" him.[17]

The section on Corsican history is, I think, still something of a mystery. Professor Tinker refers to Sir George Otto Trevelyan's estimate of Boswell's history as "By far the best account of the island that has ever yet been published."[18] And he remarks that no one is likely to assail the authority of Trevelyan. That is true. But still there is something so dull stylistically in Boswell's history of Corsica, and so little personal light in it, that one cannot help applying to it (with more justification) the criticism Dr. Johnson directed against Addison's book on Italy — that it might have been written at home. Boswell's history was like any other as Dr. Johnson said. It is evident that the work represents considerable accumulation of fact, and no small labor of organization. And as Boswell did not like ponderous bookish undertakings of the research kind, it is a question, it seems to me, how that part of Boswell's book came into being. But however that may be, the two works together, became a literary sensation, and "Corsica" made Boswell one of the best known men in the kingdom, if not in Europe.

II

At four o'clock on the afternoon of May 19th, 1770, Patrick Brydone arrived in the port of Messina, and as soon as possible, he and his friends presented themselves to the Prince of Franca Villa, who was absolute ruler of that corner of Sicily. The Prince received them with "a good deal of State,"[19] and immediately ordered guards to attend them.

And Brydone writes, "Now who do you think these trusty . . . guards are?" The "most daring, and most hardened villains . . . to be met with upon earth, who, in any other country would have been broken upon the wheel or hung in chains."[20] The Prince, having seen it would be impossible to exterminate the bandits, had declared himself their patron,

---

[17] Tinker, *op. cit.*, p. 63.
[18] *Ibid.*, p. 112.
[19] Brydone, *Sicily and Malta*, I, 67.
[20] *Ibid.*, I, 68.

and supplied any who would leave the mountains to serve him, with good pay, and uniforms of yellow and green trimmed with silver lace.

Next morning the party moved south. The Englishmen, under their umbrellas, rode kicking at their mules, and sometimes glancing at the sea, flecked with rust-colored sails of checkbecks and other small fishing boats. The guards, loaded with hangers, arquebusses and enormous pistols, went on foot, one in front of them and the other behind, and shouted accounts of the men they had killed — all of them on points of honor; but as luck would have it they had no opportunity to display their prowess.

On the way to Catania, they climbed up the precipice to Taormina, a splendid resort of the ancients and of the present day Romans, then merely a place of memories. "This famous city is now reduced to an insignificant burgh; yet even these small remains give very high ideas of its former magnificence." Mt. Aetna, rising nearly three times as high as Vesuvius made "a glorious appearance from this place."[21] And when Swinburne climbed up to Taormina, he wished he had the powers of a Salvatore Rosa. "The mountains tower to the very clouds, the castles and ruins rise on mighty masses of perpendicular rock, and seem to defy the attacks of mortal enemies; Etna with all its snowy and woody sweeps fills half the horizon; the sea is stretched out upon an immense scale."[22]

At Catania Brydone met Canon Guiseppe Recupero (1720-78), a "merry philosopher" according to Swinburne, and a vulcanologist, who had shocked the orthodox by his observations.

Recupero reasoned that if one flow of lava should be exposed for two thousand years and produce only a skim of soil by disintegration, several strata of lava with soil sandwiched between represented a history of at least two thousand years for each layer. "What shall we say," asks Brydone, "of a pit that sunk near to Jaci, of a great depth? They pierced through seven distinct lavas one over the other, and most of them covered with a thick bed of fine rich earth."[23] Evidently the first of these must have flowed from the mountain 14,000

21 *Ibid.,* I, 97.
22 Swinburne, *Travels in the Two Sicilies,* II, 361.
23 Brydone, *op. cit.,* I, 131.

years before. Moses hung "like a dead weight"[24] upon Recupero, in his studies; and the unscientific Bishop of the diocese was much annoyed. And Rev. Brian Hill, who was in that part of the world a few years later, avowed "much greater veneration for the writings of Moses, confirmed by the testimony of the most ancient authors, of Christ and his apostles, and of the whole body of the Jewish nation, than for the testimony of one Sicilian author."[25] But Brydone shared in a sporting sort of way the scientific zeal of the time. He had brought along a barometer, tape measure, thermometer, compass, electrometer, and a good deal of youthful irreverence; and when he discussed the lava flows with Recupero, he was delighted. Eight years later Dr. Johnson remarked to Mr. Fullarton, one of Brydone's touring companions in Sicily, that Brydone would have been a better author if he had been more attentive to his Bible.[26]

Probably the most spectacular part of Brydone's book is the record of his climb to the crater of Mount Aetna. On the 27th of May, 1770 at dawn, he and Fullarton and Glover, three servants, two mule tenders, and a newly acquired guide, named "Cyclops" set out from Catania. They carried blankets, warm fur coats, and axes for firewood, some tea, and bread.

At a little mountain town of Nicolosi, Brydone had an experience very much like Boswell's. A crowd gathered around him, and wanted to know why he was there. He explained, with great courtesy, that his only motive was curiosity to see Mt. Aetna. The crowd received this answer with apparent contempt. "Un bel ragione questo, non é vero?"[27] Then they asked his country, and whether they believed in Christ there. When they heard he was English, one said that he had seen several of these Inglese who had visited Mt. Aetna, and he wasn't sure why, but it seemed to him from devotion to an English Queen who had burnt in the mountain for many years. Brydone answered that this was improbable as the Inglese had very little respect for their queens living and never thought of them after they were dead; but when several

[24] *Ibid.*, I, 132.
[25] Rev. Brian Hill, *Observations and Remarks in a Journey through Sicily and Calabria*, p. 191.
[26] Boswell, *Life of Johnson*, Hill, Powell III, 356. See also II, 468, note 1.
[27] Brydone, *op. cit.*, I, 170.

others of the crowd insisted on the point, he asked the queen's name. "Anna," they said and added that her husband had been a Christian king, but afterwards, because of her, had turned heretic, so she had been condemned to burn eternally in Aetna. He asked if the king was there too. "Sicuro," they said, "and all his heretic subjects too."[28]

About two hours later they reached the lower edges of the cool forests after tramping through some ashy fields in a hot sultry air. "Every breeze was loaded with a thousand perfumes, the whole ground being covered over with the richest aromatic plants . . . If Aetna resembles hell within, it may with equal justice he said to represent paradise without."[29]

This band of encircling forest is about eight or nine miles wide, and having crossed about half of it, the party camped at a large cave, *La Spelonca del Capriole.*

Just before sunset Brydone mounted the best mule and took a solitary ride to a point from which he could see the whole panorama — the surrounding sea, the far-off dreamlike islands, the winding river Semetus, the valley of Hybla.

At eleven o'clock that night they left the comfort of their leaf beds in the cave and passed through the gloomy forests. "Universal darkness, the rustling of the trees; the heavy, dull, bellowing of the mountain; the vast expanse of ocean stretched at an immense distance below us; inspired a kind of awful horror."[30]

They were soon exhausted by the thin atmosphere. "However we determined to presevere remembering . . . that the Emperor Hadrian and the philosopher Plato underwent the same; and from the same motive too, to see the rising sun from the top of Aetna."[31] An hour before dawn they reached the wreck of an old structure, the *Torre del Filosofo,* believed to have been built by Empedocles.

"We now had time to pay our adoration in silent contemplation of the sublime objects of nature." The sky was clear, and the "immense vault of the heavens appeared in

---

28 *Ibid.,* I, 172.
29 *Ibid.,* I, 172.
30 *Ibid.,* I, 180-181.
31 *Ibid.,* I, 183.

awful majesty and splendour. The whiteness of the milky way was like a pure flame that shot across the heavens."[32]

And then, just at dawn they arrived at the crater's rim to see "the most wonderful and most sublime sight in nature." Here Brydone gives an interesting eighteenth century description.

No imagination has dared to form an idea of so glorious and so magnificent a scene. Neither is there on the surface of this globe, any one point that unites so many awful and sublime objects. — The immense elevation, from the surface of the earth, drawn as it were to a single point, without any neighboring mountain for the senses and imagination to rest upon, and recover from their astonishment in their way down to the world. . . . Add to this, the unbounded extent of the prospect, comprehending the greatest diversity and the most beautiful scenery in nature; with the rising sun, advancing in the east, to illuminate the wondrous scene.

The whole atmosphere by degrees kindled up, and shewed dimly and faintly the boundless prospect around. — Both sea and land looked dark and confused, as if only emerging from their original chaos; and light and darkness seemed still undivided; till the morning by degrees advancing, completed the separation. — The stars are extinguished, and the shades disappear. The forests, which but now seemed black and bottomless gulphs, from whence no ray was reflected to shew their form and colours, appears a new creation rising to the sight; catching life and beauty from every increasing beam. — The scene still enlarges, and the horizon seems to widen and expand itself on all sides; till the sun, like the great Creator, appears in the east, and with all his plastic ray completes the mighty scene. All appears enchantment; and it is with difficulty we can believe we are still on earth. The senses unaccustomed to such objects, are bewildered and confounded.[33]

The crater was much too hot to be inviting, and when they had made a few measurements, they began to descend to the *Torre del Filosofo.*

Old Empedocles received short shrift from Brydone. The philosopher had lived so much on the top of Aetna that he came to believe he was a god, and in order that people might think he had ascended into the heavens, he leapt into the crater, believing the deceit would never be known. "But the

---

[32] *Ibid.*, I, 184.
[33] *Ibid.*, I, 187-189.

treacherous mountain threw out his slippers, which were of brass, and announced to the world the fate of the philosopher, who, by his death as well as life only wanted to impose on mankind."[34]

But if there is such a thing as philosophy, he adds, Aetna would be a fine place for it. Thoughts are always enlarged according to the grandeur of surroundings. And when the body is released from the heavy pressure of atmosphere at ordinary levels, the mind is freer, and the soul more at liberty to act in accordance with its essential purity.

Syracuse in the eighteenth century was very much what it is now, a sleepy, picturesque town with tolerable buildings and houses, but a place preserving none of the magnificence of its great days, and nothing to detain a tourist after he had seen the ancient stadium, the latomie or sunken gardens, a cave called the ear of Dionysius, and the fountain of Arethusa.

The African and sunburnt coast of Sicily, poor, dusty, like a very old New England, with its orchards, stone walls, hills and straggling dirt roads, was not completely uncivilized. When Swinburne passed through it he was particularly surprised by what he found in Caltagirone, a very high mountain town between Ragusa and Agrigento.

As a transient he had expected nothing good. However, a servant of the Baron Rosabia [sic] happened to see him enter the city and reported to his master. Instantly the baron sent a courteous invitation to his house. Swinburne says there was no refusing such an offer, which we can easily believe, and off he went, not to a little shabby provincial house as he imagined it might be, but to a large villa furnished in the modern style with pieces which would have been admired in any refined city of Europe. The servants wore elegant livery. The plate was of the finest quality. He was told that many of the leading families had travelled.

After an excellent dinner he was carried out for an airing in a handsome lacquered coach. "It was a singular circumstance to meet a string of carriages full of well-dressed ladies on the summit of a mountain, which no vehicle can ascend, unless it be previously taken to pieces . . . We seemed to be

---

[34] *Ibid.*, I, 200.

seated among the clouds. As the vast expanse of the hills and vales grew dim with the evening vapours, our paradise resembled the amusement of the heathen gods . . . driving about Olympus, and looking down at the mortals below."[35]

At Agrigento Brydone fell in with a company of priests, who insisted that the Englishmen make up a bowl of punch, which they had often heard of, but never enjoyed. The ingredients, as soon as they were known, immediately appeared, and the mixture was so successful that, everyone preferred it to all the wines in the room. They filled the bowl often. They called the punch "Pontio," and shouted loudly to praise it, affirming that Pontio, (alluding to Pontius Pilate) was a much better fellow than they had ever suspected. One of the party, a canon, who was extremely sick after dinner, observed to Brydone, "Ah, Signor Capitano, I always knew that Pontius was a great traitor." Another when he heard this, shouted "Wait a minute there, Signor Canonico, not so fast, nothing to the prejudice of Signor Pontio, if you please. Remember that Pontius made you a Canon, and your Lordship a Bishop. You must never forget your friends." Brydone asks, "Now what do you think of these reverend fathers of the church?"[36]

The canon told him that if he would stay with them a little while, he would be convinced that they were the happiest men on earth. They had expelled everything from their religious system that had any tincture of the dismal and severe, because they were sure that if heaven indeed were the happiest of all places, the road to it must be one of the loveliest in the world. "If it is not so," he concluded, "God have mercy upon us!"[37]

From Palermo Brydone wrote, "We are now arrived at the great capital of Sicily, which, in our opinion, in beauty and elegance is greatly superior to Naples . . . It is full of people who have an air of affluence and gaiety."[38] The libraries of the nobility had the best editions of English authors — Milton, Shakespeare, Dryden, Pope, Bacon, and

---

[35] Swinburne, *op. cit.,* II, 290-292.
[36] Brydone, *op. cit.,* II, 6.
[37] *Ibid.,* II, 7.
[38] *Ibid.,* II, 23.

Bolingbroke. There was a fine opera. The stage, which like most Italian theatres was burlesque, exhibited among other ridiculous characters, those of bucks, maccaronis, London prigs, pimps, strumpets, etc.

It would appear that Brydone did very little of what might be called sight-seeing. One day he looked into the cathedral of Palermo. "The riches of this church consist principally in some bones of St. Peter, and a whole arm of St. John the Baptist. There is likewise a jaw-bone of prodigious efficacy."[39] He mentioned the porphyry monuments of the Norman kings. There is no evidence that he saw or that he was much impressed by Monreale, which is now universally admired as the chief Byzantine Norman building in Sicily, and which is certainly in its way one of the most awe inspiring cathedrals in the world — gorgeous with barbaric red and gold. Brydone merely says, "The whole is encrusted over with mosaic, at a most incredible expense."[40]

One curiosity near Palermo did impress Brydone, and other travellers too — though not for its beauty, but because of the eccentricity of its owner, an original who would have delighted Smollett. The prince of Palagonia had cleared his palace grounds of all the conventional statues erected there by his ancestors, and set out about six hundred stone monsters — animals with heads of men excellently finished, and compound animals such as mythologians never dreamed of. The interior of the Prince's house was filled with whimsical mirrors, pyramids of the finest tea cups, bowls, saucers, chamber-pots, and flower pots all cemented together, ingenious tables of *pietre commesse* like those in the Pitti at Florence, windows of colored glass cut into geometric figures and placed without apparent design, marble statues with clocks in their bosoms, statues with flickering eyes, busts with one attractive profile and an accurate skull on the other side, toads, frogs, serpents, lizards and black widows cut in marble, painted and scattered around the floor, a series of ancestors dressed in suits of semi-precious stone — suits of black marble, stockings of red, cloaks sometimes red and green, flowing lace of *giallo antico*, peruques of snow white marble. In short, modern artists, some of them, had

---

[39] *Ibid.*, II, 119.
[40] *Ibid.*, II, 120.

a notable predecessor in the Prince of Palagonia in the late eighteenth century. The Prince also drove about the city in coaches plated with heavy brass which he believed to be musket proof.[41]

Generally Brydone has no respect for religious tradition. But the story of Santa Rosalia, he tells with simplicity and without comment.

Santa Rosalia, the patroness of Palermo, was held in greater veneration there, he asserts, "than all the persons of the Trinity; and which is still much more, than even the Virgin Mary herself."[42] Brydone was curious and went through all the booksellers' shops and at last discovered an epic poem in the Sicilian language of which Santa Rosalia was the heroine. In this obscure work he found the Saint identified as a niece to King William the Good, and that at an early age she began to display symptoms of sanctity and at fifteen she deserted Palermo, renounced all society and went up into the mountains west of the city in 1159 and was not heard of again for nearly five hundred years.

In 1624 Palermo was being devastated by a terrible plague

---

[41] *Ibid.*, II, 54-60.

[42] *Ibid.*, II, 118. Brydone was a gay young man. There was another kind of tale that pleased him very well — like this one picked up from Abbe Tatti at a Prince's dinner table. The Abbe assured him that the circumstances were factual and had befallen a friend of his named Pasquale.

Now this Pasquale had been for some time a Sicilian bandit, and after difficult years in the mountains, he joined the church and became Fra Pasquale. He also shifted to Naples. In addition to going barefoot, and wearing a large rosary and a cord of discipline, and taking vows of chastity and poverty, he took a young woman, who warned him that she had another lover, who was a life-guard at the court of Naples. It was not long before the worst possible complication overtook Fra Pasquale, and he was obliged to spend a great part of one night shivering on the marble floor beneath his lady's bed. When at last he heard the snoring of his rival, he hastily dressed in the life-guard's clothes and reported to the Captain of the guards that he had seen a Capuchin Friar creep into a street at dead of night and enter the house of a well known courtesan. This news gave the life-guards an opportunity they had long been hoping for of discrediting the monks, who were constantly carping against the licentiousness of the military. The house was surrounded, and a strong detachment thrust into the woman's chamber. She jumped up screaming that she was enchanted. "Oime — siamo perduti." Her distress was great. But it was not so great as that of the life-guard discovered with all the marks of holiness about him, the crucifix, the rosary, the cord of discipline, etc. "Gentlemen, do with me what you please," he said. "I am not what I seem to be." "Ai! Se vede!" the officer replied. "We can see that. But, come, Signor Padre." By the time the lifeguard was recognized and restored to his proper character, Fra Pasquale had returned to his convent and changed into a costume more befitting the dignity of a reverend friar. See Vol. II, 70-85.

161

like that at London two generations later. In a mystical dream the whereabouts of the sacred bones of Rosalia was revealed to a holy man — also that if these bones were reverently brought down from the mountain and carried three times around the city, the plague would be lifted. After many difficulties with the unbelievers, an expedition was sent up to Monte Pellegrino which hangs spectacularly over the city, and there in a cave the bones were found. They were carried down and in a solemn procession circled the walls thrice. The plague was immediately lifted.

From the twelfth to the fifteenth of July Brydone witnessed the Festival of Santa Rosalia. A gigantic triumphal ark (a kind of Ark of the Covenant) was first dragged through the main avenues of the city surrounded by a troop of horses, and horns and drums and followed by a mob of the populace. "It appeared a great moving castle, and completely filled the street from side to side."[43] It was eighty feet high and towered above most of the villas and palaces in the city. On top was a large silver statue of Rosalia. Inside the ark was an orchestra. The whole fabric was drawn by fifty-six huge mules and managed by twenty-eight postillions dressed in gold and silver cloth and with ostrich plumes in their hats.

At night there were miles of lights and a great display of fireworks set off on the water. The viceroy went out upon the harbor in a brightly lighted galley rowed by seventy-two gleaming oars which moved in time with an orchestra in the bow. At midnight began a promenade along the Corso.

"In such an assembly, it was impossible for the heart not to dilate · · · Mine was so full, that I could hardly find utterance; and I have seen a tragedy with less emotion that I did this scene of joy." All seemed happy equals. Friendship was in every face — no proud looks. No false aloof superiority. He concluded, "I could have thrown myself down before Santa Rosalia, and blessed her for making so many people happy."[44]

---

[43] *Ibid.*, II, 157.

[44] *Ibid.*, II, 163. Brydone, *op. cit.*, I, 148 comments on the emotional Sicilian character. "I own I have sometimes envied them their feelings; and in my heart cursed the pride of reason and philosophy, with all its cool and tasteless triumphs, that lulls into a kind of stoical apathy these most exquisite sensations of the soul."

A Tuscan garden — Villa Gamberaia, Settignano near Florence.

Photo Alinari

This is quite a declaration from the man who had laughed at his Bible and called the Virgin Mary "universal legatee and executrix" of all the pagan goddesses, and told how it was wise to show to Jupiter the same respect due to the Pretender.[45]

After a happy month Brydone left Palermo with a profound regard for its affectionate people.

Brydone did for Sicily in the second half of the eighteenth century what Boswell did for Corsica. Dr. Johnson read him Mrs. Piozzi refers to his scientific observations on Mt. Aetna — measuring the temperature, the air pressure, the electrical intensity. Brydone's book seems to have become such a familiar part of the general reader's library that in 1776 when John Dryden Jr.'s *A Voyage to Sicily and Malta* was published posthumously, the printer thought it would promote sales to make it uniform with Brydone's volumes.

It may be that the readers of Brydone will be disappointed if they expect to find in him the peculiar grace and charm of Boswell's *Account of Corsica*. Brydone, I would say, is a strong, sensible, good-humored author. Sometimes his sentences are not correct; but his words and his phrases are often striking, and his attitude always pleases the reader. Brydone is certainly more conscious of the problems of writing down a clear account of an expedition than Boswell was. Boswell travelled to see people. He went to Corsica to see a famous general, and not particularly to see the island. The result is that the reader has a good character sketch of Paoli, and a very hazy idea of Boswell's journey except where he came in contact with singing sailors, a crowd of people, a jesting priest· Then his book comes to life.

Brydone has the knack of character sketches too, however. For example, his landlady at Palermo is presented in a page or so as a busy woman always talking of some prince or duke who had been delighted to stay in her modest establishment. "And we can easily learn," Brydone says, "that they were all

---

[45] *Ibid.*, I, 142; see also I, 146. "Do you remember old Huet?" Brydone asks. "One day as he passed the statue of Jupiter in the capital, he pulled off his hat, and made him a low bow. A jacobite gentleman, who observed it, asked him why he paid so much respect to that old gentleman. For the same reason, replied Huet, that you pay so much respect to the Pretender. Besides, added he, I think, there is rather a greater probability that his turn will come round again, than that of your hero."

desperately in love with her." She took it very ill that he was not struck with the same sentiments. "Ah mon Dieu! come ces Anglois sont sauvages!" They would either have to pay her more rent or more attention. But, "She is fat as a pig, and as ugly as a devil, and lays such a quantity of paint on each of her swelled cheeks, that it looks like a great plaister of red Morocco."[46] Over Brydone's writing table hung a picture of this Madame together with her deceased husband, who was posed with an open snuff box in one hand and a cup of coffee in the other, and smiling at his wife with a particularly amiable expression. The allegorical meaning was, as Brydone later found out, that although the man was very much attached to snuff and coffee, he loved his wife still more. And she was not ashamed to confess herself the originator of the conceit.

But Brydone has considered the peculiar needs of travel-writing, and as a result, his expedition around Sicily is so clearly reported that a reader has the illusion of making the journey himself. Brydone excuses himself on points of style. In one place he says "I am just now writing on the end of a barrel . . . as it is farther removed from noise. I must therefor intreat, once for all, that you will excuse incorrectness and want of method. How can one be methodical upon a barrel?"[47] In writing his travels he says, he will communicate, "as entire as possible, the same impression I myself shall receive."[48] But, he adds that few things in writing are more difficult than to be master of the reader's imagination, "to carry it along with us through every scene, and make it in a manner congenial with our own; every prospect opening upon him with the same light . . . as upon us."[49] Nevertheless he does it very well. We are with him in the sirocco at Naples before he leaves. We sail across the bay with him at sunset, and see the bold cliffs and forelands that inspired Salvatore Rosa. We see red-hot boulders vomited out of Vesuvius at night and rolling down its dark slopes. We suffer sea-sickness, make landfall, hear the roaring waters of Charybdis.

46 *Ibid.*, II, 30.
47 *Ibid.*, I, 101.
48 *Ibid.*, I, 99.
49 *Ibid.*, I, 100.

Every movement is filled in, and every adventure and prospect along the coasts and in the mountains of Sicily become part of our own experience, simply by the use of accurate daily reportage.

Other Englishmen had visited Sicily in the eighteenth century. In 1700 John Dryden Jr., second son of the poet, went down, stopping at Capri on the way. In the spring of 1725 John Breval went to see the temples at Agrigento, and Ellis Veryard, M.D. in the same year also went to the island, where he was shot at point blank by a jealous young lover, though, fortunately, the weapon "went not off." Later, as the doctor was sailing over from the south of Sicily to Malta, he was taken by Tripolitan pirates and carried to Africa. This may have happened to a good many other Englishmen, who never returned to tell of it. But Veryard was a lucky man. He had money in a shoe, and no one discovered it. He also was able to pass himself off as the servant of a Frenchman. The French king was secretly in league with Tripoli at the time. And thus he was permitted to return to Europe. Both these earlier accounts are vigorously written, graphic, and diverting, but neither of the authors appear to have been as well acquainted with Sicily as Brydone was, and later, Swinburne.

III

The beauty of Magna Graecia is legendary. After the sun has set, the clear star Hesperus guides the dreams of mankind West. In the age of Homer, the Hellenes in their thought followed this westering star across dark waves to a land still filled with light, to a land so fair and marvellous that the fruits of the trees were gold, and its flowery vales and fields fit for blessed souls to inhabit for eternity. It was the land of Orpheus, the land of the adventures (not all unhappy) of Odysseus. But until very recently only a few travellers have followed the track of Arion's wanderings among the hills and mountains of the ancient Italiotes.[50]

In 1777 Henry Swinburne began his four-year long travels in southern Italy and Sicily. He was an experienced and a

---

[50] Slaughter, *Calabria; The First Italy,* preface, pp. vi-vii.

scientific explorer having been through Spain and having written an accurate and detailed account of it. As a man of learning he packed his pages with history, geography, geology, botany, numismatics, anthropology, archeology, and architecture. In the next age after Swinburne, of course, serious scientific travelling or exploring developed specialties beyond the scope of one person. But I think it is this very inclusiveness of Swinburne's knowledge that is his most admirable quality, for although almost every particular of his work has been superseded, the range and extent of it has not been equalled. Now, however, as in the case of Boswell's *Corsica,* the author's personal recollections are the most valued part of the work.

He set out on the road through Cymetele over the uplands past apple-bearing Avella into the green bosom of the Apennines. In this pastoral scene he found, as one still may, "many traces of ancient customs in the modes and habits of the modern Italians."[51] He saw women washing their hair with a lye of wood ashes to make it yellow as they had done in Roman times. The ancient *praeficae* had their counterpart in the old women who were hired to screech and pull out their hair at burials.[52] And he found that travellers passing through vineyards were still hailed and abused by the laborers, which made him think of Horace's

> *Durus*
> *Vindemiator et invictus, cui saepe viator*
> *Cessisset, magna compellans voce cucullum.*[53]

And he remembered that even the small vessels on the Neapolitan shores had answered descriptions in the classic poets. "I believe it scarce possible," he wrote, "to enter into the spirit of the classic authors without a previous visit to Italy or Greece. I am certain that my travels on classic ground have rendered me infinitely more sensible of their beauties."[54]

Beyond Avellino by a bridge in the valley of the Calore, Swinburne's road meets the old Via Appia, the road traced by Horace in the fifth satire in his journey to Brindisium. It is a lovely green country with emerald fields and rolling hills

---

51 Swinburne, *Travels in the Two Sicilies,* I, 113.
52 *Ibid.,* I, 113.
53 *Ibid.,* I, 116.
54 *Ibid.,* I, 117.

surrounded by giant peaks, the southern skyline a grand jagged profile of the Picentine. Swinburne was not the first eighteenth century Englishman to describe this zone, however.

Sixty years before, George Berkeley, the philosopher, then in his early thirties had come into the same valley from Capua and Caserta.[55]

Berkeley's notes, I think, are interesting as they show his passion for seeing and recording everything. After passing "Monte Sarki [Sarchio] "pleasant town towards the bottom of a conical rock, on the point of which a castle," he danced to the music of "pipe and tambour," and then he went on in the dusk — "whitish stoney soil, low vale on the right, rising ground on the left: 2 or 3 bridges over the rivulet; shining flies; moonlight; bridge over a small river; Beneventum 10 at night·"[56]

From the green Vale of Calore the road leaps up to ugly Grottaminardo, dips, and then soars even higher into the evil city of Ariana, sitting like a stone tarantula upon a bare peak, where the restless winds suck forever through its filthy entrails and alleys. Swinburne saw nothing but squalor in these places, so that we can assume they have been the same these two hundred years.

And then the road comes to Puglia, where from time immemorial flocks of sheep have been driven back and forth with the seasons. It is an astonishing flat plain, where the eye penetrates sometimes for seventy or eighty miles and is lost beyond some castle poised against the sun.

As far as I am able to judge Swinburne was the only Englishman in the eighteenth century who climbed the Gargano, the "spur" of Italy. On the way out from Foggia he passed "some faint traces of walls"[57] said to be those of Arpi, a semi-mythical city, capital of a rich kingdom founded by Diomed after the siege of Troy. He was properly skeptical, but referred to Virgil who had adopted the story. At Mt. Saint Angelo Swinburne was taken to the cave of the Angel of the Gargano. He passed through a sacred grove of trees festooned with flat stones drilled through, "and hung up by

---

55 Berkeley, see the "Italian Journal" in *Works,* IV, 537.
56 *Ibid.,* IV, 538.
57 Swinburne, *op. cit.,* I, 147.

the pilgrims," just as the "pagans used to suspend little masks or images on the branches of trees in honor of Bacchus."[58] He was conducted down a flight of fifty-five steps of coarse marble into a "damp gloomy grotto, the chapel of the Archangel Michael; his statue is of the common soft stone of the country, and with all the other decorations below criticism."[59] He explained how in A.D· 491 the Angel appeared to a certain Laurence in the caves of Mount Garganus, and told him how Pope Gelasius the First might defeat his barbarian enemies and deliver Sipontum, down the coast nearby. Afterwards this cavern where the Angel had appeared became a pilgrimage center and was enriched with fabulous treasures.

From the Gargano Swinburne went westward across the weary plains of Lucera, which all his maps marked as mountainous[60] (this was in 1777), until he came to the immense castle of Frederick II, Stupor Mundi. This fortress, almost a mile around, sits on a grassy hill from which one's eye can follow all the roads from the mountains and from the sea that cross the upper Puglian plain.

Swinburne tells of hiring a guide to take him to the ruins of Salapia, a place of importance at the time of the great battle of Cannae. As they went across the fields for about nine miles, they encountered peasants who showed "some spears and heads of lances, lately turned up by the plough."[61]

The guide had heard, and in fact the whole countryside believed, that somewhere among the caves and mounds and half-buried arches there was an enchanted grotto, which concealed a massive column of solid silver and other precious things. This would some day be discovered by a man pure in heart, and would so enrich him that he could buy all the flocks that grazed in Puglia. The guide was reasonably certain of finding this treasure himself. Had he not just returned from a pilgrimage to the Madonna of Incoronata, and "taken every step enjoined by the Church for purifying his soul from all stain?"[62] He was quite sad, when, after examining the

58 *Ibid.*, I, 153.
59 *Ibid.*, I, 154.
60 *Ibid.*, I, 152.
61 *Ibid.*, I, 181.
62 *Ibid.*, I, 169.

whole place, he could not discover a single hole in the ground more than a foot deep.

Farther down the coast white cities dazzle in the sun against a post-card blue sea. Romanesque or Byzantine cathedrals with their Greek purity of line seemed rather strange. Swinburne thought they resembled the oldest Saxon churches of England, which were built before the introduction of the "lighter sort of architecture,"[63] called Gothic. And yet to show how confusing these terms were, he called the Duomo of St. Nicholas at Bari an "ugly Gothic edifice."[64]

One phenomenon that interested Berkeley was the *tarantella*. He had heard that a victim of the spider's bite might dance the poison off in a kind of frenzy. One day he went to watch a hollow-cheeked young man gyrating around a large room. Sometimes he glanced in a hand mirror, and sometimes brandished a sword, often pricking it into his side, though not so as to do himself harm. Berkeley was not impressed. He noted that a collection was taken up for the dancer's health and to pay the orchestra. Afterward he saw other dancers,[65] but came to no conclusions.

Early one May morning Swinburne hired a guide and horses and rode west along the strand of the Gulf of Taranto toward Calabria, admiring the "wild grand view of wood and water."[65] Several days in the saddle with the Ionian Sea at his left and mountains ahead brought him to the site of the extinct Greek city of Sybaris. The walls had enclosed six miles and a half and the suburbs had reached nearly seven miles along the river Crathis. None of it was left. "After retracing . . . these circumstances in my mind, I looked around me and could not help thinking myself in a dream, or that the historians must have been dreaming when they wrote of Sybaris."[66] This affluent, highly civilized, unwarlike capital was attacked and destroyed and all its people murdered 572 years before the Christian era. Swinburne wondered why it was that the ancient writers had always dealt harshly with the elegant Sybarites rather than the brutal and stupid bar-

---

[63] *Ibid.*, I, 180.
[64] *Ibid.*, I, 183.
[65] Berkeley, *op. cit.*, 543.
[66] Swinburne, *op. cit.*, I, 275.

barians who ruined them. He said he suspected that the authors were partisans of the aggressors, and even more, that those histories partook of the general weakness of all literary productions, the work "of a set of men of great poverty, sour tempers, austere morals, and much polemical irascibility." Such men would more naturally "lash the indulging voluptuary, than the bloody tyrant or ferocious ravisher . . ." He asks who is more in error "a wealthy citizen revelling in love and wine, pampered up with high seasoned viands and delicious liquors, reposing in easy carriages and beds of down" or the conqueror who may possess himself of these old riches and learn vice himself.[67]

This ancient land possessed an idyllic quality Swinburne often tried to describe. One morning he rode along the plains — "on every side, fruits and flowers, freshened by the morning air." Round heads of orange trees glowed in the first rays of the sun as it rose from Greek seas. "The whole neighborhood was enlivened by crowds of men and women singing as they descended the hill to their daily labour."[68]

In order to escape the fatigue of riding Swinburne hired a boat to bear him to the capes of lower Calabria, and he soon passed high ruins "said to be of the school of Pythagoras and a temple of Juno Lacinia with a lone column still erect, which served as a landmark to vessels and a reminder of the golden age."[69]

IV

Calabria is a place of indescribable grandeur. It is at the same time a land of mystery, and for hundreds of years, even to the Italians who lived north of the "toe," has been almost unknown. Its reputation has been and still is in a sense sinister, partly because of the fame it has had for brigands, and partly because of something, I think, which is much more difficult to define, and much more important to define. Hidden in the upland valleys are little green vales of paradise, but they are locked within mountains of such appalling violence,

---

[67] *Ibid.*, I, 299.
[68] *Ibid.*, I, 304.
[69] *Ibid.*, I, 304.

as it were, which rise in vast cliffs of bald grey almost straight from the sea to heights a mile and a half above it, that the very aspect of the land can easily work upon the awe of anyone who travels there. There is something primordial that seems to threaten the trivial and settled concepts of human life. Travellers passing through the Alps have felt it; but in Calabria something is added, for Calabria is a place of extinct cities, and an extinct civilization, a worldlost zone, once vital and splendid and the center of the Greek dream of the West. And now what is it? It is still glorious for its sun and its two seas and its pinnacle-born white towns of the Aspromonte, for its rich forests on the Sila, for the fertile vales. It is full of good people of whom no one who knows them well will say an unkind word. And yet the entire zone does not seem to have reality. It seems to have existence in the past or in timelessness. If one lives in this atmosphere long enough, he may feel, and very keenly, as did George Gissing, "The real was that long buried past . . . Today . . . an unreality . . . and an idle impertinence."[70]

In the eighteenth century this part of Italy was even less known than it is at present. The reason is not far to seek. Travel there was almost impossible. Rev. Brian Hill was heartily "grateful to the wonderful goodness of Providence," which evidently presided over him as he passed through Calabria, a country which "for its sublime and magnificent views, forests of immense chestnuts . . . mighty mountains, perhaps exceeds every other, yet affords for travellers no one convenience whatever," and on the contrary "very real danger and misery to encounter."[71] At Palmi he wrote, "so delightful a situation I have seldom seen, but here we cannot remain with any degree of comfort."[72]

And he gave a very vivid account of two inns near Cosenza. One had been stripped by two ruffians two days before, "who had used the woman who lived in it so ill," that she had ever since been confined to bed by the bruises she received. In the

---

[70] Gissing, *By the Ionian Sea*, p. 10.

[71] Brian Hill, *Observations and Remarks*, p. xi. Nugent in *Grand Tour* (3rd edition, 1778) IV, 312, says it is better to hire a boat between Messina and Naples.

[72] *Ibid.*, p. 218.

other inn was a great fire for cooking that kept them warm, but as there was no chimney, the walls and the roof were black as jet and curiously adorned with cobwebs weighted down by multitudinous soot-balls. Hill had no wish to sleep in such a room among all the people gathered there. He searched through the building and found three other rooms. "The floor of one was so full of holes, that there was danger of falling through; another was previously engaged by the pigs, one of which, that lay concealed under some dirty straw, jumped up suddenly and gave a great snort." The third room was a nearly empty granary and served very well after considerable sweeping.

Next morning when reentering the *"black hole,"* he found the rest of the company "arranged upon the floor in a very orderly manner, and all fast asleep, though several cocks that roosted overhead were crowing almost incessantly."[73]

After Swinburne's Sicilian tour he returned along the west coast of Calabria to Naples. Landing at Tropea he hired horses and passed along the Gulf of St. Eufemia for three days and came to Cosenza. He speaks of "numberless glens, from the bosom of which ascends smoke of many sequestered villages . . . A richer landscape is nowhere to be met with." The climate and the country where so many noble drives and walks might be "carried through these airy plains," and the great variety within reach would make Monteleone "a most heavenly country residence"[74] for great noblemen.

One day on the way to Cosenza, Swinburne was sharing a horse with a friar who had an endless supply of murder stories. As they went along together, the friar filled the woods with robbers, gentlemen and ladies laid low by firearms and knives. He had worked himself into a fine state of nerves, when suddenly, as they were picking their way along a sunken path over the clenched roots of thick oaks that met overhead and darkened the way, they saw ahead at a turn a man armed with a long gun and pistols. The friar, his imagination already boiling with the desperate acts he had described, gave a screech, bounded into the wood and disappeared. Swinburne said he had no time to be alarmed, for the man instantly

73 *Ibid.,* pp. 242-245.
74 Swinburne, *op. cit.,* II, 407.

informed him he was only a *sbirro,* or guard, of the neighboring baron. They shouted to the friar, but he was gone.[75]

Swinburne finally reached Cosenza and lodged at the Dominican convent where he was "loaded with attention and civilities." Some where in the vale of Crati there, in the bosom of the river, are concealed the bones of Alaric and, it is said, all his vast treasure from the sack of Rome.

From Cosenza Swinburne advanced slowly northward along the Gulf of Policastro through mountains upon the sides of which there were romantic castles. Of one of these he wrote, "It is exactly the kind of castle . . . embowered in aged groves, that Poussin and Salvatore have so often introduced into the backgrounds of their pictures." At last he came to Pæstum — easily reached now by an *auto-strada* that sweeps southward out of the suburbs of Naples on a skyway and then passes through Herculaneum, across the lower slopes of Vesuvius, through Pompeii and a luscious plain until it twists up over the promontory of Sorrento, where as Swinburne wrote:

> Stupendous cliffs, cast in the grandest mould of nature, hang majestically over the deep; romantic towers guard the coast, which is ornamented with gay villas and hanging gardens, behind which rise hills clad with verdure of a thousand tints, and . . . the extensive buildings of Salerno ascend in a pyramidal form to the ruins of an ancient castle.[76]

From Salerno it was thirty miles by water down the gulf to one of the marvels of the Mediterranean — the city of Posidonia, (Pæstum) modern Pesto.

Whoever visits this place now can still enjoy the happiness of a discoverer. There is no hotel or inn. There are no tablets or markers or advertisements of any kind. There are no guides, no boys to sell coins, no girls with flowers. There is nothing there at all — only an ideal scene of great bluish mountains, a wide green plain, lovely trees, roses[77] everywhere in the tufty fields, and the brown temples themselves.

Until the latter half of the eighteenth century no one in the civilized world seems to have noticed Pæstum. Brydone

---

[75] *Ibid.,* II, 432.
[76] *Ibid.,* II, 110-111.
[77] *Ibid.,* II, 123. The Roses of Sistilis (Pæstum) were celebrated by Virgil and Propertius for blooming twice a year and possessing a marvellous perfume.

suggests that the temples were "discovered"[78] as though they had been buried in some inaccessible wilderness as the Mayan ruins are. But they stand near the sea. They are visible from Capri. They must always have been a landmark to sailors. It is remarkable they should have been unknown so long, and that their "discovery" should have coincided so exactly with the opening up of Pompeii and Herculaneum and with the advent of Winckelmann in the æsthetic world. Numerous engravings made these temples familiar in the second half of the eighteenth century; but there was and is no substitute for seeing them. Then the power and the serenity is felt, just as the power and the serenity of Poseidon is best felt by men who sail the sea. Swinburne remarked that he thought the "best building of a different order pretty, but delicate to excess" after seeing the stark temple to the sea-god. It was "one of the noblest monuments of antiquity we have left."[79]

At this point, in those malarial fields, the eighteenth century Englishman had reached the ultimate in his Italian travels. His craving for "sublimity" was satisfied by Doric art. As an antiquity-hunter he had arrived at a relic antecedent to familiar antiquity, older than historic Rome, older than the great age of Athens. And finally those in quest of scenic majesty had come to the end of the quest.

[78] Brydone, *A Tour through Sicily and Malta,* I, 44.
[79] Swinburne, *op. cit.,* II, 128.

began with the fingers of one other one of us, though they had been clumsily broken by the terrorists which were against them

Cypresses along a road in Southern Tuscany.

CHAPTER XIII

HOME THOUGHTS

Our revels now are ended.
— Prospero.

I

Englishmen usually moved homeward with the sun. They took leave of Rome after winters among the arts and each other's fests. And when the Campagna was afire with Spring's scarlet poppies, they crossed into Tuscany, and then left behind the *uliveti,* the Val d'Arno, the villas and the castles and the sad cypresses, and so on across Lombardy toward the gleaming wall of Alps, through Haute Savoie, up the Rhone and along the Loire — or perhaps around through the Tyrol, and Germany to Cologne, Aix-la-Chapelle, Spa, Louvain, Brussels, Ghent, Bruges and Ostend to the Channel.

Mrs. Piozzi went home by way of Prague in winter. The road west from Prague to Dresden along the banks of the Elbe was "too bad to think on; while nothing literally impels one forward except the impossibility of going back." The coach was constantly slipping toward the river, but "was held up every step of the journey by men's hands," while she walked about seven miles, "suffering nothing but a little fatigue, and enjoying the most cloudless beautiful weather ever seen." At Aussig they put the shattered coach on a barge and floated the remainder of the way to Dresden, where they took some little carts "very rough and with no springs, as our very old fashioned curricles were about the year 1750."[1]

---

[1] Piozzi, *Observations and Reflections,* II, 325. William Beckford, *Italy,* p. 198, gives a poetical glimpse of the Tyrol in January 1781.

"For these ten days past I have been traversing Lapland: winds whistling in my ears, and cones showering down upon my head from the wilds of pine . . . The streams are frozen, and mankind petrified, for ought I know . . . since whole days we have journeyed on without perceiving the slightest hint of their existence . . . I wish you had been with me, exploring this savage region: wrapped in our bear-skins, we should have followed its secret avenues, and penetrated, perhaps, into some enchanted cave lined with sables, were, like the heroes of northern romances, we should have been waited upon by dwarfs."

The road to Berlin was "all of heavy sand, cut through vast forests of evergreen timber . . . rather tedious, flat, and tristful." At Berlin she remembers Genoa, Naples, Rome and Venice and remarks "If making many houses to hold many people, keeping infection away by cleanliness, and ensuring security against fire by a nice separation of almost every building from almost every other; if uniformity of appearance can compensate for elegance of architecture, and space make amends for beauty, Berlin certainly deserves to be seen·"[2] A few pages later she writes, "And now if Berlin wants taste and magnificence, here's Potsdam to shew that even with both a place may be very dismal and very disagreeable."[3] The lately deceased King of Prussia's Sans Souci she found imitated from the Colonna gallery, and the front taken from St. Peter's. In the private rooms of the king's town house she found chiefly the works of Voltaire and Metastasio. The servants showed the last book Frederick had been reading — Suetonius in French and Italian. The book mark was at the death of Augustus, "where he was reading when the same visitant called on him." She saw the spot he sat in at the last moment. The servants wept as they told the particulars, "caressing while they spoke, his favorite dogs."[4]

The road west through Germany was almost constantly dismal and depressing. The inns, however, were excellent — hot meals, clean rooms, fine clean linen. At Westphalia on the way to Brussels Mrs. Piozzi had reached the limit of patience.

> Travelling night and day through the most dismal country I ever yet beheld, brought us at length to Munster . . . Well may all our writers agree in celebrating the miseries of Westphalia! well may they, while the wretched inhabitants, uniting poverty with pride, live on their hogs, and with their hogs, and like their hogs, in mud-walled cottages . . . surrounded by black heaths, and wild uncultivated plains over which the unresisted wind sweeps with a velocity I never yet was witness to.[5]

---

2 *Ibid.,* pp. 350-352.
3 *Ibid.,* p. 356.
4 *Ibid.,* p. 360.
5 *Ibid.,* p. 370.

The tour ended, some reflections naturally presented themselves to the traveller's mind. Rev. John Owen writes:

I am disposed to think, that I have not sustained, in the varieties of my lot, an useless or unprofitable discipline. The maxim of Rousseau is frequently before me. Quiconque revient de courir le monde, est à son retour ce qu'il sera toute sa vie." I can only express my wishes, that it may be found applicable to myself, in its best interpretation. My study has been, in the route I have persued, to decipher man, under all the varieties of his natural disposition or artificial disguise. And if I have acquired any useful knowledge, or established myself in the belief of any practical truth; if I have learned to moderate my expectations, or to temper my regrets; if I have made any advances in patriotism and philanthropy, and strengthened my attachment to my country and to mankind, the great objects of my ambition will have been fully attained, and I shall neither have travelled nor suffered in vain.[6]

Sir James Edward Smith, the botanist, is a little less like Malvolio in the old play.

It is really worth while to go abroad for some time for the pleasure of coming home again. To hear every body talking English; to walk on boarded floors, without wading through — I will not say what; to be waited on by maid-servants, the general want of which must be really a most uncomfortable circumstance to female travellers — these and numberless other little particulars, forgotten during absence, recall domestic ideas, and have a wonderful effect on the spirits. . . .

Human felicity however is never without alloy. Lest Englishmen should be too happy in coming home to their dear country, it is wisely, I presume, ordained that its coasts should be furnished with a valuable and respectable set of persons called customhouse officers, whose duty it is to moderate the joy as well as the worldly affluence of all those that come in their way.[7]

But he was soon cheerful again, gathering a beautiful *Hypnum Smithii* near a watering trough on the road to Canterbury. Dr. Moore after a series of little essays on the value

---

6 Owen, *Travels*, II, 577-578.

7 Smith, *A Sketch of a Tour on the Continent*, III, 232-235. Smith has an excellent critical list of travel books on Italy at the end of Volume III.

of seeing Germany, France, Switzerland and Italy concludes
with the old lines

> Cœlum non animum mutant qui trans mare currunt,
> . . . . Quod petis hic est.[8]

Mrs. Piozzi writes:

With regard to the general effect travelling has upon the human
mind, it is different with different people. Brydone has observed,
that the magnetic needle loses her habits upon the heights of
Aetna, nor ever more regains her partiality for the *north*, till
again touched by the loadstone; it is so with many men who have
lived long from home; they find like Imogen

That there's living out of Britain:

and if they return to it after an absence of several years, bring
back with them an alienated mind — this is not well. Others
there are, who, being accustomed to live a considerable time in
places where they have not the smallest intention to fix forever,
but on the contrary firmly resolve to leave *sometime,* learn to
treat the world as a man treats his mistress, whom he likes well
enough, but has no design to marry — this is not well neither. A
third set gain the love of hurrying perpetually from place to
place; living familiarly with all, but intimately with none; till
confounding their own ideas . . . of right and wrong, they learn
to think virtue and vice ambulatory . . .; profess that climate and
constitution regulate men's actions, till they try to persuade their
companions into a belief most welcome to themselves, that the
will of God in one place is by no means his will in another; and
most resemble in their whirling fancies a boy's top I once saw
shewn by a professor who read us a lecture upon optics; it was
painted in regular stripes round like a narrow ribbon, red, blue,
green, and yellow; we set it spinning by direction of our philosopher, who whipping it merrily about, obtained as a general effect
the total privation of all the four colours, so distinct at the beginning of its *tour;* — it resembled a dirty white!

And she concludes with the following verse:

> He whom fair winds have wafted over,
> First hails his native land at Dover,
> And doubts not but he shall discover
> Pleasure in every path round Dover;
> Envies the happy crows which hover
> About old Shakespeare's cliff at Dover;
> Not once rejects that each young rover

---

8 Moore, *View of Society and Manners in Italy,* p. 512.

Feels just the same returned to Dover.
From this fond dream he'll soon recover
When debts shall drive him back to Dover,
Hoping, though poor, to live in clover,
Once safely past the estraits of Dover.
But he alone's his country's lover,
Who, absent long, returns to Dover,
And can by fair experience prove her
The best he had found since last at Dover.[9]

III

The returned traveller has always been a fine bauble of the wits. "Your idle people that leave their native country," Sterne writes, "go abroad for some reason or reasons which may be derived from one of these general causes — Infirmity of body, Imbecility of the mind, or Inevitable necessity." And with the last of these categories he lists those travelling under "benefit of clergy, either as delinquents," shipped to the colonies, "or young gentlemen transported by the cruelty of parents and guardians, and travelling under the direction of governors recommended by Oxford, Aberdeen and Glasgow." He added a fourth class, hinted at above by Mrs. Piozzi — Simple Travellers, who went abroad with the idea of saving money.[10]

Bishop Hurd wrote a serious book to prove that travel is a great waste of time. To him it was clear that Europe had nothing important to show — "Nothing but the same polished manners and artificial policies, scarcely diversified enough to take or merit our attention." If a man must travel to study human nature, he ought at least enlarge his circuit beyond the bounds of Europe. "He must go, and catch her undressed, nay quite naked, in North America."[11]

The Italian traveller was particularly ridiculous. Thomas Gray and Horace Walpole made fun of him in their letters. And James Douglas in his *Anecdotes* writes:

I have sent you a plan and drawings of Atuatuca, or Aduatica, Tungrorum, or Tongres. The drawings represent the ruins of the walls . . . Atuatica derives its name from a castle, which I con-

9 Piozzi, *op. cit.*, II, 386-389.
10 Sterne, *Sentimental Journey, Preface; in the Desobligeant.*
11 Hurd, Richard, *On the Uses of Foreign Travel* in *The Works,* IV, 197.

jecture from Caesar's expression to have been built by the Tungri, or Eubrones . . . Tungri first to cross the Rhine. *Vid. Tac.* very brave . . . charming food for a liberal mind."[12]

William Cowper satirizes the affectation of Italian manners and morals.

> *The squire, once bashful, is shamefaced no more,*
> *But teems with powers he never felt before;*
> *Whether increased momentum, and the force*
> *With which from clime to clime he sped his course*
> *(As axles sometimes kindle as they go)*
> *Chafed him, and brought dull nature to a glow;*
> *Or whether clearer skies and softer air,*
> *That made Italian flowers so sweet and fair,*
> *Freshening his lazy spirits as he ran,*
> *Unfolded genially and spread the man;*
> *Returning he proclaims by many a grace,*
> *By shrugs and strange contortions of his face,*
> *How much a dunce, that has been sent to roam,*
> *Excels a dunce, that has been kept at home.*[13]

Smollett also contributed to this ever effervescing controversy. Writing very much in the manner of Mark Twain in *Innocents Abroad*, he described the fashionable victims in Italy, "stripped perhaps in the very first partie," with an "infamous gamester," or pillaged by an antiquated "cantatrice," or "bled by a knavish antiquarian," and others who "turn fiddlers, and pretend to compose," and fops who "talk familiarly of the arts, and return finished cox-combs to their own country."[14]

Mario Praz in his retrospect on the Italian tour says that Englishmen preferred dead Romans to the living, were more interested in the flora of the Colosseum than in the fauna of the city, that their quest was all for moonbeams falling through arches and bathing battered pillars with poetic glow, for "green rays" in pellucid sunset skies, for pretty scenes in Tuscany, the land of marvels, where white oxen and "dear contadini" make such charming little figures.[15]

---

[12] Douglas, *Travelling Anecdotes Through Several Parts of Europe*, pp. 244-246.

[13] Cowper, *The Progress of Error*,

[14] Smollett, *Travels Through France and Italy*, p. 89.

[15] Praz, Mario, *Studi e Svaghi Inglesi*, "Grand Tour," p. 280.

But doubts and discussions about the value of travel will be always with us. What gives a particular interest to the Anglo-Italian relationship, is the clash of the two cultures — northern and southern, Protestant and Catholic, Puritan and Pagan. Englishmen of the eighteenth century inherited part of the Renaissance belief that Italians were subtle, treacherous creatures. Italian artistic sensibility and fine manners were admired; but the Protestant felt his own moral superiority.

An American outsider cannot help noting that many characteristics ascribed generally to the English also describe the Italians — and *vice versa*. And he cannot help observing that the English are as responsive to beauty as the Italians, and as much moved by sentiments of honor, chivalry, nobility, and affection. Take off the language, in fact, and an Englishman is as much an Italian, in many instances, as the Italian who is born in Italy. Naturally neither the English nor the Italians would subscribe to this. Both are proud of their distinguishing qualities.

But the real distinction lies in the social life of the two countries. So different are they as to suggest opposites, just as the climates suggest opposites. Italy for an Englishman is a kind of other-England, a thousand-year long dream, the land of beauty and sun, always exerting a powerful attraction to a northern mind — sometimes a too powerful and too exciting attraction. It was this that Mrs. Piozzi had in mind when she wrote of the needle losing its partiality for the north "till again touched by the loadstone," England. A great deal has always been said about the Englishman who has travelled in Italy, and returned home. But there were the renegade originals — the men who never came back.[16]

---

[16] An economic historian will doubtless remember the death of the famous John Law (1671-1729) of Lauriston at Venice. In 1694, according to the *DNB* he killed Edward "Beau" Wilson in a duel and subsequently under sentence of death fled to France. He was a great gambler worth £114,000 at one time. He participated in the Mississippi Scheme, became Controller-General of French finance, and in 1720 told Lord Stair, the British Ambassador to Paris, that he would raise France to great heights on the ruins of England and Holland, and could destroy English trade and credit whenever he wished, could break the Bank of England and the East India Company. He lost everything in the same year. In 1725 he went to Italy. In some Italian town, so the story goes, he staked his last thousand pounds against a shilling in a bet that double sixes would not be thrown six times successively. He won, and repeated the experiment before local authorities interfered. Law died poor and forgotten at Venice in 1729 — not exactly a romantic Italy-loving renegade, though something of a renegade at that.

In the eighteenth century one of the best known of these was Earl George Nassau Clavering Cowper, distant cousin of the poet, and friend of Horace Mann in Florence. Lord Cowper arrived in the city as a young man completing his tour, and was detained by the Marchioness di Corsi. His trunks were ready packed for England and remained so for many years. Religious differences prevented his marriage with the lady, although his love was genuine. Eventually he married a Miss Gore, who happened along. They had children. Later she and the children returned to England; but Lord Cowper never! He became a close friend of the Grand Duke. There are hints that the Grand Duke even became the *cicisbeo* of Lord Cowper's wife, and that it was on this account that Lord Cowper was created a Prince of the Empire, May 30, 1778, with the title of Highness in Germany, thus becoming one of the noblest noblemen in all Europe.

Perhaps the pleasantest old personage to think of in foul weather is Sir Nathaniel Thorold, who one morning sailed over the bay to Capri. As he drew near those grand cliffs rising like an incantation from the siren waters, a spell fell upon him, and he could see no reason for further life in Yorkshire. He landed, and he never left, except for excursions deeper into the Mediterranean. He took a retreat. "La premier meuble dont il se fournit pour adoucir sa solitude fut une jeune et belle fille." Many years later, probably after the middle of the century, he died; or at least his pagan soul fled west with the setting sun to the Elysian Fields across the water, his corporeal remains dissolving, where — no one knew. In time the Thorolds in England were informed of his death. They sent to Capri, together with a large sum of money, orders that Sir Nathaniel's bones be boxed up and returned for decent interment in their native soil. A dilemma for the authorities! The bones of a heretic might be almost anywhere, and yet, if they were not found, the money would be lost. According to Norman Douglas' *Late Harvest* they solved the problem by digging a nondescript Neapolitan sailor from his recent grave. If this is true the bones of Sir Nathaniel still lie under sun-flooded skies he loved, where Zephyrus draws scrolls upon the Tyrrhene, and "sea-nymphs hourly ring his knell."

CHAPTER XIV

CONCLUSION

Almost everything that sets us above savages has come to us from the shores of the Mediterranean.

— Samuel Johnson

I

Taking a long view from North America back across the Atlantic and across the centuries, one sees that England for three hundred years has been the chief foreign source of, and influence upon, our culture. Looking further, one can see that Italy has had the same relation to England's culture — not for three or four or five centuries — but ever since legions of the Cæsars came and replaced primordial British trackways with Roman roads that ran straight as blades of light through ancient fens and forests. This long view spans four centuries of military and civil domination, and a thousand years during which Britain lay on the outer verges of Christendom, looking towards Rome as the center, and it spans all the years since the Renaissance began. Not only in poetry and prose, but in other arts, and in the sciences, religion, and in politics and in manners — in all England's culture, one sees Italy like a source, from which flow clear exhilarating revelations.

After Milton and during the early eighteenth century, Italy's importance in England waned, as the political and literary influence of France increased. But by the end of the eighteenth century the attraction of Italy was felt more powerfully than ever — and very largely, in my opinion, because of the Grand Tour there. For, with all due respect to the great civilization of France, it was less complex, and less creative than that of the Italian states since the Renaissance; and the Grand Tour discovered this even while it was discovering truths about Medieval times and antiquity. The Grand Tour, more than any other single phenomenon, guided the English imagination back to Elizabethan attitudes, the fascination of Latin and Greek antiquity, and medieval mystery, and curiosity about Italy.

II

The travel-writers of the eighteenth century, who form a peculiar prose link between England's Renaissance and her Romantic ages of poetry, cultivated an extremely difficult art. The ideal travel-writer must be equal to all he meets. All history and all art should lie as open to him as the world lies open to the sun on fine days. He must be as free-minded as a great lord, as close to the earth as a farmer. He must know something of trade, be learned in the humanities, in geology, botany, numismatics, hydraulics, engineering, sociology. He must be able to go beyond the limits of his own culture. He must have simple human understanding; because without sympathy he will learn nothing. And if the country he travels in is Italy, he ought to be a poet. His sum of knowledge ought not be less than that of a novelist who writes about the lives of a highly civilized group of people. And though his problems are different from those of the novelist, the difficulties are as great. The traveller writes about actual things and facts of history. The novelist can take liberties; but the travel-writer is condemned to the torture chamber of truth, and is expected to deal with everything — all information, all thought, all description, all people — as though by chance.

Of all travel-writers who came from the North down into Italy in the eighteenth century, "a polite unassuming man," Johann Wolfgang Goethe was the most accomplished. And yet many of the English tourists of the time were the same kind of men on a smaller scale. They were balanced, integrated amateurs — lovers of as much knowledge as they could possess without pain, and not men building up partial and special knowledge for hire. It is this quality of mind, free and open on all sides, like a temple on a high place, that is most admirable in the versatile men of the Renaissance and again in the well balanced and complete English travel-writers of the eighteenth century.

It still should be a pleasure to read the best of them: acerb Smollett, Lady Mary, Addison, Peter Beckford, and his nephew

William Beckford. Mrs. Piozzi's sincerity and her literary power are still admirable. Boswell, Brydone, Swinburne and Dr. Moore will always be appreciated by those who love the past. But even the lesser writers are valuable, though much of the pleasure of reading them depends on the reader himself, who, if he knows Italy, and is familiar with the Grand Tour there, can scarcely find a book about it that is not stimulating to his imagination — or to be very precise — to his recollection.

III

One can see by looking through all these writers a long *crescendo* of Englishmen's aesthetic understanding and love of Italy. But travel writings are only one of the by-products of the great adventure of travel. What is travel after all but an intense sort of life? — so intense that sometimes the experience is like that of Saint Paul on the road to Damascus, a great light shining around him. Or it may be like the awakening of the spirit which accompanies reading oneself into the *Odyssey* — living it with one's own soul of poetry expanding over the wine-dark sea to embrace all lands, all cities, all the ways and hearts of men. Travel may be in the profoundest sense rebirth, a bringing forth of the mind to a wider life.

Much has been made of the defects of the eighteenth century tour. It was a pleasure tour. The English were poorly acquainted with the Italian people. They had stereotyped feelings about ruins (ubi sunt), looked for picturesque landscapes, and green rays in the sunsets. They thanked God, as Puritans, for being "better" than the Italians. They were monotonous and inexact about British freedom. They were "golden asses." They loved Italy. But it was a love without respect as for a gay *cocotte*. Much of this is true, and regrettable, probably. But the English traveller was learning.

His ancestors had learned about ancient poetry and philosophy, and about politics, and manners — or perhaps it is truer to say — humanity from the Italians. The eighteenth century Englishman might learn most of these things at home. But he still had to travel to learn about Italy, "the land of Art."

187

The ideal of eighteenth century Italian travel was not so far removed from the Renaissance ideal as some historians have supposed. George Turnbull in the preface to *A Treatise of Ancient Painting* (1740) reminds us that ancient philosophers travelled — after they were men of reading and experience, and that knowledge of the world and mankind can no more be acquired by abstract speculation, without studying human nature itself in its many various forms and appearances, than knowledge of the physical world by framing theories without looking into nature itself. The true business of education, he writes,

> is by cultivating and perfecting all our powers and affections, all our faculties, and all the movements by which we are set to work, to make man such as he ought to be; that is such as his greatest dignity and happiness require he should be; or in other words, to instil into him such principles, and to form within him such desires, affections and habits as will lead him right in all his pursuits and employment — to give him vigorous serviceable faculties for the good of society . . . More are ignorant of life, and quite strangers to the world and human affairs, in consequence of imploying their minds about objects that have no concern with men . . . than through mere stupidity or want of capacity. *It is false learning that is the most dangerous to the true. [Italics supplied.]*

The particular use of the arts is to understand human life better — not to be mere antiquaries or virtuosos. Travel to see the arts and to see man is really one thing. Art is "language," a noble form of conversation rich in overtones and suggestions that cannot be put into words and a way of learning and teaching truth that is peculiarly suited to the human understanding since man is a compound creature, *nexus utriusque mundi,* the spiritual and the material.

Whatever the defects of the tour, the effects were tremendous. A traveller brought back collections of statues and paintings. He re-designed his furniture, his public buildings, his houses inside and out, his gardens, his chinaware. He fired his imagination with memories of fallen columns, hills of silvery olives, flowers and villas, the blue sea, the wrecked heroic castles, the cathedrals, a different sort of people, the cypresses, the Arno at dusk in Florence, music in the streets, the cliffs of Castellammare, Sorrento and Amalfi. Eventually he re-designed his very mind. A new poetry, in some cases, was the result. But still he had not seen everything and learned everything.

The nineteenth century continued the processes of the Renaissance, so that now scores of artists are re-discovered that were virtually unheard-of through the eighteenth century. Nor is this all. At last the English love of Italy penetrated to the rock of her culture, to the character of the Italians themselves, which is their greatest glory.

IV

Ever since the eighteenth century when Englishmen eagerly sought the landscapes of Poussin, Lorrain, and Salvatore Rosa, they have loved the countryside of Italy. Pages of great beauty both in verse and prose have been written about various aspects of it, and some fine English artists have tried to capture its magic in drawings and paintings. Almost everyone feels, as Addison did, "something more particular in the face of the country . . . than can be met with in any other part of Europe." This sounds vague. By "particular" Addison meant that the country looked more lived in, that more details were formed by imagination and work — that it was a reflection of its people, a work of art itself.

No one can possibly imagine the appearance of Italian landscape without travelling to Italy. It is the result of millenial labors of the *contadini* — labors that keep in order ancient but constantly repaired terraces of olive trees, and carry them up to the sky over tops of mountains, and hang orange groves on ledges of sea-cliffs accessible only by ladders, work vines in festoons between the silk-worm trees, and then raise rich plots of grain between the trees and vines· Addison and others have talked about the "fertile clime." Some of Italy is fertile, but many of the gardens are planted on rock and are held there and made fertile because they must be — by courage, patience, harmony of man with the earth and with infinity. The ultimate achievement of the English in Italy has been to learn something of the character which makes her the land of Art, and the garden of the world — the character that suffereth long, and is kind, envieth not, vaunteth not itself, is not puffed up, beareth all things, believeth all things, hopeth all things, endureth all things.

Long before the Apostle Paul wrote, countrymen worked and loved their hills and valleys in Italy. Nothing that has happened there in two thousand years has changed it much. It takes long to make an olive grove, longer than a man can live, and it has taken long to understand the Italians, and a civilization so different from that of other countries in western Europe. But Englishmen have been in Italy for centuries, and their understanding of it is not too imperfect now.

The other day, coming back to London, an English economist wrote:

> For ever after to return to Italy will be to return home — to return to beauty, to happiness, to magic, to the life we know we are made for, the life that is so seldom ours.

APPENDICES

APPENDIX I

An account of the different ways that lead into Italy

from

Thomas Martyn's *The Gentleman's Guide in his Tour through Italy,*
London, 1787, pp. 1-26.

[I have preserved Martyn's spelling]

If you enter Italy by the way of France you will probably go to Lyons. From thence you go through Savoy and across Mt. Cenis, or pass through Province to embark at Antibes or Nice, for Genoa or Leghorn. From Swisserland [sic] you pass, St. Gotthard Mount; from Vallais, Mount St. Bernard; and from Germany, you may go through the Tyrol. From Lyons to Turin they reckon 193 English miles: the time, 56 road hours including Mt. Cenis. No sooner have you passed the frontiers of France, than you perceive a change of country, climate, and people. The mountains of Savoy afford a new scene; woods, rocks, precipices, cascades and torrents form views that charm an eye fond of rude nature: others find this journey dreary and disagreeable; the road, however, is safe and good, and in many places even beautiful . . . [p. 4] The honest, plain, and thrifty Savoyards have very little land to cultivate, and look extremely un-healthy . . . After you pass Aiguebelle, goitres are frequent . . . [p. 6] Lanslebourg is at the foot of Mount Cenis where there are about 200 houses and 100 porters on the Syndic's list who are employed in their turns. One should have the whole day for the taking apart of the coach and putting it together again in time to reach Suze. The following day from Suze it is easy to reach Turin for dinner. Lanslebourg to Novaleze requires four or five hours and is not dangerous except in a storm or after a very heavy snow. One can pass over on a mule or in Chaises-a-porteurs, which are rush bottom elbow chairs without legs, with a footboard hanging before. There is one sedan at Suze, which may be had by writing a message and sending it ahead. From six to ten men are assigned to each chair in proportion to the size of the person, and the pay of each carrier is 50 sols of Savoy or about 2 shillings and 7½d. A mule is not obliged to carry more than 350 lbs. so that if the body of the carriage weighs more, you either take more mules or pay whatever is asked for the overloaded one. At the top of the mountain is a level plain of finest turf which may be galloped over, not only with perfect safety but with a great deal of pleasure. There is a beautiful lake with excellent trout. In winter it is possible to *"se faire ramasser"* in a sled that takes you down the mountain in ten minutes. It would ordinarily take an hour. You may go from Lyon to Turin in three days and a half post, and in about 6 days by *vetturino*. [p. 13] But lay in a large stock of patience if you choose this cheap way of travel, for the driver will go 2¾ miles per hour and usually stop at only second rate inns or worse. [p. 16] The *corniche* or post *Col de Tende* is possible only by mule or horseback. The bourg of Saorgio, so singularly placed on top of a mountain that it appears to be floating in the air. The insects of Nice never sink into a winter torpor and consequently there is no sleeping without gnat-nets which are fixed to all the beds. Lodging houses are exceedingly dear, both in town and country. As for St. Gotthard, there is a little hospice at the top kept by two Capuchin friars detailed from Milan, who are to receive all travellers that way, as there are no other houses for a considerable distance. The convent on St. Bernard is 8074 English feet above the Mediterranean. Here the summer temperature is often below freezing and the famous Alpine explorer N. De Saussure has observed the thermometer below zero on the first of August at one p.m., though the sun was shining through holes in the clouds. In sheltered places small lettuces, sorry cabbage, and a little spinach may be grown. And in the summer the monks use 20 horses to provision the convent with wine, flour, cheese, dried fruits, and especially wood.

APPENDIX 2

Time and Post Table
Through the chief Grand Tour ways in Italy,
Adapted from Martyn's *Guide*, 1787

The following records the posts where the law required that horses be changed, the distance, and the time between the towns listed. Orthography by Martyn.

MOUNT CENIS TO TURIN

Mont Cenis	Posts	Miles	Time Hours	Minutes
to Novaleze	2½	14	5	10
" Susa	11	5½	1	15
" La Zaconiere	1½	9½	2	—
" S. Ambroise	1	6¾	1	15
" Rivoli	1¼	8½	2	30
" Turin	1¼	8	1	30

TURIN TO GENOA

Turin	Posts		Hours	Minutes
to Trufarello	1		1	40
" Poirino	1		1	45
" S. Michele	1		1	30
" Gabagniole	1		1	15
" Asti	1		1	30
" Annone	1		1	25
" Felissano	1		1	50
" Alessandria	1		1	50
" Novi	2		3	
" Voltaggio	2		2	45
" Campo Marone	2		3	15
" Genoa	1½		1	30

After long rains this road was impassable near Turin as there were many rivers that rose — note what happened to Sterne.

At Turin were the Auberge Royale, Hotel d'Angleterre, Hotel de France ci-devant, les Bonnes Femmes, Trois Bœufs, Deux Bœufs. The gates at Turin closed at half past six but would open on "proper application" until ten.

At Genoa the gates were shut an hour after twenty-four o'clock, or nightfall.

By land, Lerici could be reached from Genoa only on horseback. Hiring a felucca to Lerici or Leghorn was advised.

Lerici	Posts	Miles	Time Hours	Minutes
to Lesano	1	4	2	10
" Lavenza	1	6½	1	40
" Massa	1	5½	1	10
" Pietrasanta	1	7¾	1	50
" Viareggio	1	6½	1	30
" Torretta	1	8¼	1	50
" Pisa	1	5½	1	10
" Livorno	2	14¼	2	30
" Pisa to Lucca	2	14½	2	40
" Borgoborgiano	1½	12¾	2	40
" Pistoia	1½	10¾	2	45
" Prato	1½	9¼	1	55
" Firenze	1½	9½	2	10

At Pisa the gates were shut two hours after *ventiquatro* or nightfall, but were opened at any time. Going out of Florence, one had to have his baggage plumbed to avoid being detained at Siena, and to write to Rome for a *lascia-passare* to avoid being carried to the *dogana* there.

At Florence by Meggit was a superb hotel, the Locanda di Carlo, consisting of three palaces. Vanini's was also a very good hotel. Other good inns were The Post at Massa, the Croce di Malta and the Croce d'Oro at Livorno, and La Pantera at Lucca.

GENOA TO MILAN

Genoa	Posts	Miles	Time Hours	Minutes
to Tortona	2			
" Voghera	1½			
" Pavia	2	19¼		
" Bisnagio	1			
" Milano	1			

At Milan was the Albergo Reale, an excellent inn.

MILAN TO BOLOGNA

Milan	Posts	Miles	Time Hours	Minutes
to Marignana	1	10¼		
" Zurlesco	1	9¼		
" Piacenza	1			

The Sun at Lodi and the San Marco at Piacenza were good inns on this route.

For Piacenza to Bologna, see the following table.

DIRECT ROAD FROM GENOA TO BOLOGNA

Genoa	Posts	Miles	Time Hours	Minutes
to Voghera				
" Broni	2¼	14	2	30
" Castel S. Giovanni	1	9¼	1	10
" Piacenza	2	13½	2	20
" Fiorenzola	2	14	2	10
" Borgo S. Donino	1	8¼	1	10
" Castel-Guelfo	1	7½	1	5
" Parma	1	7¼	1	50
" S. Illario	1	6½	1	
" Reggio	1	10	1	30
" Rubiera	1	8½	1	30
" Modena	1	8	2	10
" Samoggia	1½	12½	2	10
" Bologna	1½	10½	2	

At Modena was the Albergo Ducale, a superb inn, and at Bologna the Locanda Reale and Il Pellegrino were both excellent. At Reggio the Lily and the Post were good, and at Parma, the Post and the Peacock.

BOLOGNA TO ROME
(by the Adriatic way)

Bologna	Posts	Miles	Time Hours	Minutes
to S. Nicolo	1¼	9¼	2	15
" Imola	1¼	11	2	10
" Faenza	1	9½	2	
" Forli	1	9½	1	35
" Cesena	1½	11½	2	15
" Savignano	1	8¼	1	30
" Rimini	1	9½	2	
" Cattolica	1½	11½	2	30
" Pesaro	1	10	2	15
" Fano	1	7	1	40
" La Marotta	1	7½	1	20
" Sinigaglia	1	6	1	
" Case-Brusciate	1	9	2	20

Continuing from Ancona to Rome

Ancona	Posts	Miles	Time Hours	Minutes
to Camerano	1	9½	2	15
" Loreto	1	8	2	
" Sambuchetto	1	10¼	3	10
" Macerata	1	6¼	1	10
" Tolentino	1½	11	2	30
" Valcimarra	1	8	1	50
" Trave	1	7½	1	45
" Serravalle	1	7	1	30
" Casenuove	1	9½	2	35
" Foligno	1	9	1	40
" La Vene	1	9	1	45
" Spoleto	1	7½	1	25
" Stettura	1	9¼	2	30
" Terni	1	8	1	55
" Narni	1	8¼	1	40
" Otricoli	1	8½	2	30
" Borghetto	¾	6¼	1	30
" Civita Castellana	¾	6	1	
" Rignano	1	7½	2	
" Castelnuovo	1	6	1	15
" Malborghetto	¾	5	1	15
" Prima Porta	¾	4½		50
" Roma	1	6	1	25

The total distance was a little more than 305 miles — about 68 hours on the road, not counting stops of any sort.

The inns on this long road were the post houses; and the choice of them was at Macerata, Foligno, Spoleto, and Narni. The roads were surprisingly good, even through the mountains. The horses were usually excellent.

In Rome, of course, there were many good lodging houses, especially in the neighborhood of the Piazza di Spagna. Among these were Dupres, Benedetto's, Meno's, Pio's, Margarita's, Damon's, Madame Steuart's, Madame Smith's, and Sarmiento's.

To Naples from Rome by the Coast —
Not through Monte Cassino

Rome	Posts	Miles	Time Hours	Minutes
to Torre Mezzavia	1	8¼	1	
" Marino	¾	6¼	1	
" Faiola	¾	4½	1	
" Velletri	1	5¼	1	10
" Casefondate	1	9½	1	40
" Sermoneta	1	8½		45
" Casenuove	1	8½	1	25
" Piperno	1	5	1	
" Maruti	1	7½	1	35

Continuing from Maruti to Naples

Maruti	Posts	Miles	Time Hours	Minutes
to Terracina	1	7½	1	25
" Fondi	1½	11½	2	30
" Itri	1	7½	1	45
" Mola di Gaeta	1	4½	1	
" Garigliano	1	8		50
" S. Agata	1	9¼	1	20
" Sparanesi	1	9¼	1	20
" Capva	1	8½	1	10
" Aversa	1	12½	1	20
" Napoli	1	11½	1	45

This journey of 152 miles required about 25 hours actual travelling time, or just a little more than an entire day. This fact, together with the very bad facilities along the way, persuaded many to drive through in one push. The only way to lodge comfortably was to obtain letters for the Ginetti palace at Velletri, and the convent of S. Erasmo near Mola di Gaeta. Once arrived in Naples, the traveller found excellent hotels delightfully situated — the Albergo Reale, Crocelli, Emanuele, Casa Isolata, Stefano di Roma.

For trips south of Naples gentlemen were advised by Nugent that, although the posts were not regulated, horses could be found all the way to Brindisi on the heel of Italy, or all the way to Reggio Calabria.

In Sicily it was stated simply that the posts were not regulated. If anyone desired to see the site of Pæstum, or Pesto, anciently Possidonia, he should pass through Nocera to Salerno and hire a boat for the last thirty miles. Possidonia was a colony of Dorian Greeks who left noble temples on the same order as those in Sicily. This excursion south of Italy was too much for most tourists, and still is.

ROME TO FLORENCE

Rome	Posts	Miles	Time Hours	Minutes
to Storta	1	9	1	20
" Baccano	1	8½	1	30
" Monte Rosa	1	6¼	1	20
" Ronciglione	1	9	1	20
" La Montagna	1	6½		
" Viterbo	¾	5	1	20
" Montefiascone	1	10	2	5
" Bolsena	1	8½	1	45
" San Lorenzo Nuovo	1	4¾	1	20
" Acquapendente	¾	6	2	
" Ponte Centino	1	5	1	
" Radicofani	1½	8½	2	35
" Ricorsi	1	5½	1	20
" Scala	1	4½	1	25
" Torrinieri	1	9	2	
" Buonconvento	1	5½	1	
" Monterone	1	7¼	1	20
" Siena	1	8½	2	

Continuing from Siena to Florence

Siena	Posts	Miles	Time Hours	Minutes
to Castiglioncello	1	10	1	30
" Poggibonsi	1	6½	1	20
" Tavernelle	1	7¼	2	
" San Casciano	1	8¼	2	
" Firenze	1½	9¾	2	30

At Viterbo, the Albergo Reale was a pretty good inn, and at Siena I Tre Re was tolerable.

APPENDIX 3

Currency Exchange from Martyn's *Guide*

Money, the most current money, or that on which there was the least loss, was the sequin of Rome, Florence, or Venice. The French Louis d'or was also very negotiable. The money of Genoa was not acceptable in any other state; it was not advisable to have more of the current coin of any state than was to be spent in that state. This was true except for the sequin·

The following values were subject to fluctuation. The word "livre" was used in the French parts of Italy instead of "lira." Again orthography is Martyn's.

Turin	a pound sterling	worth about 20 livres (or lire)
Genoa	a pound sterling	worth 28 livres
"	a Florence sequin	worth 13 pounds 10 shillings
"	a Louis d'or	worth 29 pounds 4 shillings
"	a piastre, or Spanish dollar, worth 6 pounds 10 shillings, the value varying according to the course of exchange.	
"	sequin of Florence	worth 14 pounds 10 shillings
"	pistole of Piedmont	worth 45 Milan livres current
Parma	a lira	worth 5 baiocchi or soldi
"	paolo (a paul)	worth about 6d English
"	sequin of Florence	worth 20 paoli or 44 livres of Parma
"	Louis d'or	worth 97 livres of Parma
Modena	livre	worth 6 baiocchi or soldi
"	paolo	worth 10 baiocchi of Rome
"	Roman crown	worth 10 paoli
"	Roman sequin	worth 19½ paoli
"	Florence sequin	worth 20 paoli
Rome	sequin	worth 20 paoli
"	scudo	worth 10 paoli
"	paolo	worth 10 baiocchi
"	sequin of Florence	worth 20½ paoli
"	onza of Naples	worth 24 paoli
"	Louis d'or	worth 44 paoli
"	London pound sterling	worth 42 paoli

Naples	oncia or onza	worth 3 ducats
"	1 ducat	worth 10 carlini
"	1 carlino	worth 10 grana
"	1 grano	worth 12 calli
"	oncia	worth about 25 Roman paoli
"	5 oncie made 6 sequins, and 7 oncie about 4 pounds sterling	
"	Roman crown	worth 12½ carlini
"	sequin	worth 12½ carlini
"	pound sterling	worth 52 carlini, or 2 sequins and 1 carlino
"	Naples ducat	worth 45d English
"	carlino	worth 4½ d at par, but the exchange varied 10 or 15

The carlino of Naples was the tari of Sicily.

Florence	livre	worth 1½ paolo
"	sequin	worth 20 paoli
Venice	sequin	worth 22 livres
"	filippo	worth 11 livres
"	lira or livre	worth 20 soldi
"	lirazza	worth 30 soldi

The soldo was about a farthing English.

APPENDIX 4

Sharp-Baretti Quarrel

This "book-fight," as Fanny Burney called it, was precipitated by the publication in 1766 of Dr. Samuel Sharp's *Letters from Italy*. Sharp admitted the danger "of mistaking singularities for custom," and he begged pardon of the Papists for any inadvertencies. He had no wish to offend.

First he visited Venice, where women were free, where jealousy was dead, where the nobles were all poor, where the government was perpetuated by vast numbers of spies and informers. Second he went to Rome along the Adriatic Coast, which was desolated by the Church. In the Apennines he encountered "Italian nastiness," straw beds, wet sheets, stinking floors, no privies. Once he was served "a soup like wash, with pieces of liver swimming in it; a plate full of brains, fried in the shape of fritters; a dish of livers and gizzards; a couple of fowls (always killed after your arrival) boiled to rags. . . . On their roads the chickens and fowls are so stringy, you may divide the breast into as many filaments as you can a half penny worth of thread." He suffered sour bread, rancid butter, gnats, bugs, fleas, lice night and day. The Apennines were worse than the Alps to cross.

Rome was gloomy, with narrow streets and monks and beggars and poverty everywhere except inside the churches. On the road to Naples were none but filthy inns. Dr. Sharp did like some things. He stated that he had seen four marvels: the Alps, Venice floating, St. Peters, "a meer work of Art," and fourth, and most wonderful of all, the heavens, earth, and sea of Naples. Neapolitan opera was not good. No one listened. The theatres were dark except on gala nights, and then the taper fumes were suffocating. Opera house corridors and staircase walls were stinking and slimy with filth. Beggars in the city were numberless. "What is scandalous, they are suffered to sun themselves, a great part of the day, under the palace walls, where they lie basking like dirty swine." He then commented on the misgovernment of Naples. Death and murder were unimportant. The king relaxed while the murderers did justice on one another. On the other hand, crowds in Naples were usually more sober and good natured than in London where there were always fights and "two or three dead cats hurled about from one to another." Dr. Johnson thought there was "a great deal of matter" in Sharp's *Letters*. It is true. At Naples he observed the economy of the city and many customs. Sometimes the reader discovers curious bits, such as Sharp's account of musicians going on board galleys in the port to play concerts to the slaves, who paid for the music like passengers on a ferry. He also reported that the slaves had bread, some clothes, and not much work, except at sea. And it was true, of course, that men sometimes hired themselves out as galley slaves for the comfort and security the life offered. Not all of Dr. Sharp's account is unpleasant.

When he returned from Rome to Naples, he found excellent inns. When he went into Tuscany, he noted a "remarkable change in the appearance both of the country and the people." At Siena he saw Senesino's elegant house. He was shown through it by a lovely, generous woman, who was happy at the attention paid the memory of her uncle-in-law. At Florence he praised the general cleanliness and the smooth chiselled stones of the pavement. He was amazed at the good condition of the whole populace. He defended the Florentine nobles' practice of selling wine, which Smollett decried. He took no exception to the sober and decent institution of Cicisbeos. He became acquainted at Florence with the admirable Abbe Nicolini, who had lived in England and spoke English to perfection, and who greatly admired English politics.

Dr. Sharp enjoyed the verdure of Lombardy, and, arriving at Turin in May, 1766, he praised highly the Duke of Savoy, *i.e.*, King of Sardinia. The King was regular and assiduous. He gave audience from 6 to 10 each morning, went to mass at 11:40, dined at 12:30, supped at 10 p.m. and went to bed. The King disapproved the gallantry of Cicisbeos. His government was one of the best in Europe. "The country around Turin is nearly as pleasant as that of Florence.

From this brief survey it should be seen that Sterne was not altogether right in saying that Mundungus "made the whole tour . . . without one generous connection or pleasurable anecdote to tell."

In 1768 Baretti published *An Account of the Manners and Customs of Italy, with Observations on the Mistakes of some Travellers.* He stated in his preface:

> The following work was not undertaken solely with a design to animadvert upon the remarks of Mr. Sharp and those of other English writers, who after a short tour, have ventured to describe Italy and the Italians. Much less would I pass it upon my reader for a complete and satsfactory account of that celebrated country, taken in any one of those many points of view, under which it may be considered. . . . I had long observed, with some indignation, that the generality of travel-writers are apt to turn the thoughts of those young people who go abroad, upon frivolous and unprofitable subjects, and to habituate them to premature and rash judgements, upon everything they see. I have therefore taken occasion . . . to make them sensible, if I can, of the errors they are led into, and to point out to them some objects of inquiry more worthy the curiosity of sensible persons, and caution them against being too ready to condemn every thing but what they have seen practiced at home.

Nevertheless, as the book wears on it is easy to see that Dr. Sharp was stuck like a burr in Baretti's mind. The doctor, for example, had remarked the "extreme wretchedness of the inhabitants of Ancona."

Baretti wrote:

> I should be glad to know how, and by whom, our traveller got this piece of intelligence, that those inhabitants are extremely wretched. This formidable censurer of mother church, that suffers her subjects to be so, probably formed his judgement of them all, by half a dozen country boys and girls, who followed his coach barefooted on the Loretto road, tumbling, dropping down, and kissing the dust from time to time, repeatedly crossing themselves, and singing songs in praise of their Madonna, in order to excite his liberality. But such things are common in all countries. . . . Had Mr. Sharp tarrried only a single day at Ancona, Signor Cecco Storani and I would have had the pleasure of shewing him the town: and whatever *extreme wretchedness* he may dream of in his gloomy hours, I must tell him, that he would not have been much troubled by extremely wretched beggars in the town, as I scarce saw one during the six months I lived there, though there are some in the adjacent country. He would there have seen some very good and sightly houses, the inhabitants of which would have treated him and his fair fellow-travellers, not

with a Milanese or Neapolitan profusion, but with elegance, with respect, and with kindness. He would then have, by the Anconitan gentlemen and ladies, been offered some letters to their friends along that unfrequented road to Rome, who would have occasionally accomodated him better than he was at the inns, where his *Vetturino* thought proper to carry him; to which inns few Italians of any note resort, going either to their friends, if they have any, or to convents, where hospitality is seldom denied, as at their departure it is customary to leave a little money for the celebration of two or three masses, by way of compensation for the trouble given to their entertainers.

And to conclude he suggests that Dr. Sharp might have carried killed chickens in his coach, if he did not like eating fresh-killed ones at lonely mountain inns where his coming was not divined before hand.

The true value of Baretti's book is in the variety of informaton it sets forth on the life of Italy in his time: discussions on the difficulty of a literary career there and on the activity of academies, comparisons of Italian and British painting and architecture, and on the value of church government in a land so crowded as Italy. At one point he defends the ignorance of mendicant friars by saying their function is to confess sots, listen to complaints of the sick, sweep churches, and march in processions — all things not pleasing to poets and philosophers, but very useful to keep people happy. He refers travellers to the moderation of the Church of England prayer book preface, which says, "every country should use such ceremonies as they shall think best to the setting forth of God's honour and glory." And as for church services, Baretti declares incense is very fine in a sweaty congregation. And he asks, "is there any greater sanctity in an organ than in a clarinet or a fiddle? and is the air more holily shaken by the vibration?" As a sincere Catholic, Baretti asks proof that the Protestant nations are "more tender-hearted, more hospitable, more magnanimous," than they were in older times. Baretti suggested that the Church of Rome was the only example of a long-standing government perpetuated, not by force, but by a knowledge of human character, of human needs and other political considerations. And of Rome's oft-mentioned degeneracy, he observed, "It still contains men like those who have by turns lorded it over a great part of the Pagan and Christian world." The Romans were not degenerate.

But their "art of managing nations has at last been learned by other people."

Then Baretti praises the Tuscans. It is not difficult to imagine his comments. The Tuscans have reached such perfection in cultivating the polite arts as to leave almost no hope to future cultivators ever to surpass, or even to equal them. "Tuscany was the mistress of politeness to France, as France has since been to all the western world; and this little province may justly boast of having produced (and nearly at one time) a greater number of extraordinary men than perhaps any of the most extensive European Kingdoms." Then he mentions the sensibility of the Tuscan heart, its love of poetry, even on the part of the banker-prince Lorenzo — to wit, his *Canti Carnascialeschi*. He tells of the Tuscan love of picnics, breakfasts in the fields, the love of walking, and of dancing and singing in the streets at night. He says the English may be superior to some of these simple entertainments, and yet they love to eat plain roast beef, which Italians consider fit only for the vulgar.

There was enough in Baretti's book to provoke Dr. Sharp to a defense. In 1768 he attempted an interesting trick. Baretti, as everyone knows, had been writing a paper in Italian called *Frusta letteraria,* the literary whip, in which he vented many harsh sentences against his own literary countrymen and what he felt to be shortcomings of Italian culture in general. Dr. Sharp seized on this. What could be better than to stop the mouth of this hot Italian with his own words? Accordingly he published *A View of the Customs, Manners, Drama of Italy as they are described in the Frusta Litteraria* [sic] *and in the Account of Italy in English, written by Mr. Baretti; compared with the Letters from Italy, written by Mr. Sharp.* Quite a title!

To this defense Baretti replied with considerable heat. He explained the character of the *Frusta letteraria,* and said that to use it as Sharp had done was like using Swift's bitter satires as a source of the truth and the whole truth, and that any foreigner who quoted Swift's satire to give a character of London would be guilty of saying *"the thing that is not."*

He then discussed political freedom and rejected all of Sharp's sublime stuff about the "blessings of liberty" and the "miseries of slaves." — "We who live in the monarchical governments of Italy, are very far from believing slavery to be a good thing, and full as far from believing ourselves to be slaves."

He declared the English should take fewer of their ideas of Italy from the French. Though they have written a great deal about Italian literature, Italian politics, and Italian customs "from Henricus Stephanus, down to Monsieur de Voltaire inclusively, . . . not one of the many who handled these subjects was ever so lucky as to be once right, whether he blamed or praised."

Baretti's arguments again go far beyond mere polemics and include valuable discussions of the *Comedia dell'Arte,* of Italian writers, of Italian libraries and of the civic value of church carnivals. Whatever Sharp thought of Baretti at this point, he dropped the argument, perceiving the difficulty, perhaps, of writing about subjects much less familiar to him than to a native of Italy.

LIST OF WORKS CONSULTED

BIBLIOGRAPHIC SOURCES

Cambridge Bibliography of English Literature, New York, Macmillan, 1941.

COX, EDWARD G. *A Reference Guide to the Literature of Travel*, Seattle, University of Washington, 1935-38.

HASSAL, W. D. *A Select Bibliography of Italy*, London Association of Special Libraries and Information Bureaux, 1946.

RICHARDERIE, BOUCHER DE LA, *Bibliothèque universelle des voyages*, Paris, Treuttel et Wurtz, 1808.

EIGHTEENTH CENTURY OR ORIGINAL SOURCES

ADAM, ROBERT A. *Ruins of the Palace of the Emperor Diocletian at Spalato in Dalmatia.* London, 1764.

ADDISON, JOSEPH, *Remarks on the Several Parts of Italy*, London, Tonson, 1705.

AGLIONBY, WILLIAM. *Painting Illustrated in three Dialogues*. London, 1685. the above work re-issued with the title *Choice Observations on the Art of Painting*, 1719.

ALBERTI, LEANDRO. *Descrizione di tutta l'Italia.* [first ed., 1550; ultimate ed., 1588].

AYSCOUGH, GEORGE EDWARD. *Letters from an Officer in the Guards to his Friend in England.* London, 1778. [see George Edward Lyttleton].

BARETTI, JOSEPH. *An Account of the Manners and Customs of Italy.* London, Davies, 1769.

BARRY, JAMES. *The Works.* 2 vols. London, Cadell, 1809.

BECKFORD, PETER *Familiar Letters from Italy.* 2 vols. Salisbury and London, 1787.

BECKFORD, WILLIAM. *Italy.* London, Chapman, 1928.

BELLICARD, JEROME CHARLES. *Observations upon the Antiquities of Herculaneum.* 42 plates. London, 1756. [first edition].

BERGIER, NICOLAS. *Histoire des grandes chemins de' l'Empire romain.* Bruxelles, J. Leonard, 1728. [two folio volumes, very complete and ponderous].

BERKELEY, GEORGE. "Journal of a Tour in Italy. 1717, 1718," in volume IV of *Works*, ed. Alexander Campbell Fraser. Oxford, Clarendon Press, 1871. [letters to Pope and Prior from Berkeley in Italy, vol. I of the Works of Pope, ed. Bowles. London, 1806].

BOSWELL, JAMES. *An Account of Corsica . . . and Memoires of Pascal Paoli.* London, 1768.
Private Papers of James Boswell from Malahide Castle; in the collection of Lt. Colonel Ralph Heyward Isham . . . [priv. print 1928-34, Mount Vernon, N. Y.].
Life of Samuel Johnson, L. F. Powell's revised edition. Oxford, Clarendon Press, 1934.

BOYLE, JOHN. *Letters from Italy in the Years 1754-1755*, by the late Right Honorable John Earl of Corke and Orrery. London, 1773.

BREVAL, JOHN DURANT. *Remarks on Several Parts of Europe.* 2 vols. London, 1723-26. [second edition 1738]

BROMLEY, WILLIAM. *Remarks made in Travels through France and Italy.* London, 1692. [re-issued 1705 with a burlesque table of contents].

BRYDONE, PATRICK. *A Tour through Sicily and Malta, in a Series of Letters.* 2 vols. London, Strahan and Cadell, 1773.

BURNET, GILBERT. *Some Letters containing an Account of what seemed most remarkable in . . . Italy.* Amsterdam, 1686.

CAMPBELL, JOHN. *The Travels and Adventures of Edward Brown.* [a semi-fiction based on the author's Mediterranean travels].

COLEMAN, GEORGE. *Letters.* London, 1820. [gives glimpses of Garrick's indefatigable "antiquity-hunting"].

CONDEMAINE, CHEVALIER DE LA. *An Extract from Observations made in a Tour to Italy,* translated by a Fellow of the Royal Society. London, 1768.

CORBETT, THOMAS. *Expedition of the British Fleet to Sicily,* 1718, 1719, 1720, under Sir George Byng. London, Tonson, 1729.

Critical Review, The. Vols. XXI, XXII, XXIV. London, 1766-1767.

DENNIS, JOHN. *Miscellanies in Prose and Verse.* London, 1692.

DOUGLAS, JAMES. *Travelling Anecdotes through several Parts of Europe.* London, Debrett, 1785.

DRUMMOND, ALEXANDER. *Travels through different Cities of Germany, Italy, Greece. London* [little about Italy and that dull], 1754.

DRYDEN, JOHN JR. *A Voyage to Sicily and Malta.* London, Bew, 1776. [2nd son of the poet].

DUTENS, LOUIS. *Memoires d'un Voyageur qui se repose.* Londres, 3me ed., 1807.

FERBER, JOHAN JAKOB. *Travels Through Italy, in the years 1771-1772,* translated, R. E. Raspe, London, Davis, 1776.

Florence Miscellany. Florence, privately printed, 1785.

GARDENSTONE, FRANCIS G. *Travelling Memorandums, made on the Continent of Europe.* 2 vols. Edinburgh, 1792.

GARRICK, DAVID. *The Journal of David Garrick, describing his visit to France and Italy in 1763.* New York, Mod. Lang. Ass. of America, 1939.

GIBBON, EDWARD. *Autobiography.* Oxford World Classics Series, Letters, ed. Prothero, London, Murray, 1897.

GOETHE J. WOLFGANG VON. *Italienische Reise.* herausgeben von Theodor Friedrich, Leipzig, 1921.

GRAY, THOMAS. *The Correspondence of.* ed. Toynbee and Whibley, 3 vols. Oxford, at the Clarendon Press, 1935.

GRAY, ROBERT. *Letters during the course of a tour through Germany, Switzerland, and Italy in 1791-1792.* London, F. and C. Rivington, 1794.

HAMILTON, SIR WILLIAM. *The Hamilton and Nelson Papers.* vol. I of The Collection of Autograph Letters and Historical Documents formed by Alfred Morrison, second series, 1882-1893. Printed for Private Circulation, 1893.

Collection of Etruscan, Greek, and Roman Antiquities, Naples, [colored plates — some double], 1766.

Collection of Engravings from Ancient Vases, mostly of pure Greek workmanship. 3 vols. fol. Published by D. Tischborn, director of the Royal Academy of Painting, Naples, 1791-95.

HERVEY, CHRISTOPHER. *Letters from Portugal, Spain, Italy and Germany in the Years 1759-61.* 3 vols. London, 1785.

HILL, REV. BRIAN. *Observations and Remarks in a Journey through Sicily and Calabria in the Year 1791.* London, 1792.

HOWELL, JAMES. *Epistolae Ho-Elianae,* ed. Joseph Jacobs. London, D. Nutt, 1892.

HULL, THOMAS. *Select Letters between the Late Duchess of Somerset, Lady Luxborough, Miss Dolman . . . and others.* 2 vols. London, 1778.

HURD, BISHOP WILLIAM. *On the Uses of Foreign Travel.* London, 1764. Also in Vol. IV, *The Works of.* London, Cadell, 1811.

KEATE, GEORGE. *The Alps,* a poem, London, Dodsley 1763 [ultra-pneumatic sublimity].

KEYSLER, JOHANN GEORG. *Travels through Germany, Bohemia, Hungary, Switzerland, Italy, and Lorraine.* London, 1756. [gave Smollett the headache].

210

KNIGHT, *Lady Knight's Letters from France and Italy* (1776-95), edited by Lady Eliot-Drake. London, Humphreys, 1905.

LA CONDAMINE, see Condamine above.

LA LANDE, PERE JEROME. *Voyage d'un Français en Italie, fait dans les années 1765-1766.* 10 vols. Venice, 1769.

LASSELS, RICHARD. *The Voyage of Italy.* Paris and London, 1670.

LODGE, WILLIAM. *The Painter's Voyage of Italy.* London, 1679. [translated from Barri's Viaggio Pittoresco].

LUMIDSEN, ANDREW. *Remarks on the Antiquities of Rome and its Environs.* London, 1797.

LYTTLETON, SIR THOMAS. *The Works of George Lord Lyttleton.* Published by George Edward Ayscough. 2 vols. Dublin, Faulkner, 1774.

MAJOR, THOMAS. *The Ruins of Paestum, otherwise Posidonia in Magna Grecia.* 25 copper plates. Folio. London, 1754.

MANN, HORACE. *Mann and Manners at the Court of Florence, 1740-1786,* [the letters of Horace Mann] ed. by Dr. John Doran. 2 vols. London, Bentley, 1876.

MARTYN, THOMAS. *The Gentleman's Guide in his Tour through Italy.* London, G. Kearsley, 1787.

MELMOUTH, COURTNEY. *Travels for the Heart.* 2 vols. London, 1777. [a hopeless imitation of Sentimental Journey].

MERIGOT, JASPAR. *Views and Ruins in Rome and in its Vicinity . . . from drawings on the Spot,* 62 aquatint plates. Folio, 1796 [another edition, London, 1790].

MISSON, FRANCIS MAXIMILIAN. *Nouveau Voyage d'Italie.* Hague, 1691. [English edition, London, 1695].

MONTAIGE, M. DE. *Diary of a Journey Into Italy, 1580-81.* Hazlett's translation, London, 1853.

MONTAGUE, LADY MARY WORTLEY. *Letters written during her Travels in Europe, Asia, and Africa.* 4th ed. New York, 1766.
Letters. London, Bohn's Standard Edition, 1887.

MOORE, DR. JOHN. *A View of Society and Manners in Italy.* Boston, Belknap and Young, 1792.

MORYSON, FYNES. *An Itinerary.* Folio. London, 1611, reprinted by MacLehose, 4 vols. Glasgow, 1907-08. [also reprinted under title, Shakespeare's Europe, London, 1903].

MUIRHEAD, LOCKHART. *Journey of Travels in . . . Tuscany in 1784 &1789,* London, 1803.

NORTHALL, CAPT. JOHN. *Travels through Italy.* London, 1766.

NUGENT, THOMAS. *The Grand Tour.* 4 vols. London, 1749. [one of the best guide-books of the eighteenth century].

OWEN, REV. JOHN. *Travels into different parts of Europe in the Years 1791-92.* 2 vols. London, 1796.

PARSONS, WILLIAM. *Travelling Recreations.* London, 1807.

PIOZZI, HESTER LYNCH THRALE. *Observations and Reflections made in the Course of a Journey through France, Italy, and Germany.* 2 vols. London, 1789. another ed., Dublin, 1789.

RAY, JOHN, (FRS). *Travels through the Low-Countries, Germany, Italy and France with curious Observations . . . also a Catalogue of Plants,* 2nd ed. London, 1788 [first ed. London, 1673].

RICHARDSON, JONATHAN. *An Account of some of the Statues, Bas-Reliefs, Drawings and Pictures in Italy.* London, 1720.

ROBINSON, WILLIAM. See Jones, William Powell.

RUSSELL, JONATHAN. *Letters from a Young Painter Abroad to his Friends in England.* 2 vols. London, 1750.

SALMON, J. *An Historical Description of Ancient and Modern Rome.* 2 vols. London, 1800.

SAMBER, ROBERT. *Roma Illustrata,* or a Description of the most beautiful Pieces of Painting, Sculpture and Architecture at and near Rome. Folio. London, 1676.

SHARP, DR. SAMUEL. *Letters from Italy*. London, 1766. [second printing, 1767.]

A View of the Customs and Manners, Drama of Italy as they are described in the Frusta Letteraria and in the Account of Italy, written by Mr. Baretti. London, 1768.

SHERLOCK, REV. MARTIN. *Letters from an English Traveller*. London, 1779.

SMITH, J. *Select Views in Italy* . . . with India proof engravings. 2 vols. 72 plates. London, 1796.

SMITH, SIR JAMES (M.D.). *A Sketch of a Tour on the Continent in the years 1786-87*. 3 vols. London, 1793. [Vol. III contains a list of eighteenth century books of travel in Italy with critical comments.]

SMOLLETT, TOBIAS. *Travels through France and Italy*. 2 vols. London, 1766.

SPENCE, WILLIAM. *Polymetis*. London, 1747.

STARKE, MARIANA. *Letters from Italy between the Years 1792 and 1798*. 2 vols. London, 1800. [excellent on hotels, inns, and side-trips.]

STERNE, LAURENCE. *Letters*, edited by L. P. Curtis. Oxford, Clarendon Press, 1935.

A Sentimental Journey through France and Italy, 1768.

SWINBURNE, HENRY. *Travels in the Two Sicilies in the Years 1777-80*. 2 vols. London, 1783-85. [2nd ed. 1790, 3rd ed. 1795].

THICKNESS, PHILIP. *A Years Journey through France and Part of Spain*. 2 vols. London and Bath, 1777.

TURNBULL, GEORGE, L.L.D. *A Treatise on Ancient Painting*. London, Millar, 1740.

THOMPSOM, CHARLES. *The Travels of the late Charles Thompson containing his Observations on France, Italy* . . . 3 vols. London, 1744. [another ed., 1748. This work a pastiche of other travellers]

VASARI, GIORGIO. *Le Vite de' Piu Eccellenti Pittori, Scultori e architetti*. Trieste, 1862.

VENUTI, NICCOLO' MARCELLO, MARCHESE, *A description of the ancient city of Heracles, found near Portici, a country palace belonging to the King of the Two Sicilies* . . . Done into English . . . by Wickes Skurray. London, R. Baldwin, 1750.

VENUTI, RIDOLFINO. A Collection of Some of the Finest Prospects in Italy with short remarks by . . . [the] antiquary to the Pope. Vol. I [the only one]. London, Nourse, 1762.

VERYARD, ELLIS. *An Account of Divers Choice Remarks . . . taken in a Journey through Italy . . . with the Isles of Sicily and Malta*. Oxford, 1701.

WALKER, ADAM. *Ideas suggested in an Excursion through Flanders, Germany, Italy, and France*. London, 1790.

WALPOLE, HORACE. *Letters*. 8 vols. London, Bentley, 1857.

WARCUPP, EDMUND. *Italy in its Original Glory, Ruin and Revival*. Folio. London, 1660.

WATKINS, THOMAS. *Travels in 1887-89, through Switzerland, Italy, Sicily, etc.* 2 vols. London, 1794.

WHATELY, STEPHEN. *A Short Account of a late Journey to Tuscany, Rome, and other Parts of Italy*. London, 1746.

WILKINSON, JOSHUA LUCOCK. *The Wanderer . . . in 1791-98 in France, Germany, and Italy*. 2 vols. London, 1795.

WINCKELMANN, ABBE' JOHANN JOACHIM. *Reflections on the Painting and Sculpture of the Greeks*. Translated by Henry Fusseli. London, Millar, 1767. *A Critical Account of the Situation and Destruction . . of Herculaneum, Pompeii and Stabia*. London, 1771. [compliments the travelling resolution of the English]

WRIGHT, EDWARD. *Some Observations Made in Travelling through France, Italy . . . in 1700-22*. 2 vols. 42 folding plates. London, 1730.

Wynne Diaries, ed. ANNE FREMANTLE. 3 vols. Oxford, H. Milford, 1937. [diaries in Tuscany just before the coming of Buonaparte]

YOUNG, ARTHUR. *Travels in France during the Years 1787-89*. 2 vols. Bury St. Edmonds, 1792. [references are to the Everyman reprint]

LATER CRITICAL AND HISTORICAL WORKS

ALLEN, BEVERLY SPRAGUE. *Tides in English Taste*. Cambridge, Mass., Harvard University Press, 1937.

AUBIN, ROBERT. *Topographical Poetry in XVIII Century England*. New York, The Modern Language Association of America, 1936.

BATES, E. S. *Touring in 1600*. Boston and New York, Houghton Mifflin Co., 1911.

BORENIUS, TANCRED. *English Painting in the Eighteenth Century*. London, Gifford, 1938.

COLLISON-MORLEY, LACEY. *Italy after the Renaissance*. London, Routledge, 1930.

CROCE, BENEDETTO. *Shaftesbury in Italia* (*con lettere inedite*), Critica, 1925. Un Viaggiatore in Italia nel settecento apostolo dello Shakespeare. [Martin Sherlock], Critica, 1928.

DE BEER, GAVIN R. *Early Travellers in the Alps*. London, Sidgewick and Jackson, 1930.

DOUGLAS, NORMAN. *Late Harvest*. London, Drummond, 1946. Old Calabria. London, Secker, 1923.

EINSTEIN, LEWIS. *The Italian Renaissance in England*. Columbia University Press, 1903.

FRANZ, R. W. *The English Traveller and the Movement of Ideas, 1660-1732*. University Studies, Lincoln, Nebraska. Vols. XXXII-XXXIII, 1934. [This study does not mention Italy.]

GISSING, GEORGE. *By the Ionian Sea*. London, Chapman and Hall, 1905.

GRAF, ARTURO. *L'anglomania e l'influsso inglesi in Italia nel sec. xviii*. Torino, 1911.

HAVENS, RAYMOND. "*The Romantic Aspects of the Age of Pope*," PMLA, XXVII, (1912), 297-324.

HEWLETT, MAURICE. *The Road in Tuscany*. 2 vols. London, Macmillan, 1904.

HOWARD, CLARE M. *English Travellers of the Renaissance*. New York, Columbia University Press, 1913.

HUSSEY, CHRISTOPHER. *The Picturesque*. London and New York, Putnams, 1927.

JONES, WILLIAM POWELL. *The William Robinsons in Italy*. "Huntington Quarterly," April, 1941.

KAHRL, GEORGE MORROW. *Tobias Smollett, traveller-novelist*. University of Chicago Press, 1945.

LAMBERT, R. S. ed. *Grand Tour, A Journey in the Track of the Age of Aristocracy*. London, Faber and Faber, 1935.

LEES-MILNE. *The Age of Adam*. London, Batsford, 1947.

LESLIE, CHARLES R. and TOM TAYLOR. *Life and Times of Sir Joshua Reynolds*. London, Murray, 1865.

MANWARING, ELIZ. WHEELER. *Italian Landscape in Eighteenth Century England*. New York, Oxford University Press, 1925.

MARSHALL, RODERICK. *Italy in English Literature*. New York, Columbia University Press, 1934.

MAUGHAM, H. NEVILLE. *The Book of Italian Travel*. London, 1903.

MEAD, WILLIAM EDWARD. *The Grand Tour in the Eighteenth Century*. Boston, Houghton Mifflin, 1914.

NATALI, G. *Il Settecento*. Milano, 1929.

ORTOLANI, C. *Ancora la scoperta dell'Inghilterra nel Settecento*. Marzocco, 3 Maggio, 1914.

PENROSE, BOIES. *Urbane Travellers*: 1591-1635. University of Pennsylvania, 1942.

POTTLE, FREDERICK. *The Incredible Boswell*, "Blackwood's Magazine." Vol. 218 (1929).

PRAZ, MARIO. *Studi e Svaghi Inglesi*. Firenze, G. C. Sansoni, 1937 .

PREZZOLINI, GIUSEPPE. *Come gli americani scoprirono l'Italia* (1750-1850). Milano, Treves, 1933.

RODD, SIR RENNELL. "The Italian People," *Proceedings of the British Academy*. 1920. pp. 389-404.

SHEPHERD, WILLIAM, *Historical Atlas*. New York, Henry Holland, 1929.

SITWELL, OSBERT and MARGARET BARTON. "Taste," in vol. II of *Johnson's England*. Oxford, Clarendon Press, 1933.

SLAUGHTER, GERTRUDE. *Calabria, the First Italy*. Madison, University of Wisconsin Press, 1939.

STEEGMAN, JOHN. *The Rule of Taste*. London, MacMillan, 1936.

THORPE, CLARENCE D. *Two Augustans Cross the Alps: Dennis and Addison on Mountain Scenery*," Studies in Philology, XXXII (1935), 463-482.

TINKER, CHAUNCY BREWSTER. *Young Boswell*. Boston, The Atlantic Monthly Press, 1922.

TREVELYAN, G. M. (MRS.). "Wandering Englishmen in Italy," *Proceedings of the British Academy*, 1930. pp. 61-84.

WALLASTON, G. N. *The Englishman in Italy*. Oxford, Clarendon Press, 1909. ["aurea anello fra Inghilterra" . . . a collection of English poems describing Italy]

WHITLEY, WILLIAM THOMAS. *Artists and Their Friends in England*, 1700-1799. 2 vols. London and Boston, The Medici Society, 1928.

YOUNG, G. F. (COL.). *The Medici*. New York, Modern Library, 1933.

ZANIBONI, E. *Alberghi italiani e viaggiatori stranieri, sec. XIII-XVIII*. Napoli, Detken & Rocholl, 1921. [very good for the older inns]